Since
Eve
Ate
Apples

Since Eve Ate Apples

QUOTATIONS
ON
FEASTING, FASTING & FOOD

FROM THE BEGINNING

SELECTED AND EDITED

BY

MARCH EGERTON

TSUNAMI
PRESS

Portland, Oregon

SINCE EVE ATE APPLES
Tsunami Press/December 1994

Copyright © 1994 by March Egerton
All Rights Reserved

Cover Artwork and Design by Ragtime Billy Peaches
Layout by March Egerton

Library of Congress Catalog Card Number: 94-61077
ISBN: 0-9637709-1-8

First Edition

PRINTED IN THE UNITED STATES OF AMERICA
10 8 6 4 2 1 3 5 7 9

inquiries & mail orders:
Tsunami Press
P.O. Box 80151
Portland, Oregon 97280-1151
503-245-6576

for Myrna

——✺——

and for
Ann & John

who showed me
the
way

All human history attests
That happiness for man—
the hungry sinner—
Since Eve ate apples,
Much depends on dinner!

LORD BYRON
Don Juan (1823)

ACKNOWLEDGEMENTS

Working on a book is, I imagine, a bit like building a house: fraught with pitfalls anticipated and unforseen, frequently maddening, seemingly interminable and ultimately quite satisfying. This extends even to books you don't actually write but merely edit, as does the simple truth that projects of this nature always require some outside assistance. I would like to thank the following people for their contributions:

Ann Egerton
John Egerton
Cindy Frank
Skip Higgs
Sara Holt
Carolyn James
Tim Peck
Anne Reuland
Bill Tugurian

❧ T H E   M E N U ☙

ABUNDANCE
AFRICA
AMERICANS
ANARCHY
APPETITE
AROMA
AUSTRALIA

BARBECUE
BEANS
BEEF
BEER
THE BELLY
BERRIES
BOOKS
BREAD
BREAKFAST
BRITISH
BUTTER

CAKE
CANNIBALISM
CHEESE
CHILDREN/CHILDHOOD
CHINESE
CHOCOLATE
COFFEE
COMPANY
CONDIMENTS
CONFLICT
CONVERSATION
COOKBOOKS

CONTENTS

CONTENTS

INTRODUCTION

If we drop sex from the equation—no way to win friends, certainly, but necessary to illustrate the point—it is fair to say that few things animate human beings like a choice morsel or a sharp turn of phrase. Food and words, in other words. Such commonplace articles of daily living as to seem hopelessly mundane at times, but all it takes is a little restricted access to remind us of the power they hold. Wars have been waged and civilizations transformed on their account, momentous events set in motion by nothing more complicated than a catchy slogan or the quest for a crust of bread.

I have long been interested in this connection between words and food. Often neutral in and of themselves (certain varieties of peppers notwithstanding), they become riveting tools of expression when placed in the proper hands. It is easy enough to cite examples of plain language used to extraordinary effect—Lou Gehrig's farewell, a Hemingway short story, Billie Holiday warbling "Strange Fruit," Neil Armstrong's lunar proclamation—but food is more ephemeral. As a way of understanding the depth of meaning in our meals, consider how Escoffier or Julia Child have used cuisine as a vehicle for artistic statement; now contrast that with the way someone like Gandhi or Bobby Sands has used food, or more precisely the refusal of it, as a political tool. If that sounds too academic, think in terms closer to home: parents and grandparents have found few more effective mediums for expressing caring and devotion to their offspring. Nothing says lovin', you will recall, like something from the oven.

So then, you begin to realize that the implications of food in our world are as multifaceted as any diamond. And just as it is our nature to elevate food above the animal plane of simple sustenance—to pledge our allegiance to it, rhapsodize about it, experiment with it, debate, photograph, fondle it—we likewise are predisposed toward celebrating the linguistic skill of others. Understandably titillated by this sort of gastro-literary symbiosis, I thought it might be worthwhile to examine what exactly has been said about food and eating over the centuries. This eventually led to the book you now hold.

The material included here, the result of many months' research, spans five millennia. Some of the quotations, such as those enunciating the once dim view of modernly mundane foods like milk and tomatoes, are interesting because they offer a glimpse at how things have changed; others, like the passage on barbecue from Homer's *Odyssey*, are compelling for precisely the opposite reason, underscoring the existence of certain constants in the culinary equation.

A collection of quotations is by its very nature an arbitrary volume. This is true enough of many reference works, but becomes particularly noticeable when one aims at compiling the noteworthy sayings of others on a given topic. Rather than try and escape this inescapable truth, I have attempted within these pages to embrace it. *Since Eve Ate Apples* is intended first and foremost as a serious reference book, but it is also meant to appeal to the casual browser. Toward that end, I was determined to avoid the usual dour, classics-heavy tone of many a quotation collection, in favor of a more eclectic and colorful assortment. Thus, you will find ever-quotable Shakespearean verse sidling up against the gastronomic wisdom of everyone from Buddy Hackett to Madame Chiang Kai-Shek. Have fun with it.

A NOTE TO THE READER

To maximize your enjoyment of *Since Eve Ate Apples*, be mindful of the following:

- The quotations are divided into 161 categories, which are listed in the table of contents and arranged alphabetically.

- Within each category, quotations are listed chronologically, with anonymous entries and proverbs placed at the end of each category.

- In cases where the author is known but neither the actual source nor the year is known, the author's year of birth and, if applicable, death, are listed and the quotation is placed chronologically according to when that person flourished. A slightly inexact but unavoidable circumstance, which I think you will find to be quite functional.

- Finally, this book is indexed by author, with each sub-entry listed by category as well as page number.

And ye shall eat the fat of the land.
GENESIS 45:18
(c. 700 B.C.)

Come ye, say they, I will fetch wine, and we will fill
ourselves with strong drink; and tomorrow shall be as this
day, and much more abundant.
ISAIAH 56:12
(c. 700 B.C.)

A land of wheat, and barley, and vines, and fig trees, and
pomegranates; a land of oil, olive, and honey; a land
wherein thou shalt eat bread without scarceness, thou shalt
not lack any thing in it.
DEUTERONOMY 8:8-9
(c. 650 B.C.)

Surfeit has killed more men than famine.
THEOGNIS
Sententiae (c. 500 B.C.)

Their tables were stor'd full, to glad the sight,
And not so much to feed on as delight.
WILLIAM SHAKESPEARE
Pericles (1608-09)

Some people have food, but no appetite. Others have
appetite, but no food. I have both—the Lord be praised.
OLIVER CROMWELL
(1599-1658)

The folds shall be full of sheep: the valleys also shall
stand so thick with corn, that they shall laugh and sing.
THE BOOK OF COMMON PRAYER 66:11
(1662)

The country abounds with grapes, large figs and peaches;
the woods with deer, conies, turkeys, quails, curlues,
plovers, teile, herons. . . . The rivers are stored plentifully
with fish that we saw play and leap.
WILLIAM HILTON
Voyage to the Carolina Coast (1664)

I told him . . . that we ate when we were not hungry, and drank without the provocation of thirst.
JONATHAN SWIFT
Gulliver's Travels (1726)

In giving a dinner, the error is usually on the side of abundance.
THOMAS COOPER
Domestic Cookery (1824)

Soochow, the good place. At dawn
The bamboo is cut smooth as jade,
Sweet and intense on an earthenware plate.
Soochow, the good place. The arbutus,
Sweet like heavenly dew,
Filling my cheeks with juice.
Soochow, the good place. Big beans
Picked when the flowers bend low
And munched when tea is served.
Soochow, the good place—when the shad
Come by. River globefish
In spring we cook with ginger and chives.
Soochow, the good place. In summer
Plump fish dart about the river
Avoiding the fisherman's boat.
Purple crabs and red wine dregs
Make the autumn pass.
When waxy meats and sturgeon appear,
Carp and bream leap into the pot.
KU TIEH CHING
Soochow, the Good Place (c. 1850)

Four more years of the full dinner pail.
REPUBLICAN CAMPAIGN SLOGAN
(1900)

They sat down to tables that well might have groaned, even howled, such was the weight that they carried.
MARTHA MCCULLOCH-WILLIAMS
Dishes and Beverages of the Old South (1913)

The food came out in caravans; it came in flotillas; it came in argosies.
IRVIN S. COBB
Red Likker (1929)

Let there be more corn and more meat, and let there be no hydrogen bombs at all.
NIKITA KHRUSHCHEV
while visiting an Iowa farm (1959)

In a city full of misers the cheats have plenty to eat.
INDIAN PROVERB

A F R I C A

We remember the fish, which we did eat in Egypt freely; the cucumbers, and the melons, and the leeks, and the onions, and the garlic.
NUMBERS 11:5
(c. 700 B.C.)

But, first or last,
Your fine Egyptian cookery
Shall have the fame.
I have heard that Julius Caesar
Grew fat with feasting there.
WILLIAM SHAKESPEARE
Antony and Cleopatra (1606-07)

Along much of the west coast the yam is not only a food of vast importance but also a kind of symbol. The yam has helped many West Africans to survive. Accordingly, his gratitude is so great that eating it is almost a religious exercise.
LAURENS VAN DER POST
African Cooking (1970)

Bedouin hospitality dictates that a guest must always be offered the best portion of any meal; the guest's politeness, however, ensures that he in turn must refuse this honor, ceding it to the oldest person at the table.
PAUL WILLIAM ROBERTS
River in the Desert (1993)

AMERICANS

The Americans are not accustomed to what we call grand feasts; they treat strangers as they treat themselves every day, and they live well. They say they are not anxious to starve themselves the week, in order to gormandize on Sunday. This trait will paint you a people at their ease, who wish not to torment themselves for show.
J.P. BRISSOT DE WARVILLE
New Voyage into the United States (1791)

The predominance of grease in the American kitchen, coupled with the habits of hearty eating, and constant expectoration, are the causes of the diseases of the stomach which are so common in America.
JAMES FENIMORE COOPER
(1789-1851)

A man accustomed to American food and American domestic cookery would not starve to death suddenly in Europe; but I think he would gradually waste away, and eventually die.
MARK TWAIN
A Tramp Abroad (1879)

The average American's simplest and commonest form of breakfast consists of coffee and beefsteak.
MARK TWAIN
A Tramp Abroad (1879)

The American does not drink at meals as a sensible man should. Indeed, he has no meals. He stuffs for ten minutes thrice a day.
RUDYARD KIPLING
American Notes (1891)

America knows nothing of food, love or art.
ISADORA DUNCAN
(1878-1927)

One finds the same endless amateurishness, so characteristic
of everything American, from politics to cookery—the same
astounding lack of training and vocation.
H.L. MENCKEN
A Book of Prefaces (1917)

The national taste for bad food seems all the more remarkable when one recalls that the United States, more than
any other country of the modern world, has been enriched
by immigrant cuisines.
H.L. MENCKEN
in the Chicago Tribune (1926)

Has America ever developed any indigenous dishes worth
eating? It has, but they are all Aframerican. . . . The black
cooks of the Chesapeake littoral invented stewed terrapin,
chicken a la Maryland, fried soft crabs and panned oysters,
not to mention strawberry shortcake and crab soup. These
are the delicatessen that a Nordic Americano orders when
he is in the mood for feasting, and has money in his jeans.
H.L. MENCKEN
in American Mercury (1927)

What ails our victualry, principally, is the depressing
standardization that ails everything American. . . . The
public cooks have all abandoned specialization, and everyone of them seems bent upon cooking as nearly as possible
like all the rest.
H.L. MENCKEN
Prejudices: Sixth Series (1927)

If in its diverse manifestations, the American table is
distinctly different from ours, that in no way means that
it is fundamentally bad.
PROSPER MONTAGNE
Larousse Gastronomique (1938)

Americans will eat garbage, provided you sprinkle it
liberally with ketchup, mustard, chili sauce, Tabasco sauce,

cayenne pepper, or any other condiment which destroys the original flavor of the dish.
HENRY MILLER
(1891-1980)

At Monticello and the White House, ⌈Thomas Jefferson and his chef, James Hemming⌉ introduced ice cream, macaroni, spaghetti, savoye, cornbread stuffing, waffles, almonds, raisins, vanilla and many more dishes and foods to America. James Hemming and other of Jefferson's servants from these two great houses handed down to generations of Negro and white families alike the repertory of the American table.
LEONARD E. ROBERTS
The Negro Chef Cookbook (1960)

Food, one assumes, provides nourishment; but Americans eat it fully aware that small amounts of poison have been added to improve its appearance and delay its putrefaction.
JOHN CAGE
Silence (1961)

More die in the United States of too much food than too little.
JOHN KENNETH GALBRAITH
(1908 -)

At the time Columbus discovered America, the Indians were using two thousand different foods derived from plants, a figure Europe could hardly have matched.
WAVERLEY ROOT
Eating in America (1976)

Hawaii is probably the only state that ever entered the Union because of food.
WAVERLEY ROOT AND RICHARD DE ROCHEMONT
Eating in America (1976)

The history of American food is the history of the destruction of its taste.
JOHN AND KAREN HESS
The Taste of America (1977)

The United States—a stewpot of cultures—has developed a gastronomy more varied, more distinctive, and more colloquially fascinating than that of any other in the world.
JOHN MARIANI
The Dictionary of American Food and Drink (1983)

Today one hears a lot about 'American cuisine' and I think it is high time we took proper pride in it.
RICHARD NELSON
Richard Nelson's American Cooking (1983)

There is nothing as American as a French chef from the Bronx.
SUSAN HELLER ANDERSON AND DAVID W. DUNLAP
in the New York Times (1985)

The dinner table in America is becoming a trap. People are so scared they don't have any butter or anything. When they talk about healthy food, they usually mean things that don't taste very good.
JULIA CHILD
(1989)

Eating in America is like taking medicine.
ELLEN GOODMAN
(1990)

Something about food is eating us in America today. Something about food unsettles us, makes us nervous. For some strange reason, I think we're afraid of food.
COLMAN ANDREWS
Everything on the Table (1992)

A hungry people listens not to reason, nor cares for justice, nor is bent by any prayers.
SENECA
The Shortness of Life (c. 49 A.D.)

ANARCHY

Who ever heard of a fat man heading a riot, or herding together in turbulent mobs?
WASHINGTON IRVING
(1783-1859)

Principles have no real force except when one is well fed.
MARK TWAIN
(1835-1910)

People of brains are justified in supplying the mob with
the food it likes.
GEORGE GISSING
New Grub Street (1891)

Hunger does not breed reform; it breeds madness and all
the ugly distempers that make an ordered life impossible.
WOODROW WILSON
address to Congress (1918)

Hunger is the mother of anarchy.
HERBERT HOOVER
in a speech (1919)

The first need of the world, more urgent even than bread,
is order. And the second need is food. Hungry people
abandon all restraint, and defy all order.
HERBERT HOOVER
in a speech (1919)

Hungry men have no respect for law, authority or human life.
MARCUS GARVEY
Philosophy and Opinions (1923)

How long would we remain free in a daily, desperate,
overpopulated scramble for bread?
DAVID BRINKLEY
(1920 -)

No bread—no authority.
TURKISH PROVERB

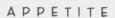

APPETITE Put a knife to thy throat, if thou be a man given to appetite.
PROVERBS 23:2
(c. 350 B.C.)

All the labor of man is for his mouth, and yet the appetite
is not filled.
ECCLESIASTES 6:7
(c. 200 B.C.)

The appetites of the belly and the palate, far from dimin-
ishing as men grow older, go on increasing.
CICERO
To Caelium (c. 50 B.C.)

Reason should direct and appetite obey.
CICERO
On Duties (44 B.C.)

Wisdom does not show itself so much in precept as in
life—a firmness of mind and mastery of appetite.
SENECA
Moral Letters (c. 63 A.D.)

Let the first satisfaction of appetite be always the measure
to you of eating and drinking; and appetite itself the sauce
and the pleasure.
EPICTETUS
Encheiridion (c. 110 A.D.)

Appetite comes with eating . . . but thirst goes away with
drinking.
FRANCOIS RABELAIS
Gargantua (1535)

And through the hall there walked to and fro
A jolly yeoman, marshall of the same,
Whose name was Appetite; he did bestow
Both guests and meate, whenever in they came . . .
EDMUND SPENSER
The Faerie Queene (1590)

O, who can hold a fire in his hand
By thinking on the frosty Caucasus?
Or cloy the hungry edge of appetite
By bare imagination of a feast?
WILLIAM SHAKESPEARE
Richard II (1595-96)

Doth not the appetite alter? A man loves the meat in his youth, that he cannot endure in his age.
WILLIAM SHAKESPEARE
Much Ado About Nothing (1598-99)

Will is the pimp of appetite.
LOPE DE VEGA
The Crazy People of Valencia (c. 1600)

I find no abhorring in my appetite.
JOHN DONNE
Devotions upon Emergent Occasions (1624)

All things require skill but an appetite.
GEORGE HERBERT
Outlandish Proverbs (1640)

'Tis not the meat, but 'tis the appetite
Makes eating a delight.
SIR JOHN SUCKLING
Ballade Upon a Wedding (1641)

If a man want an Appetite to his Victuals, the smell of the Earth new turned up, by digging with a Spade, will procure it.
WILLIAM COLES
The Art of Simpling (1656)

Govern well thy appetite, lest Sin
Surprise thee, and her black attendant Death.
JOHN MILTON
Paradise Lost (1667)

New meat begets a new appetite.
JOHN RAY
English Proverbs (1670)

No man's body is as strong as his appetites, but Heaven has corrected the boundlessness of his voluptuous desires by stinting his strength and contracting his capacities.
JOHN TILLOTSON
(1630-1694)

Keen appetite
And quick digestion wait on you and yours.
JOHN DRYDEN
Cleomenes: The Spartan Hero (1692)

If thou rise with an appetite thou art sure never to sit
down without one.
WILLIAM PENN
Fruits of Solitude (1693)

His thirst he slakes at some poor neighboring brook,
Nor seeks for sauce where Appetite stands cook.
CHARLES CHURCHILL
Gotham (1764)

Now to the meal
Of silence, grandeur, and excess, he drags
His palled unwilling appetite.
PERCY BYSSHE SHELLEY
Queen Mab (1813)

Here is neither want of appetite nor mouths,
Pray heaven we be not scant of meat or mirth.
SIR WALTER SCOTT
(1771-1832)

Our appetites, of one or another kind, are excellent spurs
to our reason, which might otherwise but feebly set about
the great ends of preserving and continuing the species.
CHARLES LAMB
(1775-1834)

And gazed around them to the left and right
With the prophetic eye of appetite.
LORD BYRON
Don Juan (1823)

Conquer your passions, boys, and don't be eager after vittles.
Subdue your appetites, my dears, and you've conquered
human nature.
CHARLES DICKENS
Nicholas Nickleby (1838-39)

Town seems to sharpen a man's appetite.
CHARLES DICKENS
David Copperfield (1849-50)

These appetites are very humiliating weaknesses. That our grace depends so largely upon animal condition is not quite flattering to those who are hyperspiritual.
HENRY WARD BEECHER
(1813-1887)

The best bill of fare I know is a good appetite.
JOSH BILLINGS
His Works Complete (1876)

The appetite is sharpened by the first bites.
JOSE RIZAL
(1861-1896)

Appetite: An instinct thoughtfully implanted by Providence as a solution to the labor question.
AMBROSE BIERCE
The Devil's Dictionary (1906)

When one has an honest appetite all food tastes good: shrimps Newburg with hot rolls and alligator pear salad, or black bread and sour cheese.
KATHLEEN THOMPSON NORRIS
Hands Full of Living (1931)

I have never been able to sacrifice my appetite on the altar of appearance.
ROBERT MORLEY
(1908-1992)

It is difficult to restrain one's appetite by painting pictures of cakes.
CHINESE PROVERB

A waiting appetite kindles many a spite.
ENGLISH PROVERB

One man has no appetite for his food, while another has no food for his appetite.
JEWISH PROVERB

I had rather live
With cheese and garlic in a windmill, far,
Than feed on cates and have him talk to me
in any summer-house in Christendom.
WILLIAM SHAKESPEARE
1 Henry IV (1597-98)

When from a long distant past nothing subsists, after the
people are dead, after the things are broken and scattered,
still, alone, more fragile, but with more vitality, more
unsubstantial, more persistent, more faithful, the smell and
taste of things remain poised for a long time, like souls,
ready to remind us . . .
MARCEL PROUST
(1871-1922)

In our opinion food should be sniffed lustily at table, both
as a matter of precaution and as a matter of enjoyment,
the sniffing of it to be regarded in the same light as the
tasting of it.
E.B. WHITE
Every Day Is Saturday (1934)

In the window I smelled all the food of San Francisco.
There were seafood places out there where the buns were
hot, and the baskets were good enough to eat too; where
the menus themselves were soft with foody esculence as
though dipped in hot broths and roasted dry and good
enough to eat too. Just show me the bluefish spangle on a
seafood menu and I'd eat it; let me smell the drawn butter
and lobster claws. There were places where they special-
ized in thick red roast beef au jus, roast chicken basted in
wine. There were places where hamburgs sizzled on grills
and the coffee was only a nickel. And oh, that pan-fried
chow mein flavored the air that blew into my room from
Chinatown, vying with the spaghetti sauces of North
Beach, the soft-shell crabs of Fisherman's Wharf—nay, the

ribs of Fillmore turning on spits! Throw in the Market
Street chili beans, red hot, and frenchfried potatoes of the
Embarcadero wino night, and steamed clams from
Sausalito across the bay, and that's my ah-dream of San
Francisco. Add fog, hunger-making raw fog, and the throb
of neons in the soft night, the clack of high-heeled beauties,
white doves in a Chinese grocery window...
JACK KEROUAC
On the Road (1957)

Whiffs of burnt sugar drift into the room, the smell of
roasted peanuts, Chinese soups, roast meat, herbs, jasmine,
dust, incense, charcoal fires, they carry fire about in baskets here, it's sold in the streets, the smell of the city is
the smell of the villages upcountry, the smell of the forest.
MARGUERITE DURAS
The Lover (1985)

A rich man's sickness and a poor man's pancake are smelt
a long way off.
BELGIAN PROVERB

The good supper is known by its odor.
MOROCCAN PROVERB

AUSTRALIA If it be true that, while the French eat, the English only
feed, we may fairly add that the Australians 'grub'.
RICHARD TWOPENY
Town Life in Australia (1883)

Of course meat is the staple of Australian life. A working-
man whose whole family did not eat meat three times a
day would indeed be a phenomenon. High and low, rich
and poor, all eat meat to an incredible extent, even in the
hottest weather.
RICHARD TWOPENY
Town Life in Australia (1883)

Australia is inhabited by a people largely carnivorous and addicted to tea.

PHILIP EDWARD MUSKETT
The Art of Living in Australia (1894)

Is it not strange that so far ingenuity, universal approval, or general consensus of opinion, call it what you will, has not up till the present given us an Australian national dish?

PHILIP EDWARD MUSKETT
The Art of Living in Australia (1894)

The Australians stand pretty well alone in being a people who have never invented a new dish or a new drink.

JOHN ROTHENSTEIN
The Life and Death of Conder (1938)

The kings are gone; were never here, anyway.
    Even the aborigines couldn't afford them
In a meagre country with a pantry of grubs and
    white-ants.

JOHN BLIGHT
Larder (c. 1970)

Our eating shows us to be a singularly working-class society, whose food had to be portable and profitable.

MICHAEL BROOK SYMONS
One Continuous Picnic (1982)

BARBECUE

So they broke ⌈a heifer⌉ up forthwith, and cut out the rump-slices in proper form, and wrapped them one slice between two pieces of fat, and laid other slices of raw flesh upon these. The old King burnt them upon the faggots, and poured over them sparkling wine; the young men stood by his side, holding their five-prong forks in their hands. Then, after the rump-slices were burnt, and they had divided the tripes, they chopped up the rest and ran the pieces on spits, and grilled them holding the ends of the spits in their hands.

HOMER
Odyssey (c. 800 B.C.)

And they shall eat the flesh in that night, roast with fire, and unleavened bread; and with bitter herbs they shall eat it.

EXODUS 12:8
(c. 700 B.C.)

The capon burns, the pig falls from the spit,
The clock hath strucken twelve.

WILLIAM SHAKESPEARE
The Comedy of Errors (1592-93)

Weke, weke! so cries a pig prepared to the spit.

WILLIAM SHAKESPEARE
Titus Andronicus (1593-94)

It is no exaggeration to say that many a gubernatorial election in Georgia has been carried by means of votes gained at barbecues.

JOHN R. WATKINS
in The Strand (1898)

Grilling, broiling, barbecuing—whatever you want to call it—is an art, not just a matter of building a pyre and throwing on a piece of meat as a sacrifice to the gods of the stomach.

JAMES BEARD
Beard on Food (1974)

Going to a white-run barbeque is, I think, like going to a gentile internist: It might turn out all right, but you haven't made any attempt to take advantage of the percentages.

CALVIN TRILLIN
(1935 -)

About 27,000 years ago, according to paleontologists, man discovered fire. Later that same day, along about suppertime, it's very likely that he invented barbecue.

GREG JOHNSON AND VINCE STATEN
Real Barbecue (1988)

Barbecue is more than a meal; it's a way of life.

GREG JOHNSON AND VINCE STATEN
Real Barbecue (1988)

You can't reach the pinnacle of true barbecue without hardwood smoke, a slow fire, and time, precious time. No matter how you cut it, slice it, chop it, or pull it, you can't make real barbecue in a hurry.

JOHN EGERTON
in Southern Living (1990)

If the spit is right, then the meat is right.

INDIAN PROVERB

The man with meat seeks fire.

NIGERIAN PROVERB

B E A N S

If pale beans bubble for you in a red earthenware pot, you can often decline the dinners of sumptuous hosts.

MARTIAL
Epigrams (c. 95 A.D.)

Abstain from beans.

PLUTARCH
Of the Training of Children (c. 100 A.D.)

That which Pythagoras said to his scholars of old, may be forever applied to melancholy men: A fabis abstinete, eat no beans.

ROBERT BURTON
The Anatomy of Melancholy (1651)

I was determined to know beans.

HENRY DAVID THOREAU
Walden (1854)

There is no dignity in the bean. Corn, with no affectation of superiority, is, however the child of song. It waves in all literature. But mix it with beans and its high tone is gone. Succotash is vulgar.

CHARLES DUDLEY WARNER
My Summer in a Garden (1870)

Inhabitants of undeveloped nations and victims of natural disasters are the only people who have ever been happy to see soybeans.
FRAN LEBOWITZ
(1950 -)

Beans are not equal to meat.
NAMIBIAN PROVERB

Manchuria produces two products: soya beans and bandits.
CHINESE PROVERB

A bean in liberty is better than a comfit in prison.
ENGLISH PROVERB

Hunger makes beans taste like almonds.
ITALIAN PROVERB

B E E F

Bring hither the fatted calf, and kill it.
LUKE 15:23
(c. 75 A.D.)

What say you to a piece of beef and mustard?
WILLIAM SHAKESPEARE
The Taming of the Shrew (1593-94)

Give then great meals of iron and beef and steel, they will eat like wolves and fight like devils.
WILLIAM SHAKESPEARE
Henry V (1598-99)

I am a great eater of beef, and I believe that does harm to my wit.
WILLIAM SHAKESPEARE
Twelfth Night (1601-02)

He is a terrible fastener on a piece of beef, and you may have hope to stave the guard off sooner.
JOHN EARL
Microcosmographie (1628)

For its merit I will knight it, and then it will be Sir-loin.
KING CHARLES II OF ENGLAND
(1630-1685)

Any of us would kill a cow rather than not have beef.
SAMUEL JOHNSON
Boswell's Life of Johnson (1778)

One far Sir Loin possesses more sublime
Than all the airy castles built by rhyme.
PETER PINDAR
Bozzy and Piozzi (1786)

There's nothing picturesque in beef.
WILLIAM COMBE
Doctor Syntax in Search of the Picturesque (1812)

Please, I wish you would have the cook give me only a six-
ounce steak instead of the regular man-sized one. It's a
terrible sentence the doctor has imposed on me.
WILLIAM HOWARD TAFT
to the White House housekeeper (c. 1910)

Roast Beef, Medium, is not only a food. It is a philosophy.
EDNA FERBER
Roast Beef, Medium (1911)

Beauty will buy no beef.
ENGLISH PROVERB

B E E R

Their beer was strong; their wine was port;
Their meal was large; their grace was short.
MATTHEW PRIOR
An Epitaph (1703)

I have fed purely upon ale; I have eat my ale, drank my
ale, and I always sleep upon ale.
GEORGE FARQUHAR
The Beaux' Stratagem (1707)

They who drink beer will think beer.
WASHINGTON IRVING
The Sketch Book (1820)

Life is with such all beer and skittles;
They are not difficult to please
About their victuals.
C.S. CALVERLEY
Contentment (1872)

Who invented beer only God knows. The books say that
the ancient Egyptians made and drank it, but that seems
somewhat improbable, for there is no sign of maltiness in
their literature, or in their theology.
H. L. MENCKEN
in American Mercury (1931)

All but the desserts in this book goes good with the beer . . .
an' speakin' o' beer, you can stir up most o' these dishes
with one arm an' hold a beer in the other.
MARY LASWELL
Mrs. Rasmussen's Book of One-Arm Cookery (1946)

The Pilgrims landed at Plymouth Rock because they ran
out of beer. A statement from their ship's log: 'For we
could not now take time for further search or consideration; our victuals being much spent, especially beer.'
GEORGE AND BERTHE HERTER
Bull Cook and Authentic Historical Recipes and Practices (1960)

Nothing ever tasted any better than a cold beer on a
beautiful afternoon with nothing to look forward to but
more of the same.
HUGH HOOD
(1924 -)

Beer isn't food; don't be content with it.
UGANDAN PROVERB

T H E
B E L L Y

There's no worse life for a man than to tramp it. It's this
damned belly that gives a man his worst troubles.
HOMER
Odyssey (c. 800 B.C.)

My belly has long been crying cupboard.
TERENCE
The Eunuch (161 B.C.)

It is a hard matter, my fellow citizens, to argue with the
belly, since it has no ears.
PLUTARCH
(46-120 A.D.)

A bellyful is a bellyful.
FRANCOIS RABELAIS
Gargantua (1535)

A full belly doth not engender a subtle wit.
GEORGE PETTIE
Civil Conversations of Stefano Guazzo (1581)

The master of art or giver of wit,
Their belly.
BEN JONSON
The Poetaster (1601)

The rebellions of the belly are the worst.
FRANCIS BACON
(1561-1626)

This ravening fellow has a wolf in his belly.
JOHN FLETCHER
Women pleas'd (1619)

Cold comfort to fill their hungry bellies.
WILLIAM BRADFORD
Of Plymouth Plantation (1620-1647)

He who does not mind his belly will hardly mind any-
thing else.
SAMUEL JOHNSON
Boswell's Life of Johnson (1763)

I can reason down or deny everything except this perpetual
Belly: feed he must and will, and I cannot make him
respectable.
RALPH WALDO EMERSON
Representative Men (1850)

The belly is the coward of the body.
VICTOR HUGO
(1802-1885)

The belly is the reason why man does not mistake himself for God.
FRIEDRICH NIETZSCHE
Beyond Good and Evil (1886)

There's nothing worse than working your belly to no purpose.
ALEXANDER SOLZHENITSYN
One Day in the Life of Ivan Denisovich (1962)

The belly is a demon.
ALEXANDER SOLZHENITSYN
One Day in the Life of Ivan Denisovich (1962)

Grinding one's teeth does not fill one's belly.
ARAB PROVERB

The belly hates a long sermon.
ENGLISH PROVERB

When the belly is full the mind is among the maids.
ENGLISH PROVERB

An empty belly is the best cook.
ESTONIAN PROVERB

The belly is an exacting bailiff.
ESTONIAN PROVERB

The belly overreaches the head.
FRENCH PROVERB

If it were not for the belly, the back might wear gold.
GERMAN PROVERB

An empty belly knows no songs.
GREEK PROVERB

A fat belly did not invent gunpowder.
GREEK PROVERB

A full belly makes a heavy head.
INDIAN PROVERB

A hungry belly and a full belly do not walk the same path.
JAMAICAN PROVERB

What a fat belly cost, I wish I had; what a fat belly does,
I wish on my enemies.
JEWISH PROVERB

The belly is ungrateful—it always forgets we already gave
it something.
RUSSIAN PROVERB

A full belly is deaf to learning.
RUSSIAN PROVERB

The belly rules the mind.
SPANISH PROVERB

BERRIES

A man will pass his summers in health, who will finish
his luncheon with black mulberries.
HORACE
Satires (c. 30 B.C.)

For my part, I confess I fairly swill
And stuff myself with strawberries; and abuse
The doctors all the while, draught, powder, and pill,
And wonder how any sane head can choose
To have their nauseous jalaps, and their bill,
All which, like so much poison, I refuse,
Give me a glut of strawberries; and lo!
Sweet through my blood, and very bones, they go.
LEIGH HUNT
quoting an unidentified Italian poet (1840)

I came across excellent blackberries, and ate of them
heartily. It was mid-day, and when I left the brambles,

I found I had a sufficient meal so that there was no need to go to an inn. Of a sudden it struck me as an extraordinary thing. Here had I satisfied my hunger, without payment, without indebtedness to any man. The vividness with which I felt that this was extraordinary seems to me a shrewd comment on a social state which practically denies a man's right to food unless he have money.

GEORGE GISSING
Commonplace Book (1903)

The Strawberry is not everyone's fruit. To some it brings a sudden rash, and to others twinges of rheumatism. This fact must be admitted and faced.

EDWARD BUNYARD
The Anatomy of Dessert (1934)

⌈The wild blueberry has⌉ a tartness which takes the edge off its sweetness and makes it more interesting, like a beauty spot on the face of a plain woman.

WAVERLEY ROOT
Food (1980)

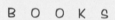

B O O K S

And I took the little book out of the angel's hand, and ate it up; and it was in my mouth sweet as honey: and as soon as I had eaten it, my belly was bitter.

REVELATION 10:10
(c. 95 A.D.)

When I have a little money, I buy books; if any is left, I buy food and clothing.

DESIDERIUS ERASMUS
Familiar Colloquies (1518)

Sir, he hath never fed of the dainties that are bred in a book. He hath not eat paper, as it were; he hath not drunk ink; his intellect is not replenished; he is only an animal, only sensible in the duller parts.

WILLIAM SHAKESPEARE
Love's Labour's Lost (1594-95)

The readers and the hearers like my books,
But yet some writers cannot them digest;
But what care I? for when I make a feast
I would my guests should praise it, not the cooks.
SIR JOHN HARINGTON
Against Writers Who Carp at Other Men's Books (1618)

Many people believe that it is enough to supply the body,
insatiable as it is, with victuals. Far from it—the spirit
requires nourishment just as much as the body, but it
receives it from the printer rather than from the cook. In
short: what a little cake is for the stomach, a little book is
for the soul.
ABRAHAM A SANCTA CLARA
Something for Everybody (1699)

A man may as well expect to grow stronger by always
eating, as wiser by always reading.
JEREMY COLLIER
(1650-1726)

To read without reflecting, is like eating without digesting.
EDMUND BURKE
Letters (1744-1797)

It is no more necessary that a man should remember the
different dinners and suppers which have made him
healthy, than the different books which have made him
wise. Let us see the result of good food in a strong body,
and the result of great reading in a full and powerful mind.
SYDNEY SMITH
Elementary Sketches of Moral Philosophy (1806)

There is more reason for saying grace before a new book
than before dinner.
CHARLES LAMB
Essays of Elia (1823)

To expect a man to retain everything that he has ever read
is like expecting him to carry about in his body everything
that he has ever eaten.
ARTHUR SCHOPENHAUER
Parerga and Paralipomena (1851)

Next to eating good dinners, a healthy man with a benevolent turn of mind must like, I think, to read about them.
WILLIAM MAKEPEACE THACKERAY
(1811-1863)

The man who reads everything is like the man who eats everything: he can digest nothing, and the penalty for cramming one's mind with other men's thoughts is to have no thoughts of one's own.
WOODROW WILSON
in a letter to Ellen Axson (1884)

What is literature compared with cooking? The one is shadow, the other is substance.
E.V. LUCAS
Three Hundred and Sixty-Five Days (And One More) (1926)

More eating of corn bread would I'm sure make a better foundation for an American literature. The white bread we eat is to corn bread what Hollywood will be to real American dramatic literature when it comes.
SHERWOOD ANDERSON
Memoirs (1942)

God have mercy on the sinner
Who must write with no dinner,
No gravy and no grub,
No pewter and no pub,
No belly and no bowels,
Only consonants and vowels.
JOHN CROWE RANSOM
Survey of Literature (1945)

There is a communion of more than our bodies when bread is broken and wine is drunk. And that is my answer, when people ask me: Why do you write about hunger, and not wars or love?
M.F.K. FISHER
(1908-1992)

Howard Nolan, 20, an undergraduate at Brasenose College, Oxford, yesterday finished eating the 566 pages of a copy of the University Examination Statutes, which he began six days earlier.

ANONYMOUS
in the London Daily Telegraph (1966)

Ink runs from the corners of my mouth.
There is no happiness like mine.
I have been eating poetry.

MARK STRAND
Eating Poetry (1968)

BREAD

In the sweat of thy face shalt thou eat bread, till thou return unto the ground; for out of it wast thou taken: for dust thou art, and unto dust shalt thou return.

GENESIS 3:19
(c. 700 B.C.)

Man doth not live by bread only, but by every word that proceedeth out of the Lord doth man live.

DEUTERONOMY 8:3
(c. 650 B.C.)

A crust eaten in peace is better than a banquet partaken in anxiety.

AESOP
The Town Mouse and the Country Mouse (c. 550 B.C.)

If thine enemy be hungry, give him bread to eat.

PROVERBS 25:21
(c. 350 B.C.)

Cast thy bread upon the waters: for thou shalt find it after many days.

ECCLESIASTES 11:1
(c. 200 B.C.)

Christ our passover is sacrificed for us: therefore let us keep the feast, not with the old leaven, neither with the

leaven of malice and wickedness; but with the unleavened bread of sincerity and truth.
I CORINTHIANS 5:7
(c. 35 A.D.)

Give us this day our daily bread.
MATTHEW 6:11
(c. 75 A.D.)

What man is there of you, whom if his son ask bread, will he give him a stone?
MATTHEW 7:9
(c. 75 A.D.)

If your slave commits a fault, do not smash his teeth with your fists; give him some of the hard biscuit which famous Rhodes has sent you.
MARTIAL
Epigrams (c. 95 A.D.)

Two things only the people anxiously desire—bread and circuses.
JUVENAL
Satires (c. 120 A.D.)

You shall find out how salt is the taste of another man's bread, and how hard is the way up and down another man's stairs.
DANTE ALIGHIERI
The Divine Comedy (c. 1320)

I know on which side my bread is buttered.
JOHN HEYWOOD
Proverbs (1546)

Acorns were good 'til bread was found.
FRANCIS BACON
Colours of Good and Evil (1597)

Better halfe a loafe than no bread.
WILLIAM CAMDEN
Remaines (1605)

All sorrows are less with bread.
MIGUEL DE CERVANTES
Don Quixote (1605-15)

Bread made only of the branny part of the meal, which
the poorest sort of people use, especially in time of dearth
and necessity, giveth a very bad and excremental nourishment to the body: it is well called panis canicarius, because
it is more fit for dogs than for men.
TOBIAS VENNER
Via recta (1620)

Yea, even mine own familiar friend, whom I trusted: who
did also eat of my bread, hath laid great wait for me.
THE BOOK OF COMMON PRAYER 41:9
(1662)

This bread of life dropped in thy mouth doth cry:
Eat, eat me, soul, and thou shalt never die.
EDWARD TAYLOR
Poetical Works (c. 1700)

Bread is the staff of life; in which is contained, inclusive,
the quintessence of beef, mutton, veal, venison, partridge,
plum-pudding, and custard: and to render all complete,
there is intermingled a due quantity of water, whose
crudities are also corrected by yeast or barm, through
which means it becomes a wholesome fermented liquor,
diffused through the mass of bread.
JONATHAN SWIFT
A Tale of a Tub (1704)

Bachelor's fare: bread and cheese, and kisses.
JONATHAN SWIFT
Polite and Ingenious Conversation (1738)

I won't quarrel with my bread and butter.
JONATHAN SWIFT
Polite and Ingenious Conversation (1738)

Their learning is like bread in a besieged town: every man gets a little, but no man gets a full meal.

SAMUEL JOHNSON
Boswell's Life of Johnson (1775)

Bread is the fruit of the earth, but it is blessed by the sun's rays.

FRIEDRICH HOLDERLIN
Bread and Wine (1800)

Children should not eat these ⌈beaten⌉ biscuits—nor grown persons either, if they can get any other sort of bread.

ELIZA LESLIE
Directions for Cookery in its Various Branches (1837)

In heaven I hope to bake my own bread and clean my own linen.

HENRY DAVID THOREAU
Journal (1841)

'A loaf of bread,' the Walrus said,
'Is what we chiefly need:
Pepper and vinegar besides
Are very good indeed—
Now if your ready, Oysters dear,
We can begin to feed.'

LEWIS CARROLL
Through the Looking Glass (1871)

I never had a piece of toast
Particularly long and wide,
But fell upon the sanded floor,
And always on the buttered side.

JAMES PAYN
Chamber's Journal (1884)

I have eaten your bread and salt.
I have drunk your water and wine.
The deaths ye died I have watched beside
And the lives ye led were mine.

RUDYARD KIPLING
Departmental Ditties (1886)

The smell of buttered toast simply talked to Toad, and
with no uncertain voice; talked of warm kitchens, of
breakfasts on bright frosty mornings, of cozy parlour
firesides on winter evenings, when one's ramble was over
and slippered feet were propped on the fender; of the
purring of contented cats, the twitter of sleepy canaries.
KENNETH GRAHAME
The Wind in the Willows (1908)

The peasants of Sicily, who have kept their own wheat
and make their own natural brown bread, ah, it is amazing how fresh and sweet and clean their loaf seems, so
perfumed, as home-made bread used all to be before the war.
D.H. LAWRENCE
Sea and Sardinia (1921)

This bread I break was once the oat,
This wine upon a foreign tree
Plunged in its fruit;
Man in the day or wind at night
Laid the crops low, broke the grape's joy.
DYLAN THOMAS
This bread I break (1933)

You can travel fifty thousand miles in America without
once tasting a piece of good bread.
HENRY MILLER
(1891-1980)

Man does not live by bread alone, even presliced bread.
D.W. BROGAN
in Forbes (1964)

If you dip bread into fresh milk and suck before swallow-
ing, it tastes like a feast.
BERNARD MALAMUD
The Fixer (1966)

Good bread is the most fundamentally satisfying of all foods;
and good bread with fresh butter, the greatest of feasts.
JAMES BEARD
Beard on Bread (1973)

Why buy the loaf when you can get free slices?
MATT GROENING
citing an 'old baked goods proverb' in Love is Hell (1984)

Where there's smoke, there's toast.
ANONYMOUS

When you have only two pennies left in the world, buy a loaf of bread with one, and a lily with the other.
CHINESE PROVERB

Bread is better than the song of birds.
DANISH PROVERB

The second side of the bread takes less time to toast.
ENGLISH PROVERB

Bread and salt make the cheeks red.
GERMAN PROVERB

What God gives hard bread he gives sharp teeth.
GERMAN PROVERB

Labor is bitter, but sweet is the bread which it buys.
INDIAN PROVERB

Make your head into a cart and your feet into wheels and you'll get bread.
INDIAN PROVERB

Everything revolves around bread and death.
JEWISH PROVERB

If thou canst not offer wheaten bread, at least offer kind words.
KURDISH PROVERB

However bad the bread it is better than cattle dung.
NIGERIAN PROVERB

A piece of bread in one's pocket is better than a feather in one's hat.
SWEDISH PROVERB

Woe to thee, O land, when thy king is a child, and thy princes eat in the morning!
ECCLESIASTES 10:16
(c. 200 B.C.)

Sixty runners will not overtake him who breakfasts early.
TALMUD: BABA KAMMA
(c. 200 A.D.)

Be uppe betyme and breake thy faste.
JOHN FITZHERBERT
The Boke of Husbandry (1523)

Breakfast makes good memory.
FRANCOIS RABELAIS
Gargantua (1535)

Read o'er this;
And after this; and then to breakfast, with
What appetite you have.
WILLIAM SHAKESPEARE
Henry VIII (1612-13)

I advertise all such as have plethoric and full bodies, especially living at rest, and which are of a phlegmatic temperament, that they not only eschew the use of breakfasts, but also oftentimes content themselves with one meal in a day.
TOBIAS VENNER
Via recta (1620)

Hope is a good breakfast, but it is a bad supper.
FRANCIS BACON
Apophthegms New and Old (1624)

A good, honest, wholesome, hungry breakfast.
IZAAK WALTON
The Compleat Angler (1653)

If I were to fast for my life I would eat a good breakfast in the morning.
JOHN RAY
English Proverbs (1670)

I am one
Who eats breakfast
Gazing at morning-glories.
MATSUO BASHO
(1644-94)

For her own breakfast she'll project a scheme,
Nor take her tea without a stratagem.
EDWARD YOUNG
Love of Fame: The Universal Passion (1725-28)

Thy morning bounties ere I left my home,
The biscuit, or confectionary plum.
WILLIAM COWPER
On the Receipt of My Mother's Picture (1790)

A late breakfast deranges the whole business of the day,
and throws a portion of it on the next, which opens the
door for confusion to enter.
MARY RANDOLPH
The Virginia House-Wife (1824)

His breakfast, water-porridge, humble food:
A barley crust he in his wallet flings;
On this he toils and labours in the wood,
And chops his faggot, twists his band, and sings
As happily as princes and as kings,
With all their luxury: blest is he.
JOHN CLARE
The Woodsman (1830)

He will bring his nightcap with him, for where the
M.F.H. dines he sleeps, and where the M.F.H. sleeps he
breakfasts.
R.S. SURTEES
Handley Cross (1843)

Before breakfast, a man feels but queasily,
And a sinking at the lower abdomen
Begins the day with indifferent omen.
ROBERT BROWNING
The Flight of the Duchess (1844)

Life, within doors, has few pleasanter prospects than a neatly arranged and well-provisioned breakfast table.
NATHANIEL HAWTHORNE
The House of the Seven Gables (1851)

'No business before breakfast, Glum!' says the King. 'Breakfast first, business next.'
WILLIAM MAKEPEACE THACKERAY
The Rose and the Ring (1855)

A meager, unsubstantial breakfast causes a sinking sensation of the stomach and bowels.
PYE HENRY CHAVASSE
Advice to a Wife on the Management of Herself (c. 1870)

Why, sometimes I've believed as many as six impossible things before breakfast.
LEWIS CARROLL
Through the Looking Glass (1871)

If you have to work before breakfast, get your breakfast first.
JOSH BILLINGS
(1818-1885)

In England people actually try to be brilliant at breakfast. This is so dreadful of them. Only dull people are brilliant at breakfast.
OSCAR WILDE
An Ideal Husband (1895)

I am convinced that the Muses and the Graces never thought of having breakfast anywhere but in bed.
MARY ARNIM
Elizabeth and Her German Garden (1898)

The critical period in matrimony is breakfast-time.
A.P. HERBERT
Uncommon Law (1935)

We plan, we toil, we suffer—in the hope of what? A camel-load of idol's eyes? The title deeds of Radio City? The empire of Asia? A trip to the moon? No, no, no, no. Simply to wake just in time to smell coffee and bacon and eggs. And, again I cry, how rarely it happens! But when it does happen—then what a moment, what a morning, what a delight!

J.B. Priestley
(1894-1984)

All happiness depends on a leisurely breakfast.

John Gunther
(1958)

I hadn't eaten anything that morning so I walked over to a restaurant and made short Schrafft of breakfast.

Goodman Ace
The Fine Art of Hypochondria (1966)

BRITISH

Oh! The roast beef of England,
And old England's roast beef.

Henry Fielding
The Grub Street Opera (1731)

In England there are sixty different religions but only one sauce.

Voltaire
(1694-1778)

If an earthquake were to engulf England tomorrow, the English would manage to meet and dine somewhere among the rubbish, just to celebrate the event.

Douglas Jerrold
quoted in Blanchard Jerrold's Life of D. Jerrold (1859)

Dr. Johnson's morality was as English an article as a beefsteak.

Nathaniel Hawthorne
Our Old Home (1863)

The English diet, compared with the German, even with the French, is a sort of back-to-nature diet, a return to cannibalism. This diet, I think, gives heavy feet to the mind—Englishwomen's feet.

Friedrich Nietzsche
Ecce Homo (1888)

Naturally enough, the American colonists, being of English birth and habit, brought English cooking with them . . . its weakness for large chunks and its antipathy to sauces.
H.L. MENCKEN
in the Baltimore Evening Sun (1910)

You are offered a piece of bread and butter that feels like a damp handkerchief and sometimes, when cucumber is added to it, like a wet one.
SIR COMPTON MACKENZIE
describing an English tea party in Vestal Fire (1927)

The tragedy of English cooking is that 'plain' cooking cannot be entrusted to 'plain' cooks.
COUNTESS MORPHY
English Recipes (1935)

To eat well in England you should have breakfast three times a day.
SOMERSET MAUGHAM
(1874-1965)

An Englishman teaching an American about food is like the blind leading the one-eyed.
A.J. LIEBLING
(1904-1963)

It takes some skill to spoil a breakfast—even the English can't do it.
JOHN KENNETH GALBRAITH
(1908 -)

You just put everything in hot water and take them out again after a little while.
ARTHUR HAWKINS
quoting a French chef on English cooking in Who Needs a Cookbook (1968)

British tourists are always happy abroad so long as the natives are waiters.
ROBERT MORLEY
(1908-1992)

Tea to the English is really a picnic indoors.
ALICE WALKER
The Color Purple (1982)

B U T T E R He asked water, and she gave him milk; she brought forth butter in a lordly dish.
JUDGES 5:2
(c. 500 B.C.)

She looketh as butter would not melt in her mouth.
JOHN HEYWOOD
Proverbs (1546)

Honest bread is very well—it's the butter that makes the temptation.
DOUGLAS JERROLD
The Catspaw (1850)

'It was the best butter,' the March Hare meekly replied.
LEWIS CARROLL
Alice's Adventures in Wonderland (1865)

The King said
'Butter, eh?'
And bounced out of bed.
A.A. MILNE
The King's Breakfast (1924)

Guns will make us powerful; butter will only make us fat.
HERMANN GOERING
in a radio broadcast (1936)

He who has overmuch butter greases his boots.
BULGARIAN PROVERB

Be not a baker if your head be of butter.
ENGLISH PROVERB

Butter is gold in the morning, silver at noon, and lead at night.
ENGLISH PROVERB

There are many eatables in the buttery that can't be placed on the table.
ICELANDIC PROVERB

Butter is life.
INDIAN PROVERB

He who has butter on his bread should not go into the sun.
JEWISH PROVERB

C A K E

You've baked this cake;
Even eat it for your pains.
TERENCE
Phormio (161 B.C.)

Would you both eat your cake and have your cake?
JOHN HEYWOOD
Proverbs (1546)

My cake is dough: but I'll in among the rest,
Out of hope of all, but my share of the feast.
WILLIAM SHAKESPEARE
The Taming of the Shrew (1593-94)

He that will have a cake out of the wheat must needs
    tarry the grinding.
Have I not tarried?
Ay, the grinding: but you must tarry the bolting.
Have I not tarried?
Ay, the bolting: but you must tarry the leavening.
Still have I tarried.
Ay, to the leavening: but here's yet in the word 'hereafter'
    the kneading, the making of the cake, the heating of
    the oven and the baking:
Nay, you must stay the cooling too, or you may chance to
    burn your lips.
WILLIAM SHAKESPEARE
Troilus and Cressida (1601-02)

Dost thou think because thou art virtuous, there shall be no more cakes and ale?
WILLIAM SHAKESPEARE
Twelfth Night (1601-02)

There is a thing called wheaten flour, which the sulphury necromantic cooks do mingle with water, eggs, spice and other tragical magical enchantments, and then they put it little by little into a frying-pan of boiling suet, where it is transformed into the form of a flapjack, which in our translation is called a pancake.
JOHN TAYLOR
Jack-a-Lent (1630)

It's food too fine for angels; yet come, take
And eat thy fill! It's Heaven's sugar cake.
EDWARD TAYLOR
Poetical Works (c. 1700)

At length I recollected the thoughtless saying of a great princess, who, on being informed that the country people had no bread, replied, 'Let them eat cake.'
JEAN JACQUES ROUSSEAU
Confessions (1788)

One time I saw two of my young mistresses and some lady visitors eating ginger cakes, in the yard. At that time those cakes seemed to me to be absolutely the most tempting and desireable things that I had ever seen; and I then and there resolved that, if I ever got free, the height of my ambition would be reached if I could get to the point where I could secure and eat ginger cakes in the way that I saw those ladies doing.
BOOKER T. WASHINGTON
(1856-1915)

It is impossible, perhaps under existing laws, to prohibit the sale of spongecake altogether, but there is certainly plenty of warrant . . . for compelling its vendors to label it plainly.
H.L. MENCKEN
in the Baltimore Evening Sun (1910)

The black stove, stoked with coal and firewood, glows like a lighted pumpkin. Eggbeaters whirl, spoons spin round in bowls of butter and sugar, vanilla sweetens the air, ginger spices it; melting, nose-tingling odors saturate the kitchen, suffuse the house, drift out to the world on puffs of chimney smoke. In four days our work is done. Thirty-one cakes, dampened with whiskey, bask on window sills and shelves.
TRUMAN CAPOTE
A Christmas Memory (1956)

You can't eat your cake and have it.
ENGLISH PROVERB

One can get sick of cake, but never of bread.
RUSSIAN PROVERB

CANNIBALISM

Cannibals have the same notion of right and wrong that we have. . . . Eating fallen enemies is only an extra ceremonial. The wrong does not consist in roasting them, but in killing them.
VOLTAIRE
Letter to Frederick the Great (1737)

Go to the meat-market of a Saturday night and see the crowds of live bipeds staring up at the long rows of dead quadrupeds. Does not the sight take a tooth out of the cannibal's jaw? Cannibals? Who is not a cannibal?
HERMAN MELVILLE
Moby Dick (1851)

Cannibal: A gastronome of the old school.
AMBROSE BIERCE
The Devil's Dictionary (1906)

And please don't cook me, kind sirs! I am a good cook myself, and cook better than I cook, if you see what I mean. I'll cook beautifully for you, a perfectly beautiful breakfast for you, if only you won't have me for supper.
J.R.R. TOLKIEN
The Hobbit (1937)

Cannibal: A guy who goes into a restaurant and orders the waiter.
JACK BENNY
(1894-1974)

I believe in compulsory cannibalism. If people were forced to eat what they kill, there would be no more war.
ABBIE HOFFMAN
Revolution for the Hell of It (1968)

I believe that if I ever had to practice cannibalism, I might manage if there were enough tarragon around.
JAMES BEARD
(1903-1985)

Is it progress if a cannibal uses a knife and fork?
STANISLAW LEM
(1921 -)

Cannibals aren't vegetarians, they're humanitarians.
ANONYMOUS

CHEESE

My cheese, my digestion.
WILLIAM SHAKESPEARE
Troilus and Cressida (1601-02)

Digestive cheese, and fruit there sure will be.
BEN JONSON
Epigrams (1616)

As after cheese, nothing to be expected.
THOMAS FULLER
The Church-History of Britain (1655)

Cheese it is a peevish elf,
It digests all things but itself.
JOHN RAY
English Proverbs (1670)

A woman had such an antipathy against cheese that if she did but eat a piece of bread, cut with a knife which a little

before had cut cheese, it would cause a deliquium.
INCREASE MATHER
Remarkable Providences (1684)

Cheese, that the table's closing rites denies,
And bids me with the unwilling chaplain rise.
JOHN GAY
Trivia (1716)

Cheese and salt meat should be sparingly eat.
BENJAMIN FRANKLIN
Poor Richard's Almanac (1733)

To Make an Excellent Winter Cheese—To a cheese of 2
gallons of new milke, take 10 quarts of stroakings and 2
quarts of cream, put it to 4 spoonfuls of rennit, set it
together as hot as ye can from ye Cow . . .
MARTHA WASHINGTON
Booke of Cookery (1749)

Hellish dark, and smells of cheese!
R.S. SURTEES
Handley Cross (1843)

His intimate friends call him 'Candle-ends',
And his enemies, 'Toasted-cheese'.
LEWIS CARROLL
The Hunting of the Snark (1876)

Many's the long night I've dreamed of cheese—
toasted, mostly.
ROBERT LOUIS STEVENSON
Treasure Island (1883)

Poets have been mysteriously silent on the subject of cheese.
G.K. CHESTERTON
(1874-1936)

as I was crawling
through the holes in
a swiss cheese
the other
day it occurred to

me to wonder
what a swiss cheese
would think if
a swiss cheese
could think and after
cogitating for some
time I said to myself
if a swiss cheese
could think
it would think that
a swiss cheese
was the most important
thing in the world
just as everything that
can think at all
does think about itself.

DON MARQUIS
archy does his part (1935)

Never commit yourself to a cheese without having first examined it.

T.S. ELIOT
(1888-1965)

How can you be expected to govern a country that has 246 kinds of cheese?

CHARLES DE GAULLE
(1890-1970)

A cheese may disappoint. It may be dull, it may be naïve, it may be oversophisticated. Yet it remains cheese—milk's leap toward immortality.

CLIFTON FADIMAN
Any Number Can Play (1957)

A poet's hope: to be,
like some valley cheese,
local, but prized elsewhere.

W.H. AUDEN
Shorts II (1976)

An apple pie without some cheese
Is like a kiss without a squeeze.
ANONYMOUS

It is better to scrape the cheese than to peel it.
DANISH PROVERB

Who satisfieth thy mouth with good things; so that thy youth is renewed like the eagle's.
**PSALMS 103:5
(c. 150 B.C.)**

Begin, baby boy: if you haven't had a smile for your parent, then neither will a god think you worth inviting to dinner, nor a goddess to bed.
**VIRGIL
Eclogues (42-37 B.C.)**

Young children and chickens would ever be eating.
**THOMAS TUSSER
Five Hundred Points of Good Husbandry (1557)**

He that is manned with boys and horsed with colts shall have his meat eaten and his work undone.
**WILLIAM CAMDEN
Remaines Concerning Britain (1636)**

I have been assured by a very knowing acquaintance in London, that a young healthy child well nursed is at a year old a most delicious, nourishing, and wholesome food, whether stewed, roasted, baked, or boiled, and I make no doubt that it will equally serve in a fricassee, or a ragout.
**JONATHAN SWIFT
A Modest Proposal for Preventing the Children of Poor People from
    Being a Burden to their Parents or Country (1729)**

Little Jack Horner sat in the corner,
Eating a Christmas pie.

He put in his thumb, and pulled out a plum,
And said, 'What a good boy am I!'
ANONYMOUS
Little Jack Horner (c. 1764)

The youth who follows his appetites too soon seizes the
cup, before it has received its best ingredients, and by
anticipating his pleasures, robs the remaining parts of life
of their share, so that his eagerness only produces a man-
hood of imbecility and an age of pain.
OLIVER GOLDSMITH
(1730-1774)

Oliver Twist has asked for more!
CHARLES DICKENS
Oliver Twist (1837-38)

In order to know whether a human being is young or old,
offer it food of different kinds at short intervals. If young,
it will eat anything at any hour of the day or night.
OLIVER WENDELL HOLMES
(1809-1894)

The first six years of our life make us; all that is added
later is veneer; and yet some say, if a woman can cook a
dinner or dress herself well she has culture enough.
OLIVE SCHREINER
The Story of an African Farm (1883)

It is amusing to see boys eat—when you have not got to
pay for it.
JEROME K. JEROME
The Idle Thoughts of an Idle Fellow (1889)

What is patriotism but the love of good things we ate in
our childhood?
LIN YUTANG
(1895-1976)

Inherent in every adult masculine heart there remains
some of the qualities of a small boy. He is secretly plagued
by a spirit of pyromania and he delights in playing with

fires. In common with the small boy, he enjoys food, lots of food, especially when it is prepared and eaten in an atmosphere of cheerful informality out-of-doors.
ESQUIRE'S HANDBOOK OF FOOD
(1949)

Phone for the fish knives, Norman,
As Cook is a little unnerved;
You kiddies have crumpled the serviettes
And must have things daintily served.
SIR JOHN BETJEMAN
How to Get on in Society (1954)

Over the years since I left home, I have kept thinking about the people I grew up with and about our way of life. I realize how much the bond that held us had to do with food.
EDNA LEWIS
The Taste of Country Cooking (1976)

As a child my family's menu consisted of two choices: take it, or leave it.
BUDDY HACKETT
(1924 -)

A boy is an appetite with a skin pulled over it.
ANONYMOUS

A growing boy has a wolf in his belly.
GERMAN PROVERB

Nowadays, [Chinese] people tend to eat too much. Besides feeding themselves they like to look at a lot of food. How can it please them to lounge about all day for the sake of some delicacies, soiling their mouths with roasts and smoked meats?
ANONYMOUS
(c. 350 A.D.)

CHINESE

Given extensive leisure, what do not the Chinese do? They eat crabs, drink tea, taste spring water, sing operatic airs, fly kites, play shuttle cock, match grass blades, make paper boxes, solve complicated wire puzzles, play mahjongg, gamble and pawn clothing, stew ginseng, watch cock-fights, romp with their children, water flowers, plant vegetables, graft fruits, take afternoon naps, have three meals in one, guess fingers, play at palmistry, gossip about fox spirits, go to operas, beat drums and gongs, play the flute, practise on calligraphy, munch duck gizzards, salt carrots, fondle walnuts, fly eagles, feed carrier pigeons, quarrel with their tailors, go on pilgrimages, visit temples, climb mountains, watch boat races, hold bull fights, take aphrodisiacs, smoke opium, gather at street corners, shout at aeroplanes, fulminate against the Japanese, wonder at the white people, criticize their politicians, read Buddhist classics, practise deep-breathing, hold Buddhist seances, consult fortune tellers, catch crickets, eat melon seeds, gamble for moon cakes, hold lantern competitions, burn rare incense, eat noodles, solve literary riddles, train pot-flowers, send one another birthday presents, kow-tow to one another, produce children, and sleep.

LIN YUTANG
(1895-1976)

If there is anything ⌈the Chinese⌉ are serious about, it is neither religion nor learning, but food.

LIN YUTANG
My Country and My People (1935)

The Chinese do not draw any distinction between food and medicine.

LIN YUTANG
The Importance of Living (1937)

We ⌈the Chinese⌉ eat food for its texture, the elastic or crisp effect it has on our teeth, as well as for fragrance, flavor and color.

LIN YUTANG
(1895-1976)

Food is always better eaten in little doleful pinchfuls off the ends of chopsticks, no gobbling, the reason why Darwin's law of survival applies best to China: if you don't know how to handle a chopstick and stick it in that family pot with the best of them, you'll starve.
JACK KEROUAC
The Dharma Bums (1958)

Cantonese will eat anything in the sky but airplanes, anything in the sea but submarines, and anything with four legs but the table.
AMANDA BENNETT
in the Wall Street Journal (1983)

When it comes to Chinese food I have always operated under the policy that the less known about the preparation the better. . . . A wise diner who is invited to visit the kitchen replies by saying, as politely as possible, that he has a pressing engagement elsewhere.
CALVIN TRILLIN
Third Helpings (1983)

Them Chinamen eat with two little sticks an it is almost impossible to shovel any food in your mouth with em, an so a lot of it wind up on my clothes. No wonder you do not see a lot of fat Chinamen aroun. You would think they would of learnt to use a fork by now.
WINSTON GROOM
Forrest Gump (1986)

Please understand the reason why Chinese vegetables taste so good. It is simple. The Chinese don't cook them, they just threaten them!
JEFF SMITH
The Frugal Gourmet Cooks with Wine (1986)

CHOCOLATE The superiority of the article both for health and nourishment will soon give it the same preference over tea and
coffee in America which it has in Spain.
THOMAS JEFFERSON
in a letter to John Adams (1785)

One lacquey carried the chocolate pot into the sacred
presence; a second, milled and frothed the chocolate with
the little instrument he bore for that function; a third,
presented the favoured napkin; a fourth (he of the two
gold watches), poured the chocolate out. It was impossible
for Monseigneur to dispense with one of these attendants
on the chocolate and hold his high place under the admir-
ing Heavens. Deep would have been the blot upon his
escutcheon if his chocolate had been ignobly waited upon
by only three men; he must have died of two.
CHARLES DICKENS
A Tale of Two Cities (1859)

Tea, although an Oriental,
Is a gentleman at least;
Cocoa is a cad and coward,
Cocoa is a vulgar beast.
G.K. CHESTERTON
The Song of Right and Wrong (1915)

Cocoa? Cocoa! Damn miserable puny stuff, fit for kittens
and unwashed boys.
SHIRLEY JACKSON
The Bird's Nest (1974)

Research tells us that fourteen out of any ten individuals
like chocolate.
SANDRA BOYNTON
Chocolate: The Consuming Passion (1982)

Clear accounts and thick chocolate.
ARGENTINIAN PROVERB

One must drink ⌈Turkish coffee⌉ hot, but in several installments, otherwise it is no good. One takes it in little swallows for fear of burning one's self—in such fashion that in a cafe one hears a pleasant little musical sucking sound.

JEAN DE THEVENOT
The Travels of Monsieur de Thevenot into the Levant (1687)

Coffee is not as necessary to ministers of the reformed faith as to Catholic priests. The latter are not allowed to marry, and coffee is said to induce chastity.

DUCHESS CHARLOTTE-ELISABETH OF ORLEANS
(1652-1722)

Coffee (which makes the politician wise,
And see through all things with his half-shut eyes)
Sent up vapours to the Baron's brain
New stratagems, the radiant lock to gain.

ALEXANDER POPE
The Rape of the Lock (1714)

It is disgusting to note the increase in the quantity of coffee used by my subjects and the amount of money that goes out of the country in consequence. Everybody is using coffee. If possible this must be prevented. My people must drink beer. His Majesty was brought up on beer, and so were his officers. Many battles have been fought and won by soldiers nourished on beer; and the King does not believe the coffee-drinking soldiers can be depended upon to endure hardships or to beat his enemies in case of the occurrence of another war.

FREDERICK THE GREAT
(1777)

Coffee:
Black as the devil,
Hot as hell,

Pure as an angel,
Sweet as love.
CHARLES MAURICE DE TALLEYRAND
(1754-1838)

Coffee detracts nothing from your intellect; on the contrary, your stomach is freed by it and no longer distresses your brain; it will not hamper your mind with troubles but give freedom to its workings. Suave molecules of Mocha stir up your blood, without causing excessive heat; the organ of thought receives from it a feeling of sympathy; work becomes easier and you will sit down without distress to your principal repast which will restore your body and afford you a calm delicious night.
CHARLES MAURICE DE TALLEYRAND
(1754-1838)

Coffee, though a useful medicine, if drunken constantly will at length induce a decay of health, and hectic fever.
JESSE TORREY
The Moral Instructor (1819)

If you want to improve your understanding, drink coffee.
SYDNEY SMITH
(1771-1845)

Sarah Shute
1803-1840
Here lies, cut down like unripe fruit,
The wife of Deacon Amos Shute.
She died of drinking too much coffee,
Anno Dominy eighteen forty.
TOMBSTONE
located in Canaan, New Hampshire (1840)

Coffee is perhaps more nutritious and certainly more permanent in its stimulating effects, than tea. But its influences, on the whole, are less genial. Taken in large quantities, at once, it not only produces morbid vigilance, but affects the brain, so as to occasion vertigo, and a sort of altered consciousness, or confusion of ideas, not amounting to delirium; which I can compare to nothing so well as the feeling when one is lost amid familiar objects, which look strange, and seem to have their positions, in reference to the points of the compass, changed.

DR. DANIEL DRAKE
Principal Diseases of the Interior Valley of North America (1850)

A cup of coffee—real coffee—home-browned, home-ground, home-made, that comes to you dark as a hazel-eye, but changes to a golden bronze as you temper it with cream that never cheated, but was real cream from its birth, thick, tenderly yellow, perfectly sweet, neither lumpy nor frothing on the Java: such a cup of coffee is a match for twenty blue devils, and will exorcise them all.

HENRY WARD BEECHER
Eyes and Ears (1862)

No coffee can be good in the mouth that does not first send a sweet offering of odor to the nostrils.

HENRY WARD BEECHER
Eyes and Ears (1862)

The best proof that tea or coffee are favorable to intellectual expression is that all nations use one or the other as aids to conversation.

PHILIP G. HAMERTON
The Intellectual Life (1873)

The egesta of the whale, found in lumps weighing several pounds in the sea on the coast of Zanzibar, is sold at a high price being held a potent aphrodisiac. A small hollow is drilled in the bottom of the cup and the coffee is poured upon the bit of ambergris it contains; when the oleaginous matter shows in dots amidst the kaymagh, the bubbly froth which floats upon the surface, an expert 'coffee servant' distributes it equally among the guests.

SIR RICHARD BURTON
Love, War and Fancy (c. 1885)

Look here, Steward, if this is coffee, I want tea; but if this is tea, then I wish for coffee.

ANONYMOUS
cartoon caption in Punch (1902)

If you can make a good cup of coffee, you can make any man glad he has left his mother.

MRS. W.T. HAYES
Kentucky Cook Book (1912)

I have measured out my life with coffee spoons.

T.S. ELIOT
The Love Song of J. Alfred Prufrock (1915)

Nothing'll make a father swear before the children quicker than a cup of poor coffee.

KIN HUBBARD
Abe Martin on Things in General (c. 1920)

In Europe the most obstreperous nations are those most addicted to coffee. . . . We rightly speak of a storm in a teacup as the tiniest disturbance in the world, but out of a coffee cup come hurricanes.

ROBERT LYND
The Blue Lion (1923)

In the interim he takes out of another rag-knot a few aromatic seeds called heyl, an Indian product, but of whose scientific name I regret to be wholly ignorant, or a little saffron, and after slightly pounding these ingredients, throws them into the simmering coffee to improve its flavour, for such an additional spicing is held indispensable in Arabia though often omitted elsewhere in the East. Sugar would be a totally unheard of profanation.

FRANCIS TURNER PALGRAVE
quoted in William Ukers' All About Coffee (1935)

The coffee was so strong it snarled as it lurched out of the pot.

BETTY MACDONALD
The Egg and I (1945)

I think if I were a woman I'd wear coffee as a perfume.
JOHN VAN DRUTEN
(1901-1957)

English coffee tastes like water that has been squeezed out of a wet sleeve.
FRED ALLEN
Treadmill to Oblivion (1954)

After insisting on coffee, I realized why the English are big tea drinkers. Just taste their coffee and you'll see the reason.
JOEY ADAMS
Cindy and I (1957)

Even the Turkish coffee turned out to be deadly. If you don't believe me, make it at home some time. Dig up some dirt from your backyard, add a teaspoon of mud, a drop of fertilizer, add hot water, presto!—instant Turkish coffee.
JOEY ADAMS
Cindy and I (1957)

A real art student wears coloured socks, has a fringe and a beard, wears dirty jeans and an equally dirty seaman's pullover, carries a sketch-book, is despised by the rest of society, and loafs in a coffee bar.
JOHN BRATBY
Breakdown (1960)

Actually this seems to be the basic need of the human heart in nearly every great crisis—a good hot cup of coffee.
ALEXANDER KING
I Should Have Kissed Her More (1961)

Coffee in England is just toasted milk.
CHRISTOPHER FRY
in the New York Post (1962)

Never drink black coffee at lunch; it will keep you awake in the afternoon.
JILLY COOPER
How to Survive from Nine to Five (1970)

As with art it is prepared, so one should drink it with art.
ARAB PROVERB

Coffee has two virtues: it is wet and warm.
DUTCH PROVERB

Coffee and tobacco are complete repose.
TURKISH PROVERB

COMPANY

One finds many companions for food and drink, but in a serious business a man's companions are very few.
THEOGNIS
Elegies (c. 500 B.C.)

We should look for someone to eat and drink with before looking for something to eat and drink, for dining alone is leading the life of a lion or wolf.
EPICURUS
Aphorisms (c. 300 B.C.)

You must consider carefully beforehand with whom you are to eat and drink, rather than what you are to eat and drink. For a dinner of meats without the company of a friend is like the life of a lion or a wolf.
EPICURUS
Fragments (c. 285 B.C.)

If you don't know how to live right, give way to those who are expert at it. You have had enough fun, eaten and drunk enough: time you were off.
HORACE
Epistles (c. 20 B.C.)

Always remember if a friend be dining with one, to help him to the choicest parts. Do not, however, press your friend too warmly to eat or drink, but receive him well, and give him good cheer.
BONVESIN DE LA RIVA
Concerning Fifty Gentilities for the Table (c. 1300)

Wife, make us a dinner, spare flesh neither corn;
Make wafers and cakes, for our sheep must be shorn.
At sheep-shearing neighbours none other things crave
But good cheer and welcome, like neighbours to have.
Good fellow, good neighbour, that fellowly guest,
With heartile welcome should have of the best.
Three dishes well dressed, and welcome with all,
Both pleaseth thy friend and becometh thy hall.

THOMAS TUSSER
Five Hundred Points of Good Husbandry (1557)

For whom he means to make an often guest
One dish will serve, and welcome make the rest.

JOSEPH HALL
Virgidemarium (1597)

Sit down and feed, and welcome to our table.

WILLIAM SHAKESPEARE
As You Like It (1599-1600)

I charge thee, invite them all; let in the tide
Of knaves once more: my cook and I'll provide.

WILLIAM SHAKESPEARE
Timon of Athens (1607-08)

Not with whom thou art bred, but with whom thou
art fed.

MIGUEL DE CERVANTES
Don Quixote (1605-15)

With the bread eaten, up breaks the company.

MIGUEL DE CERVANTES
Don Quixote (1605-15)

Tis not the food, but the content,
That makes the table's merriment.

ROBERT HERRICK
Hesperides (1648)

A cheerful look makes a dish a feast.

GEORGE HERBERT
Jacula Prudentum (1651)

He showed me his bill of fare to tempt me to dine with him; poh, said I, I value not your bill of fare, give me your bill of company.
JONATHAN SWIFT
Journal to Stella (1711)

Then from the Mint walks forth the man of rhyme,
Happy to catch me just at dinner-time.
ALEXANDER POPE
Epistle to Dr. Arbuthnot (1735)

When serving a guest, the proper thing is to let him choose his own food. From each dish let him choose the lean, fat, savory or crisp parts. Let him be comfortable. Why 'force-feed' him? I often notice a host piling food upon the guest's bowl and plate, to his annoyance. He is neither a child nor a bride enduring hunger pangs out of modesty. Do not be the provincial woman when waiting upon your guests.
YUAN MEI
The Menu (1797)

With their plain dinner, and pleasant conversation, they pass half an hour and even more; sometimes sitting until 1 o'clock, especially if they have company. If the most illustrious visitors are present, they add nothing to the bread and potatoes, or whatever plain dishes they happen to have on the table, except perhaps some one kind of the best fruit of the season; and they never make any apologies.
WILLIAM A. ALCOTT
Ways of Living (1837)

You can hardly call that house a home to which a man dares not carry a friend without previous notice to his wife or daughter, for fear of finding an ill-dressed, ill-served dinner, together with looks of dismay at the intrusion.
A LADY OF CHARLESTON
The Carolina Housewife (1847)

Who has but once dined his friends, has tasted what it is
to be Caesar.
HERMAN MELVILLE
Moby Dick (1851)

If one guest came he sometimes partook of my frugal meal,
and it was no interruption to conversation to be stirring a
hasty-pudding, or watching the rising and maturing of a
loaf of bread in the ashes, in the meanwhile. But if twenty
came and sat in my house there was nothing said about
dinner. We naturally practised abstinence, as if eating were
a foresaken habit.
HENRY DAVID THOREAU
Walden (1854)

The rule for hospitality and Irish help, is, to have the
same dinner every day throughout the year. At last, Mrs.
O'Shaughnessy learns to cook it to a nicety, the host learns
to carve it, and the guests are well-starved.
RALPH WALDO EMERSON
The Conduct of Life (1860)

Philosopher, whom dost thou most effect,
Stoics austere, or Epicurus' sect?
Friend, 'tis my grave infrangible design
With those to study and with these to dine.
RICHARD GARNETT
Idylls and Epigrams (1869)

It isn't so much what's on the table that matters, as what's
on the chairs.
W.S. GILBERT
(1836-1911)

I hate guests who complain of the cooking and leave bits
and pieces all over the place and cream-cheese sticking to
the mirrors.
SIDONIE COLETTE
Cheri (1920)

Taking food alone tends to make one hard and coarse. . . .
it is only in company that eating is done justice; food must
be divided and distributed if it is to be well received.
WALTER BENJAMIN
One-Way Street (1928)

Lunching with poets, dining late with peers,
I felt that I had come into my own.
SIR JOHN BETJEMAN
Oxford Ode (1938)

What greater restoratives have we poor mortals than a
good meal taken in the company of loving friends?
FLORA THOMPSON
Lark Rise to Candleford (1945)

A freeloader is a confirmed guest. He is the man who is
always willing to come to dinner.
DAMON RUNYON
Short Takes (1946)

While two are eating, one would not know even though
the other should die.
KOREAN PROVERB

A smiling face is half the meal.
LATVIAN PROVERB

CONDIMENTS
At mealtime come thou hither, and eat of the bread, and
dip thy morsel in the vinegar.
RUTH 2:14
(c. 700 B.C.)

The sweetest wine turneth to the sharpest vinegar.
JOHN LYLY
Euphues and His England (1580)

No store-room should be without tarragon vinegar.
COLONEL KENNEY-HERBERT
Culinary Jottings from Madras (1885)

Condiments are like old friends—highly thought of, but often taken for granted.
MARILYN KAYTOR
in Look (1963)

Marmalade in the morning has the same effect on taste buds that a cold shower has on the body.
JEANINE LARMOTH
in Town & Country (1986)

From three things may the Lord preserve us:
From valets much too proud to serve us;
From women smeared with heavy fard, good grief!
From lack of mustard when we eat corned beef.
ANONYMOUS

Mustard makes a weak man wise.
ANONYMOUS

A dull vinegar and a lenient master are good for nothing.
SERBIAN PROVERB

CONFLICT

If thine enemy be hungry, give him bread to eat; and if he be thirsty, give him water to drink: For thou shalt heap coals of fire upon his head.
PROVERBS 25:21-22
(c. 350 B.C.)

Strange to see how a good dinner and feasting reconciles everybody.
SAMUEL PEPYS
Diary (1665)

If thou be hungry, I am angry; let us go fight.
JOHN RAY
English Proverbs (1670)

Oh! God! that bread should be so dear,
And flesh and blood so cheap!
THOMAS HOOD
The Song of the Shirt (1846)

Never argue at the dinner table, for the one who is not hungry always gets the best of it.

RICHARD WHATELY
(1787-1863)

'Let's fight till six, and then have dinner,' said Tweedledum.

LEWIS CARROLL
Through the Looking Glass (1871)

When you get me a good man made out of arguments, I will get you a good dinner with reading you the cookery-book.

GEORGE ELIOT
Middlemarch (1872)

There is nothing to which men, while they have food and drink, cannot reconcile themselves.

GEORGE SANTAYANA
Interpretations of Poetry and Religion (1900)

It is a good rule never to start an argument just before breakfast or enter into a quarrel just before supper. A quarrel that is unavoidable then is likely to be less bitter if the battlers hold off long enough to take a bite of food.

ARTHUR T. JERSILD
in Educational Psychology (1936)

The business of eating, which in common with a crisis or danger brings heterogenous incompatibilities comfortably together, was over and now suddenly we were all fallen apart.

NADINE GORDIMER
The Lying Days (1953)

No one ever filed for divorce on an empty stomach.

MAMA LEONE
in Viva (1977)

Better to have bread and an onion with peace than stuffed fowl with strife.

ARAB PROVERB

He who cannot cut the bread evenly cannot get on well
with people.
CZECH PROVERB

Spread the table and contention will cease.
ENGLISH PROVERB

Quarrel is not a food which is eaten.
GHANIAN PROVERB

In a fight sweetmeats are not distributed.
INDIAN PROVERB

Better to eat bread in peace, than cake amidst turmoil.
SLOVAKIAN PROVERB

CONVERSATION

Do not talk while eating, lest the windpipe act before the
gullet, and life be endangered.
TALMUD: TAANIT
(c. 200 A.D.)

The words of his mouth were softer than butter, having
war in his heart: his words were smoother than oil, and
yet they be very swords.
THE BOOK OF COMMON PRAYER 55:22
(1662)

Dinner was made for eatin', not for talkin'.
WILLIAM MAKEPEACE THACKERAY
Fashnable Fax and Polite Annygoats (1837)

You'll have no scandal while you dine,
But honest talk and wholesome wine.
ALFRED, LORD TENNYSON
To the Rev. F.D. Maurice (1855)

Eating without conversation is only stoking.
MARCELINE COX
Ladies' Home Journal (1943)

A dog will carry his bone to a private nook and do his gnawing undisturbed, but civilized man wants companions who can talk, to nourish his mind as well as his body.
JOHN ERSKINE
The Complete Life (1943)

Women eat when they talk, men talk when they eat.
MALCOLM DE CHAZAL
(1949)

Conversation is the enemy of good wine and food.
ALFRED HITCHCOCK
(1978)

All food is good to eat, but all words are not fit to speak.
HAITIAN PROVERB

Eat, don't ask.
MOORISH PROVERB

COOKBOOKS

The Receipts of cookery are swelled to a Volume, but a good Stomach excels them all.
WILLIAM PENN
Fruits of Solitude (1693)

Even the finest of cookbooks is no substitute for the poorest of dinners.
ALDOUS HUXLEY
(1894-1963)

Judging by the vast amount of cookbooks printed and sold in the United States one would think the American woman a fanatical cook. She isn't.
MARLENE DIETRICH
(1904-1992)

In fact, cookbooks ⌈in the South⌉ outsell everything but the Holy Bible.
JACK AND OLIVIA SOLOMON
Cracklin' Bread and Asfidity (1979)

The novice should call up the best cook he or she knows and listen to what that person says. A friend beats a cookbook hands down; you can't cross-examine a cookbook.
LAURIE COLWIN
Home Cooking (1988)

Cooking has become an art, a noble science; cooks are gentlemen.
ROBERT BURTON
The Anatomy of Melancholy (1651)

As we brew, we must bake.
WILLIAM GODWIN
Caleb Williams (1794)

Cooking may be acquired; roasting is a gift of nature.
ANTHELME BRILLAT-SAVARIN
The Physiology of Taste (1825)

The influence of cookery on domestic happiness must be evident to all those who have had experience of the toils and troubles of married life.
PRUDENCE SMITH
Modern American Cookery (1831)

Not on morality, but on cookery, let us build our strong-hold: there brandishing our frying-pan, as censer, let us offer sweet incense to the Devil, and live at ease on the fat things he has provided for his elect!
THOMAS CARLYLE
Sartor Resartus (1834)

Kissing don't last; cookery do.
GEORGE MEREDITH
The Ordeal of Richard Feverel (1859)

Everything changes. The only thing that remains immovable across the centuries and fixes the character of an individual or a people is cooking.
VICTOR HUGO
(1802-1885)

Cookery means the knowledge of Medea and Circe and of Helen and of the Queen of Sheba. It means the knowledge of all herbs and fruits and balms and spices, and all that is healing and sweet in the fields and groves and all that is savory in meats.

JOHN RUSKIN
(1819-1900)

Progress in civilization has been accompanied by progress in cookery.

FANNIE MERRITT FARMER
The Boston Cooking-School Cook Book (1896)

The culinary art depends on the psychological state of society . . . wherever life is easy and comfortable, it always experiences a considerable development.

AUGUSTE ESCOFFIER
(1847-1935)

Cookery is high art; let us think of it as such, and we shall be properly proud of such triumphs as we achieve. Who would not rather make a delicate strawberry short-cake than play The Maiden's Prayer on the piano? Where is the painted table-scarf that can compare with an honest loaf of milk-white bread?

KATE DOUGLAS WIGGIN
A Book of Dorcas Dishes & Family Recipes (1911)

The chief objection to the New England Puritans, of course, is not that they burned Indians at the stake . . . but that they cursed the country with crude cookery and uneatable victuals.

H.L. MENCKEN
in the Baltimore Evening Sun (1910)

As one star differs from another in glory, so does one family, one region, differ from all the others in its manner of eating, drinking, and cooking.

MARTHA McCULLOCH-WILLIAMS
Dishes and Beverages of the Old South (1913)

Some people make too much of a business of cooking. Properly managed, cooking is the simplest of work, but nowhere is an efficiency expert so needed as in the kitchen

G.F. SCOTSON-CLARK
Eating Without Fears (1924)

In cooking, as in all the arts, simplicity is the sign of perfection.

CURNONSKY
(1873-1956)

Once learnt, this business of cooking was to prove an ever growing burden. It scarcely bears thinking about, the time and labor that man and womankind have devoted to the preparation of dishes that are to melt and vanish in a moment like smoke or a dream, like a shadow, and as a post that hastes by, and the air closes behind them, and afterwards no sign where they went is to be found.

ROSE MACAULAY
Personal Pleasures (1936)

Cooking I look upon as one of the real pleasures of life, and I always chafe a little when my wife assumes complete charge and I am edged out of the kitchen.

LEWIS MUMFORD
quoted in Marian Squire's The Stag at Ease (1938)

Don't think—cook!

LUDWIG WITTGENSTEIN
(1889-1951)

To a large extent we can let others do our cooking for us . . . but unless we too know how to cook, those who prepare our food will prepare it any way they like and we must take what we get.

JOHN ERSKINE
The Complete Life (1943)

All cooking is a matter of time. In general, the more time the better.

JOHN ERSKINE
The Complete Life (1943)

Cooking is like love—it should be entered into with abandon, or not at all.

HARRIET VAN HORNE
in Vogue (1956)

Men do not have to cook their food; they do so for symbolic reasons to show they are men and not beasts.

EDMUND LEACH
(1910-1989)

When I cook, I never measure or weigh anything. I cook by vibration. I can tell by the look and smell of it.

VERTAMAE GROSVENOR
Vibration Cooking (1970)

Cooking is a way of giving and of making yourself desirable.

MICHAEL BOURDIN
(1978)

The only real stumbling block is the fear of failure. In cooking you've got to have a what-the-hell attitude.

JULIA CHILD
(1912 -)

The old White Trash tradition of cooking is still very much alive, especially in the country.

ERNEST MATTHEW MICKLER
White Trash Cooking (1986)

It is better for food to be raw than burnt.

KENYAN PROVERB

You can't cook porridge with a fool.

RUSSIAN PROVERB

Before cooking, one must have provisions.

SENEGALESE PROVERB

Prince Hui's cook was cutting up a bullock. Every blow of his hand, every heave of his shoulders, every tread of his foot, every thrust of his knee, every whshh of rent flesh, every chhk of the chopper, was in perfect rhythm—like the dance of the Mulberry Grove, like the harmonious chords of Ching Shou.
CHUANG TZU
(c. 369-286 B.C.)

Your true cook differs nothing from a poet;
For both have mind, and both
Make it their trade to show it.
EUPHORION
Fabulae Incertae (c. 185 B.C.)

A cook should double one sense have: for he should taster for himself and master be.
MARTIAL
Epigrams (c. 95 A.D.)

I seem to you cruel and too much addicted to gluttony, when I beat my cook for sending up a bad dinner. If that appears to you too trifling a cause, say for what cause you would have a cook flogged.
MARTIAL
Epigrams (c. 95 A.D.)

Food prepared by two cooks is neither hot nor cold.
TALMUD: ERUBIN
(c. 200 A.D.)

Cooks are not to be taught in the kitchen.
JOHN LYLY
Euphues and His England (1580)

'Tis burnt; and so is all the meat.
What dogs are these? Where is the rascal cook?
WILLIAM SHAKESPEARE
The Taming of the Shrew (1593-94)

Sirrah, go hire me twenty cunning cooks.
WILLIAM SHAKESPEARE
Romeo and Juliet (1594-95)

'Tis an ill cook that cannot lick his own fingers.
WILLIAM SHAKESPEARE
Romeo and Juliet (1594-95)

Would the cook were of my mind!
WILLIAM SHAKESPEARE
Much Ado About Nothing (1598-99)

God sends meat and the Devil sends cooks.
THOMAS DELONEY
Works (1600)

Occasional examples of bad temper are inevitable in the case of men and women cooks.
SAINT VINCENT DE PAUL
(1581-1660)

Too many cooks spoil the broth.
SIR BALTHAZAR GERBIER
Discourse of Building (1662)

His cook is his chief merit. The world visits his dinners, not him.
MOLIERE
The Misanthrope (1666)

If something is not right, this is due to carelessness, and it is the cook's fault. If something is good, say why, and when it is bad, pick out its faults. If one does not keep the cook in line, he becomes insolent. Before the food comes, send word down that the food tomorrow must be better.
YUAN MEI
The Menu (1797)

Nowadays, common cooks will put chickens, geese, ducks and pork all in one pot, so that all taste the same. I am afraid that their ghosts must be filing their complaints in the city of the dead.
YUAN MEI
The Menu (1797)

Then receive him as best such an advent becomes,
With a legion of cooks, and an army of slaves!
LORD BYRON
The Irish Avatar (1821)

Yet smelt roast meat, beheld a clear fire shine,
And cooks in motion with their clean arms bared.
LORD BYRON
Don Juan (1823)

A good cook is the peculiar gift of the gods. He must be a
perfect creature from the brain to the palate, from the
palate to the finger's end.
WALTER SAVAGE LANDOR
Imaginary Conversations (1824-53)

We may live without poetry, music and art;
We may live without conscience, and live without heart;
We may live without friends; we may live without books;
But civilized man cannot live without cooks.
EDWARD R. BULWER-LYTTON
Lucile (1860)

Many excellent cooks are spoiled by going into the arts.
PAUL GAUGUIN
(1848-1903)

The cook was a good cook, as cooks go; and as cooks go
she went.
H.H. "SAKI" MUNRO
Reginald (1904)

It is sheer foolhardiness to be arrogant to a cook.
AGNES REPPLIER
Americans and Others (1912)

'But why should you want to shield him?' cried Egbert;
'the man is a common murderer.'

'A common murderer, possibly, but an uncommon cook.'
H.H. "SAKI" MUNRO
Beasts and Super-Beasts (1914)

To the old saying that man built the house but woman made of it a 'home' might be added the modern supplement that woman accepted cooking as a chore but man has made of it a recreation.

EMILY POST
Etiquette (1922)

Neither knowledge or diligence can create a great chef. Of what use is conscientiousness as a substitute for inspiration?

SIDONIE COLETTE
Prisons and Paradise (1932)

The true cook is the perfect blend, the only perfect blend, of artist and philosopher. He knows his worth: he holds in his palm the happiness of mankind, the welfare of generations yet unborn.

NORMAN DOUGLAS
An Almanac (1945)

Too many cooks spoil the brothel.

POLLY ADLER
A House is Not a Home (1953)

A good cook is like a sorceress who dispenses happiness.

ELSA SCHIAPARELLI
Shocking Life (1956)

Monsieur Bourgignon, our chef saucier, told me that by the time a cook is forty he is either dead or crazy.

DAVID OGILVY
Confessions of an Advertising Man (1963)

Anybody can make you enjoy the first bite of a dish, but only a real chef can make you enjoy the last.

FRANCOIS MINOT
in the New York Times (1964)

Almost any woman can cook well if she has plenty to do with. The real test of a cook is to be able to produce a good meal with but little out of which to make it.

BEATRICE VAUGHAN
The Old Cook's Almanac (1966)

Not that there isn't a lot of drudgery in any art—and more in cooking than in most—but if a man has never been pleasantly surprised at the way custard sets or flour thickens, there is not much hope of making a cook of him.
ROBERT FARRAR CAPON
The Supper of the Lamb (1969)

Murder is commoner among cooks than among members of any other profession.
W.H. AUDEN
Forewords and Afterwords (1973)

It is a fundamental fact that no cook, however creative and capable, can produce a dish of a quality any higher than that of its raw ingredients.
ALICE WATERS
Chez Panisse Menu Cookbook (1982)

One cook's a cook, two cooks are half a cook, and three cooks are no cook at all.
ANONYMOUS

When the cook and the steward fall out we hear who stole the butter.
DUTCH PROVERB

The cook and butler are never enemies.
ITALIAN PROVERB

Even were a cook to cook a fly, he would keep the breast for himself.
POLISH PROVERB

Jacob saw that there was corn in Egypt.
GENESIS 42:1
(c. 700 B.C.)

C O R N

Thou shalt offer for the meat offering of thy firstfruits green ears of corn dried by the fire, even corn beaten out

of full ears. And thou shalt put oil upon it, and lay
frankincense thereon: it is a meat offering.
LEVITICUS 2:14-15
(c. 700 B.C.)

Corn shall make the young men cheerful, and new wine
the maids.
ZECHARIAH 9:17
(c. 520 B.C.)

Corne, which is the staffe of life.
EDWARD WINSLOW
Good News from New England (1624)

The corn was orient and immortal wheat, which never
should be reaped, nor was ever sown. I though it had stood
from everlasting to everlasting.
THOMAS TRAHERNE
Centuries of Religious Meditations (c. 1675)

Her corn-cake, in all its varieties of hoe-cake, dodgers,
muffins, and other species . . . was a sublime mystery to
all less practiced compounders.
HARRIET BEECHER STOWE
Uncle Tom's Cabin (1852)

There is a partiality in the North for yellow meal, which
the Southerners regard as only fit for chicken and cattle
feed. The yellow may be sweeter, but I acknowledge I have
never succeeded in making really nice bread from it.
MARION HARLAND
Common Sense in the Household (1893)

The corn that makes the holy bread
By which the soul of man is fed,
The holy bread, the food unpriced,
Thy everlasting mercy, Christ.
JOHN MASEFIELD
The Everlasting Mercy (1911)

A Garth Negro or white cropper would relish corn pone
for dinner or supper, but to have had to eat it for breakfast

would have broken his spirit and made him feel that he
had been cast into the outer darkness by the Cap'n.
WILLIAM BRADFORD HUIE
Mud on the Stars (1942)

Never call it 'Hominy Grits'
Or you will Give Charlestonians fits!
When it comes from the mill, it's 'grist';
After you cook it well, I wist,
You serve 'hominy'! Do not skimp;
Serve butter with it and lots of shrimp.
JUNIOR LEAGUE OF CHARLESTON
Charleston Receipts (1950)

To try to cook without cornmeal in the South is a lost
cause.
SALLIE F. HILL
The Progressive Farmer's Southern Cookbook (1961)

Southern political personalities, like sweet corn, travel
badly. They lose flavor with every hundred yards away
from the patch.
A.J. LIEBLING
The Earl of Louisiana (1961)

Grits
Sits
Right.
ROY BLOUNT, JR.
Song to Grits (1982)

Grits is the first truly American food.
TURNER CATLEDGE
in the New York Times (1982)

Selu came into the world singing. From the top of a
cornstalk she came—strong, ripe, tender. A grown woman.
Kanati, the first man, heard the song. It sounded like
company. Then she gave Kanati her hand and stepped
down. They went home together. Selu took the corn and
went into the kitchen. Soon the kettle was bubbling and

Kanati smelled the most delicious aroma he'd ever known—
the sweet heart of the corn. Kanati felt in harmony with
all that lives.
MARILU AWIAKTA
Selu: Seeking the Corn-Mother's Wisdom (1993)

CUISINE Cuisine is when things taste like themselves.
CURNONSKY
(1873-1956)

After endless luncheons in smart restaurants, endless
tasting, endless talking about food, one inevitably develops
a certain apathy toward elegant cuisine.
JAMES BEARD
Delights and Prejudices (1964)

Dietitians are the worst enemy of the great cuisine. It is
impossible to have low calories in excellent food.
LOUIS VAUDABLE
in Life (1966)

For art, there is no future, it's the living moment, then it's
dead. That's wonderful. Cuisine is like a fireworks display,
nothing remains. It is une fete, rapid, ephemeral.
PAUL BOCUSE
(1978)

DAIRY Every one that useth milk is unskilled in the word of
righteousness: for he is a babe.
HEBREWS 5:13
(c. 65 A.D.)

Good sooth, she is
The queen of curds and cream.
WILLIAM SHAKESPEARE
The Winter's Tale (1610-11)

Milk . . . causeth the body to wax gross, and for amending
of a dry constitution, and for them that are extenuated by

long sickness, or are in a consumption, it is by reason of
the excellent moistening, cooling and nourishing faculty of
it, of singular efficacy.

TOBIAS VENNER
Via recta (1620)

Little Miss Muffet
Sat on a tuffet,
Eating some curds and whey.
Along came a spider,
And sat down beside her,
And frightened Miss Muffet away.

ANONYMOUS
Little Miss Muffet (c. 1805)

Bread, milk, and butter are of venerable antiquity. They
taste of the morning of the world.

LEIGH HUNT
The Seer (1840)

Things are seldom what they seem,
Skim milk masquerades as cream.

W.S. GILBERT
H.M.S. Pinafore (1878)

What the French call Christian milk—milk which has
been baptized.

MARK TWAIN
A Tramp Abroad (1879)

That delightful substance ⌈milk⌉ which comes out of the
wonderful chemistry which God has given the cow for the
delight of the world and the sustenance of children.

CHAUNCEY DEPEW
in a speech to the U.S. Senate (1902)

Milk before wine
I would 'twere mine;
Milk taken after,
Is poison's daughter.

ANONYMOUS

Who drinks boiled buffalo milk will keep his strength
through life.
INDIAN PROVERB

Each glass of curdled milk contains an extra year of life.
IRANIAN PROVERB

D E A T H   Death in all its shapes is hateful to unhappy man, but the
worst is death from hunger.
HOMER
Odyssey (c. 800 B.C.)

But of the tree of the knowledge of good and evil, thou
shalt not eat of it: for in the day that thou eatest thereof
thou shalt surely die.
GENESIS 2:17
(c. 700 B.C.)

They that be slain with the sword are better than they
that be slain with hunger.
LAMENTATIONS 4:9
(c. 575 B.C.)

There is death in the pot.
II KINGS 4:40
(c. 500 B.C.)

Let us eat and drink; for tomorrow we die.
I CORINTHIANS 15:32
(c. 35 A.D.)

More people die from overeating than from under-
nourishment.
TALMUD: SHABBATH
(c. 200 A.D.)

Men dig their Graves with their own Teeth and die more
by those fatal instruments than the Weapons of their
Enemies.
THOMAS MOFFETT
Health's Improvement (1590)

Your worm is your only emperor for diet; we fat all
creatures else to fat us, and we fat ourselves for maggots.
WILLIAM SHAKESPEARE
Hamlet (1600-01)

One doth but breakfast here, another dines, he that liveth
longest doth but sup; we must all go to bed in another
world.
JOSEPH HENSHAW
Horae Succisivae: or, Spare Hours of Meditation (1631)

Decapitation is a gruesome affair but I am condemned to
die that way. . . . Be sure not to forget to eat dried bean
curd with fried peanuts. The two give you the taste of the
best ham.
CHIN SHENG-TAN
instructions to his son in his will (c. 1650)

You've time to get hungry, while you're waiting for
someone's death to get a living.
MOLIERE
The Physician in Spite of Himself (1666)

Hunger is as leisurely a death as breaking upon the wheel.
DANIEL DEFOE
Colonel Jack (1722)

I saw few die of hunger; of eating, a hundred thousand.
BENJAMIN FRANKLIN
Poor Richard's Almanac (1735)

Hanging is an easier death than starving.
WILLIAM DONALDSON
The Life and Adventures of Sir Bartholomew Sapskull (1768)

He hath a fair sepulcher in the grateful stomach of the
judicious epicure—and for such a tomb might be content to
die.
CHARLES LAMB
Essays of Elia (1823)

They put arsenic in his meat
And stared aghast to watch him eat;

They poured strychnine in his cup
And shook to see him drink it up.

A.E. HOUSMAN
A Shropshire Lad (1896)

Here lie the bones
of Joseph Jones
Who ate while he was able;
But once o'er fed
He dropt down dead,
And fell beneath the table.
When from the tomb
To meet his doom
He rises amidst sinners:
Since he must dwell
In heav'n or hell
Take him—which gives best dinners.

TOMBSTONE
Wolverhampton, Staffordshire, England (c. 1900)

Statistics show that of those who contract the habit of
eating very few survive.

WALLACE IRWIN
(1876-1959)

More people will die from hit-or-miss eating than from
hit-and-run driving.

DUNCAN HINES
Adventures in Good Eating (1936)

Now hopping-john was F. Jasmine's very favorite food. She
had always warned them to wave a plate of rice and peas
before her nose when she was in her coffin, to make
certain there was no mistake; for if a breath of life was
left in her, she would sit up and eat, but if she smelled
the hopping-john, and did not stir, then they could just
nail down the coffin and be certain she was truly dead.

CARSON McCULLERS
The Member of the Wedding (1946)

A nuclear power plant is infinitely safer than eating
because 300 people choke to death on food every year.
WASHINGTON GOVERNOR DIXY LEE RAY
(1977)

The heads of parrots, tongues of nightingales,
The brains of peacocks, and of ostriches,
Shall be our food; and, could we get the phoenix,
Though nature lost her kind, she were our dish.
BEN JONSON
Volpone (1606)

My footboy shall eat pheasants, calver'd salmons,
Knots, godwits, lampreys. I myself will have
The beards of barbels serv'd instead of salads,
Oil'd mushrooms, and the swelling unctuous paps
Of a fat pregnant sow, newly cut off.
BEN JONSON
The Alchemist (1610)

What will not luxury taste? Earth, sea, and air,
Are daily ransack'd for the bill of fare.
Blood stuffed in skins is British Christian's food,
And France robs marshes of the croaking brood.
JOHN GAY
Trivia (1716)

If shark's fins remain unyielding it is a fiasco. The Wu
family uses only the upper half of the fins. This is rather
chic.
YUAN MEI
The Menu (1797)

You first parents of the human race . . . who ruined
yourself for an apple, what might you not have done for a
truffled turkey?
ANTHELME BRILLAT-SAVARIN
The Physiology of Taste (1825)

To eat ⌈small birds⌉ a la Brillat Savarin: Take hold of the bird by the bill; open your mouth wide enough to introduce the whole bird into it easily; then shut it, at the same time biting off the bill just at its base; chew properly and swallow.

PIERRE BLOT
Handbook of Practical Cookery (1867)

To eat the lotus of the Nile
And drink the poppies of Cathay.

JOHN GREENLEAF WHITTIER
The Tent on the Beach (1867)

If I can't have too many truffles, I'll do without.

SIDONIE COLETTE
(1873-1954)

Five muffins are enough for any man at any one meal, and the breast and wing of a chicken should suffice without attacking the fibrous legs. Very different, however, is the case of pate de fois gras, sandwiches, oysters, and meringues. I cannot eat too many of these. I make it, therefore, my rule to consume very limited quantities of plain food in order to leave as much room as possible for delicacies.

E.V. KNOX
(1881-1971)

One of the easiet forms of pretense to break down is the pretense of enthusiasm for exotic foods. Just bring on the exotic foods.

ROBERT BENCHLEY
Benchley—or Else! (1947)

A pate is nothing more than a French meat loaf that's had a couple of cocktails.

CAROL CUTLER
Pate: The New Main Course for the 80's (1983)

I sometimes feel that more lousy dishes are presented under the banner of pate than any other.

KINGSLEY AMIS
in the London Illustrated News (1986)

⌈Truffles⌉ are an event, a food that lends an air of luxury to any meal. The first truffle-eaters, citizens of fourteenth-century France, believed that truffles enhanced love. In those days, nearly every new food was considered an aphrodisiac, although the truffle never quite shook off that lovely reputation.
JACQUELINE DEVAL
Reckless Appetites (1993)

The cost takes away the taste.
FRENCH PROVERB

DESSERT

I will make an end of my dinner; there's pippins and cheese to come.
WILLIAM SHAKESPEARE
The Merry Wives of Windsor (1600-01)

Coleridge holds that a man cannot have a pure mind who refuses apple dumplings, I am not certain but he is right.
CHARLES LAMB
Essays of Elia (1823)

A dessert without cheese is like a beautiful woman with only one eye.
ANTHELME BRILLAT-SAVARIN
The Physiology of Taste (1825)

The friendly cow all red and white,
I love with all my heart:
She gives me cream with all her might,
To eat with apple tart.
ROBERT LOUIS STEVENSON
A Child's Garden of Verses (1885)

⌈Shortcake⌉ is a confection of amazing lightness and delicacy—a victual of the fourth dimension, and of such extreme attenuation that its texture suggests that of an evening mist.
H.L. MENCKEN
in the Baltimore Evening Sun (1910)

Should I, after tea and cakes and ices,
Have the strength to force the moment to its crisis.
T.S. ELIOT
The Love Song of J. Alfred Prufrock (1915)

DIETING At the end of every diet, the path curves back to the trough.
MASON COOLEY
(1927 -)

If you wish to grow thinner, diminish your dinner,
And take to light claret instead of pale ale;
Look down with utter contempt upon butter,
And never touch bread till it's toasted—or stale.
H.S. LEIGH
Carols of Cockayne (1869)

I go up and down the scale so often that if they ever perform an autopsy on me they'll find me like a strip of bacon—a streak of lean and a streak of fat.
TEXAS GUINAN
(1884-1933)

It is possible to be so busy going on or off a diet that there isn't time left to enjoy life. Once people ate everything set before them, and had the courage to digest it too.
MARCELENE COX
in Ladies' Home Journal (1942)

Eat, drink and be merry, for tomorrow ye diet.
LEWIS COPELAND
5000 Quotations for All Occasions (1945)

If you want to feel important, go on a diet.
JOEY ADAMS
(1911 -)

I feel about airplanes the way I feel about diets. It seems to me they are wonderful things for other people to go on.
JEAN KERR
The Snake Has All the Lines (1960)

In two decades I've lost a total of 789 pounds. I should be hanging from a charm bracelet.

ERMA BOMBECK
(1927 -)

I've been on a diet for two weeks and all I've lost is two weeks.

TOTIE FIELDS
(1931-1978)

So far I've kept my diet secret but now I might as well tell everyone what it is. Lots of grapefruit throughout the day and plenty of virile young men.

ANGIE DICKINSON
(1932 -)

Cleer eir and walking make good digestioun.

ANONYMOUS
A Diatorie (1430)

Unquiet meals make ill digestions.

WILLIAM SHAKESPEARE
The Comedy of Errors (1592-93)

Born merely for the purpose of digestion.

JEAN DE LA BRUYERE
(1645-1696)

The fate of a nation has often depended on the good or bad digestion of a prime minister.

VOLTAIRE
(1694-1778)

A good eater must be a good man; for a good eater must have a good digestion, and a good digestion depends upon a good conscience.

BENJAMIN DISRAELI
The Young Duke (1831)

Digestion is the great secret of life.

SYDNEY SMITH
Letter to Arthur Kinglake (1837)

DIGESTION

If we could by any means appropriate to our use some of the extraordinary digestive power that a boa constrictor has in his gastric juices, there is really no manner of reason why we should not comfortably dispose of as much of an ox as our stomachs will hold, and one might eat French dishes without the wretchedness of thinking what's to follow.

GEORGE MEREDITH
The Ordeal of Richard Feverel (1859)

Cheerfulness of mind is essential to a good digestion, as a good digestion is essential to cheerfulness of mind.

ABBY MERRILL ADAMS
Sense in the Kitchen (1884)

Happiness is for me largely a matter of digestion.

LIN YUTANG
(1895-1976)

DINING IN

Feed your animals before you sit down to eat.

TALMUD: BERAKOTH
(c. 200 A.D.)

My servant wakes me: 'Master, it is broad day.
Rise from bed. I bring you bowl and comb.
Winter comes and the morning air is chill:
Today Your Honor must not venture abroad.'
When I stay at home, no one comes to call;
What must I do with the long, idle hours?
Setting my chair where a faint sunshine falls
I have warmed wine and opened my poetry-books.

PO CHU-I
My Servant Wakes Me (c. 825 A.D.)

Where's the cook? Is supper ready, the house trimmed, rushes strewed, cobwebs swept?

WILLIAM SHAKESPEARE
The Taming of the Shrew (1593-94)

To feed were best at home;
From thence the sauce to meat is ceremony;
Meeting were bare without it.
WILLIAM SHAKESPEARE
Macbeth (1605-06)

Home, and, being washing-day, dined upon cold meat.
SAMUEL PEPYS
Diary (1666)

No meal is as good as when you have your feet under
your own table.
SCOTT NEARING
(1970)

Better than a feast elsewhere is a meal at home of tea and rice.
JAPANESE PROVERB

Only from your own table can you go away full.
JEWISH PROVERB

Philo swears that he has never dined at home, and it is so:
he never dines at all unless invited out.
MARTIAL
Epigrams (c. 95 A.D.)

**D I N I N G
O U T**

To eat at another man's table is your ambition's height.
JUVENAL
Satires (c. 120 A.D.)

First come, first served.
HENRY BRINKLOW
Complaint of Roderyck Mors (1614)

Who depends upon another man's table often dines late.
JOHN RAY
English Proverbs (1670)

I have heard that people eat most heartily of another
man's meat, that is, what they do not pay for.
WILLIAM WYCHERLEY
The Country Wife (1675)

Ever a glutton, at another's cost,
But in whose kitchen dwells perpetual frost.
JOHN DRYDEN
The Fourth Satire of Persius (1695)

When a man is invited to dinner, he is disappointed if he does not get something good.
SAMUEL JOHNSON
Boswell's Life of Johnson (1777)

Ye diners-out from whom we guard our spoons.
THOMAS BABINGTON MACAULAY
Political Georgics (c. 1850)

Solomon of saloons, and philosophic diner-out.
ROBERT BROWNING
Mr. Sludge, "The Medium" (1864)

After the coffee has been served, the lights are turned down or extinguished, brulee is brought in and placed in the centre of the table upon a pedestal surrounded by flowers. A match is lighted, and after allowing the sulphur to burn entirely off is applied to the brandy, and as it burns it sheds its weird light upon the faces of the company, making them appear like ghouls in striking contrast to the gay surroundings. The stillness that follows gives an opportunity for thoughts that break out in ripples of laughter which pave the way for the exhilaration that ensues.
LAFCADIO HEARN
La Cuisine Creole (1885)

It is very poor consolation to be told that a man who has given one a bad dinner, or poor wine, is irreproachable in private life. Even the cardinal virtues cannot atone for half-cold entrees.
OSCAR WILDE
The Picture of Dorian Gray (1891)

My dinners have never interfered with my business. They have been my recreation. . . . A public banquet, if eaten

with thought and care, is no more of a strain than a
dinner at home.
CHAUNCEY DEPEW
(1834-1928)

Tourists are free spenders and 'eating out' amid country
surroundings is the modern vogue—the prevailing recre-
ational fashion.
DUNCAN HINES
Adventures in Good Eating (1936)

Why should so vast a national expenditure be left entirely
to chance?
DUNCAN HINES
Adventures in Good Eating (1936)

Let us consider for a moment lunch in the country. I do
not mean lunch in the open air, for it is obvious that there
is no meal so heavenly as lunch thus eaten, and I have no
time to dwell upon the obvious.
A.A. MILNE
(1882-1956)

Dining-out is a vice, a dissipation of spirit punished by
remorse.
CYRIL CONNOLLY
The Unquiet Grave (1944)

It's like in posh places, you get to like avocado and spinach
and other way-out foods. So you have them every time. You
learn about wine and that's the scene for awhile. When
you've done all that, then you can go back. You realize that
the waiter's just there to ask you what you want, not what
anyone expects you to want. So if you feel like cornflakes
for lunch, you ask for them, without feeling like a north-
ern comedian.
PAUL MCCARTNEY
(1942 -)

In eating other people's food, one eats until the perspira-
tion flows.
CHINESE PROVERB

DINNER   A puzzle dinner—where you'd be puzzled which dish to try first.
TERENCE
Phormio (161 B.C.)

Givers of great dinners know few enemies.
MARTIAL
Epigrams (c. 95 A.D.)

It is the hope of a good dinner that beguiles you.
JUVENAL
Satires (c. 120 A.D.)

Dinners cannot be long where dainties want.
JOHN HEYWOOD
Proverbs (1546)

He that hath a good dinner knows better the way to supper.
ANONYMOUS
Fair Maid of Bristow (1605)

His dinner is his other work, for he sweats at it as much as at labor.
JOHN EARL
Microcosmographie (1628)

Corydon and Thyrsis met,
Are at their savoury dinner set,
Of herbs, and other country messes,
Which the neat-handed Phillis dresses.
JOHN MILTON
L'Allegro (1632)

At dinner my man appears.
GEORGE HERBERT
Jacula Prudentum (1651)

My wife had got ready a very fine dinner—viz., a dish of marrow-bones; a leg of mutton; a loin of veal; a dish of fowl; three pullets and two dozens of larks all in a dish;

a great tart, a neat's tongue, a dish of anchovies, a dish of prawns, and cheese.
SAMUEL PEPYS
Diary (1660)

A good dinner, and company.
SAMUEL PEPYS
Diary (1668)

In my own memory dinner has crept by degrees from twelve to three, and where it will fix nobody knows.
RICHARD STEELE
in The Tatler (1710)

We were to do more business after dinner; but after dinner is after dinner—an old saying and a true.
JONATHAN SWIFT
Journal to Stella (1711)

Nice eaters seldom meet with a good dinner.
THOMAS FULLER
Gnomologia (1732)

This was a good dinner enough, to be sure; but it was not a dinner to ask a man to.
SAMUEL JOHNSON
Boswell's Life of Johnson (1763)

A man is in general better pleased when he has a good dinner upon his table, than when his wife talks Greek.
SAMUEL JOHNSON
Boswell's Life of Johnson (1773)

Before dinner men meet with great inequality of understanding.
SAMUEL JOHNSON
Boswell's Life of Johnson (1777)

A man seldom thinks with more earnestness of anything than he does of his dinner.
SAMUEL JOHNSON
in Mrs. Piozzi's Anecdotes (1786)

A dinner lubricates business.
WILLIAM SCOTT
Boswell's Life of Johnson (1791)

One would risk disgust if one saw politics, justice, and one's dinner in the making.
SEBASTIEN CHAMFORT
Maxims and Considerations (1796)

Dinnertime is the most wonderful period of the day and perhaps its goal—the blossoming of the day. Breakfast is the bud.
NOVALIS
(1772-1801)

The dinner in its turn was highly admired; And Mr. Collins begged to know which of his fair cousins the excellence of its cookery was owing. But here he was set right by Mrs. Bennet, who assured him with some asperity that they were very well able to keep a good cook, and that her daughters had nothing to do in the kitchen. He begged pardon for having displeased her. In a softened tone she declared herself not at all offended; but he continued to apologize for about a quarter of an hour.
JANE AUSTEN
Pride and Prejudice (1813)

The hour of dinner includes everything of sensual and intellectual gratification which a great nation glories in producing.
SYDNEY SMITH
in the Edinburgh Review (1819)

When dinner has oppress'd one,
I think it is perhaps the gloomiest hour
Which turns up out of the sad twenty-four.
LORD BYRON
(1788-1824)

That all-softening, over-powering knell,
The tocsin of the soul—the dinner bell.
LORD BYRON
Don Juan (1821)

Always contented with his life,
and with his dinner, and his wife.
ALEXANDER PUSHKIN
(1823)

All human history attests
That happiness for man—the hungry sinner—
Since Eve ate apples, much depends on dinner!
LORD BYRON
Don Juan (1823)

A rich soup; a small turbot; a saddle of venison; an apricot
tart: this is a dinner fit for a king.
ANTHELME BRILLAT-SAVARIN
The Physiology of Taste (1825)

What were a day without a dinner? A dinnerless day!
Such a day had better be a night.
HERMAN MELVILLE
White Jacket (1850)

You need not rest your reputation on the dinners you
give.
HENRY DAVID THOREAU
Walden (1854)

Truth that peeps
Over the glass's edge when dinner's done,
And body gets its sop, and holds its noise,
And leaves soul free a little.
ROBERT BROWNING
Bishop Blougram's Apology (1855)

Oh, better no doubt is a dinner of herbs,
When season'd by love, which no rancor disturbs
And sweeten'd by all that is sweetest in life
Than turbot, bisque, ortolans, eaten in strife!
But if, out of humor, and hungry, alone
A man should sit down to dinner, each one
Of the dishes of which the cook chooses to spoil
With a horrible mixture of garlic and oil,

The chances are ten against one, I must own,
He gets up as ill-tempered as when he sat down.
EDWARD R. BULWER-LYTTON
Lucile (1860)

O hour of all hours, the most bless'd upon earth,
Blessed hour of our dinners.
EDWARD R. BULWER-LYTTON
Lucile (1860)

Dinner was large, luminous, sumptuous.
THOMAS CARLYLE
Reminiscences of Sundry (1867)

A good dinner sharpens wit, while it softens the heart.
JOHN DORAN
(1807-1878)

Drinking, and no thinking, at dinner.
GEORGE MEREDITH
The Adventures of Harry Richmond (1871)

Bad dinners go hand-in-hand with total depravity, while a
well-fed man is already half saved.
ANONYMOUS
The New Kentucky Home Cookbook (1884)

A good dinner is not to be despised. It paves the way for
all the virtues.
LOUISE IMOGEN GUINEY
Goose-Quill Papers (1885)

Jim said you mustn't count the things you are going to
cook for dinner, because that would bring bad luck.
MARK TWAIN
The Adventures of Huckleberry Finn (1885)

All people are made alike—
of bones and flesh and dinner—
Only the dinners are different.
GERTRUDE LOUISE CHENEY
People (1927)

If you knew how your dinner was made, you'd lose your lunch.
SLOGAN OF PEOPLE FOR THE ETHICAL TREATMENT OF ANIMALS (c. 1980)

A good breakfast is no substitute for a large dinner.
CHINESE PROVERB

For a good dinner and a gentle wife you can afford to wait.
DANISH PROVERB

Better a good dinner than a fine coat.
FRENCH PROVERB

New sleeves get a good dinner.
IRANIAN PROVERB

Every dog knows his dinner time.
JAMAICAN PROVERB

DINNER PARTIES

Annius has some two hundred tables, and servants for every table. Dishes run hither and thither, and plates fly about. Such entertainments as these keep to yourselves, ye pompous; I am ill pleased with a supper that walks.
MARTIAL
Epigrams (c. 95 A.D.)

You praise, in three hundred verses, Sabellus, the baths of Ponticus, who gives such excellent dinners. You wish to dine, Sabellus, not to bathe.
MARTIAL
Epigrams (c. 95 A.D.)

A friendly swarry, consisting of a boiled leg of mutton with the usual trimmings.
CHARLES DICKENS
Pickwick Papers (1836-37)

Of all dinners, when it can be managed in any way, the impromptu one is ranked as the most infallibly successful; the enjoyment therein is proportioned to the absence of ceremony, and to the cordial feeling each guest brings with him.
CHARLES PIERCE
The Household Manager (1857)

[Thoreau] declined invitations to dinner-parties, there each was in everyone's way, and he could not meet the individuals to any purpose. 'The make their pride,' he said, 'in making their dinner cost much; I make my pride in making my dinner cost little.' When asked at table what dish he preferred, he answered, 'The nearest.'
RALPH WALDO EMERSON
Thoreau (1862)

The golden rule for giving dinners is, let all dinners be according to the means of the givers. It is a great mistake for people of moderate means to attempt to imitate the dinners of the rich. Also, the smaller the dinner, the better will be the chance of its being well-cooked.
JOHN TIMBS
Lady Bountiful's Legacy (1862)

'O Looking-Glass creatures,' quoth Alice, 'draw near!
'Tis an honor to see me, a favor to hear;
'Tis a privilege high to have dinner and tea
Along with the Red Queen, the White Queen and me!'
LEWIS CARROLL
Through the Looking Glass (1871)

It may be received as an axiom that the social progress of a community is in direct proportion to the number of its dinner parties.
ABBY MERRILL ADAMS
Sense in the Kitchen (1884)

A dinner invitation, once accepted, is a sacred obligation. If you die before the dinner takes place, your executor must attend.
WARD MCALLISTER
Society as I Have Found It (1890)

At a dinner party one should eat wisely but not too well, and talk well but not too wisely.

SOMERSET MAUGHAM
in his diary (1896)

Where the guests at a gathering are well-acquainted, they eat 20 percent more than they otherwise would.

EDGAR WATSON HOWE
Country Town Sayings (1911)

A revolution is not the same as a dinner party.

MAO TSE-TUNG
in a report (1927)

I think this is the most extraordinary collection of talent, of human knowledge, that has ever been gathered together at the White House, with the possible exception of when Thomas Jefferson dined alone.

JOHN F. KENNEDY
address to Nobel Prize winners (1962)

The social dinner is of medieval inefficiency.

JEAN-JACQUES SERVAN-SCHREIBER
in the New York Times (1968)

DISORDERS

As houses well stored with provisions are likely to be full of mice, so the bodies of those that eat much are full of diseases.

DIOGENES THE CYNIC
(c. 390-320 B.C.)

If the bowels be costive, limpet and common shellfish will dispel the trouble, or low-growing sorrel.

HORACE
Satires (c. 30 B.C.)

If you are surprised at the number of our maladies, count our cooks.

SENECA
(4 B.C.-65 A.D.)

Many dishes bring many diseases.
PLINY THE ELDER
(23-79 A.D)

The glutton is like a dog who is never satiated; he becomes disgusting to everyone and, being subject to diarrhea, his body becomes like a sieve.
SAADIA BEN JOSEPH
(892-942 A.D.)

I can not eat but little meat,
My stomach is not good.
WILLIAM STEVENSON
Gammer Gurton's Needle (1566)

The head anointed with the juice of leeks preserveth the hair from falling out. A mouse roasted and given to children to eat remedieth pissing the bed.
ANONYMOUS
The Widdowes Treasure (1595)

Great and late suppers are very offensive to the whole body, especially to the head and eyes, by reason of the multitude of vapors that ascend from the meats that have been plentifully received.
TOBIAS VENNER
Via recta (1620)

The choleric drinks, the melancholic eats, the phlegmatic sleeps.
GEORGE HERBERT
Outlandish Proverbs (1640)

A depraved taste in food is gratified with that which disgusts other people: it is a species of disease.
VOLTAIRE
Philosophical Dictionary (1764)

The allegory of Adam and Eve eating of the tree of evil, and entailing upon their posterity the wrath of God and the loss of everlasting life, admits of no other explanation

than the disease and crime that have flowed from unnatu-
ral diet.
PERCY BYSSHE SHELLEY
Queen Mab (1813)

'There's nothing like eating hay when you're faint,' the
King remarked to her, as he munched away. 'I should
think throwing cold water over you would be better,' Alice
suggested: 'or some sal-volatile.'
'I didn't say there was nothing better,' the King replied. 'I
said there was nothing like it.' Which Alice did not
venture to deny.
LEWIS CARROLL
Through the Looking Glass (1871)

Many are suffering, and many are going into the grave,
because of the indulgence of appetite. They eat what suits
their perverted taste, thus weakening the digestive organs
and injuring their power to assimilate the food that is to
sustain life. This brings on acute disease, and too often
death follows. The delicate organism of the body is worn
out by the suicidal practices of those who ought to know
better.
ELLEN G. WHITE
Testimonies (1900)

Sedentary life, rich and sophisticated food, laziness, and
comfortable chairs conduce to a slackness of the large
bowel, with manifold troubles as a result.
V.H. MOTTRAM
Food and the Family (1925)

I wish my ulcers and I could get together on a mutually
satisfactory diet.
IRVIN S. COBB
(1876-1944)

Schizophrenia beats dining alone.
ANONYMOUS

D I V I N E

A land flowing with milk and honey.
Exodus 3:8
(c. 700 B.C.)

Behold, a virgin shall conceive, and bear a son, and shall call his name Immanuel. Butter and honey shall he eat, that he may know to refuse the evil, and choose the good.
Isaiah 7:14
(c. 700 B.C.)

O nights and suppers of gods!
Horace
Satires (c. 30 B.C.)

When someone asked him how it was possible to eat acceptably to the gods, he said, If it is done graciously and fairly and restrainedly and decently, is it not also done acceptably to the gods?
Epictetus
Discourses (c. 110 A.D.)

Miracles do occur, but they rarely provide food.
Talmud: Shabbath
(c. 200 A.D.)

In comparison with the stars, what is more trifling a matter than my dinner?
Saint Augustine
Soliloquies (c. 387 A.D.)

My soul tasted that heavenly food, which gives new appetite while it satiates.
Dante Alighieri
The Divine Comedy (c. 1320)

A dish fit for the gods.
William Shakespeare
Julius Caesar (1599-1600)

He rained down manna also upon them for to eat: and
gave them food from heaven. So man did eat angels' food:
for he sent them meat enough.
**THE BOOK OF COMMON PRAYER 78:25
(1662)**

They eat, they drink, and in communion sweet
Quaff immortality and joy.
**JOHN MILTON
Paradise Lost (1667)**

Who never ate his bread in sorrow,
Who never spent the darksome hours
Weeping and watching for the morrow
He knows ye knot, ye heavenly powers.
**JOHANN WOLFGANG VON GOETHE
Willhelm Meister's Apprenticeship (1795-96)**

For he on honey-dew hath fed,
And drunk the milk of Paradise.
**SAMUEL TAYLOR COLERIDGE
Kubla Khan (1797)**

Eat, drink, and play, and think that this is bliss.
There is no heaven but this;
There is no hell
Save earth, which serves the purpose doubly well.
**ARTHUR HUGH CLOUGH
Easter Day (1849)**

The food of the soul is light and space.
**HERMAN MELVILLE
(1819-1891)**

Oh, dainty and delicious!
Food for the gods! Ambrosia for Apicius!
Worthy to thrill the soul of sea-born Venus,
Or titillate the palate of Silenus!
**W.A. CROFFUT
Clam Soup (c. 1910)**

Who but a god could have come up with the divine fact of okra?
JAMES DICKEY
Jericho (1974)

Rely on Heaven for your meals.
CHINESE PROVERB

Fine rice, buffalo's milk, a good wife, white clothes; these are the four marks of Heaven.
INDIAN PROVERB

Eating is heaven.
KOREAN PROVERB

DYSPEPSIA

Behold, my belly is as wine which hath no vent; it is ready to burst like new bottles.
JOB 32:19
(c. 325 B.C.)

A surfeit of the sweetest things,
The deepest loathing to the stomach brings.
WILLIAM SHAKESPEARE
A Midsummer Night's Dream (1595-96)

'Tis not her coldness, father
That chills my labouring breast;
It's that confounded cucumber
I've ate and can't digest.
R.H. BARHAM
The Confession (1835)

Often has the affectionate wife caused her husband a sleepless night and severe distress because she has prepared for him food which did not agree with his constitution or habits.
SARAH JOSEPHA HALE
The Ladies' New Book of Cookery (1852)

When the barbarous practise of stuffing one's guests shall have been abolished, a social gathering will not necessarily imply hard work, and dyspepsia.

A.M. DIAZ
Papers Found in the School Master's Trunk (1875)

In the matter of diet—I have been persistently strict in sticking to the things which didn't agree with me until one or the other of us got the best of it.

MARK TWAIN
(1835-1910)

If Australia is to become in the future, as we all hope it may, a power in the world second to none, the wives and mothers of her husbands and sons must understand the necessity of providing them with a diet which shall make them strong and brave, and root out what now seems to be the curse of the land—dyspepsia—brought on in great measure by badly cooked and therefore indigestible food.

PHILIP EDWARD MUSKETT
The Art of Living in Australia (1894)

Indigestion: A disease which the patient and his friends frequently mistake for deep religious conviction and concern for the salvation of mankind.

AMBROSE BIERCE
The Devil's Dictionary (1906)

I would like to find a stew that will give me heartburn immediately, instead of at 3 o'clock in the morning.

JOHN BARRYMORE
(1882-1942)

E A T I N G

And the people sat down to eat and to drink, and rose up to play.

EXODUS 32:6
(c. 700 B.C.)

Other men live to eat, whereas I eat to live.
SOCRATES
(469-399 B.C.)

If you are a rich man, eat whenever you please; and if you
are a poor man, eat whenever you can.
DIOGENES THE CYNIC
(c. 390-320 B.C.)

A man hath no better thing under the sun, than to eat,
and to drink, and to be merry.
ECCLESIASTES 8:15
(c. 200 B.C.)

There is much in a person's mode of eating.
OVID
(43 B.C.-17 A.D.)

Who planteth a vineyard, and eateth not of the fruit
thereof? Who feedeth a flock, and eateth not of the milk
of the flock?
I CORINTHIANS 9:7
(c. 35 A.D.)

If any would not work, neither should he eat.
II THESSALONIANS 3:10
(c. 50 A.D.)

Take no thought for your life, what ye shall eat or what
ye shall drink.
MATTHEW 6:25
(c. 75 A.D.)

Preach not to them what they should eat, but eat as
becomes you, and be silent.
EPICTETUS
Discourses (c. 110 A.D.)

Such whose sole bliss is eating, who can give but that one
brutal reason why they live.
JUVENAL
Satires (c. 120 A.D.)

Chew well with your teeth and you'll feel it in your toes.
Talmud: Shabbath
(c. 200 A.D.)

The art of dining well is no slight art, the pleasure not a slight pleasure.
Michel de Montaigne
Essays (1588)

Eat enough and it will make you wise.
John Lyly
Midas (1589)

And do as adversaries do in law,
Strive mightily, but eat and drink as friends.
William Shakespeare
The Taming of the Shrew (1593-94)

It was an odd saying of a mad Fellow, who having well dined, clapt his hand upon the board, and protested, that this eating and drinking was a very pretty invention, who ever first found it out.
Sir Thomas Mayerne
Excellent & Approved Experiments in Cookery (1658)

Fame is at best an unperforming cheat;
But 'tis substantial happiness to eat.
Alexander Pope
Prologue Design'd for Mr. D'Urfey's Last Play (1713)

Eat-well is drink-well's brother.
James Kelly
Complete Collection of Scottish Proverbs (1721)

Judicious drank, and greatly daring din'd.
Alexander Pope
The Dunciad (1728)

He that eats well and drinks well should do his duty well.
Thomas Fuller
Gnomologia (1732)

Alas! in truth the man but chang'd his mind,
Perhaps was sick, in love, or had not din'd.
ALEXANDER POPE
Epistle to Several Persons (1734)

He was an ingenious man that first found out eating and drinking.
JONATHAN SWIFT
Polite and Ingenious Conversation (1738)

Their various cares in one great point combine,
The business of their lives—that is, to dine.
EDWARD YOUNG
(1683-1765)

Nothing would be more tiresome than eating and drinking if God had not made them a pleasure as well as a necessity.
VOLTAIRE
(1694-1778)

I take care never to eat anything without knowing what it is.
THOMAS DAY
The History of Sandford and Merton (1789)

Think in the morning. Act in the noon. Eat in the evening. Sleep in the night.
WILLIAM BLAKE
The Marriage of Heaven and Hell (1793)

A man should eat slowly, properly, even if he eats alone.
RABBI NACHMAN OF BRATSLAV
(1772-1811)

I eat well, and I drink well, and I sleep well—but that is all.
THOMAS MORTON
A Roland for an Oliver (1819)

Tell me what you eat, I'll tell you what you are.
ANTHELME BRILLAT-SAVARIN
The Physiology of Taste (1825)

Let the stoics say what they please, we do not eat for the good of living, but because the meat is savory and the appetite is keen.
RALPH WALDO EMERSON
Nature (1836)

Con-found all presents wot eat!
R.S. SURTEES
Handley Cross (1843)

He was a kind and thankful toad, whose heart dilated in proportion as his skin was filled with good cheer; and whose spirits rose with eating, as some men's do with drink.
WASHINGTON IRVING
(1783-1859)

Sense is but an afterbirth; we eat and drink many months before we are conscious of thoughts.
HERMAN MELVILLE
Mardi (1849)

He who dines latest is the greatest man; and he who dines earliest is accounted the least.
HERMAN MELVILLE
White Jacket (1850)

Have we not stood here like trees in the ground
    long enough?
Have we not groveled here long enough, eating and
    drinking like mere brutes?
WALT WHITMAN
Leaves of Grass (1855-1892)

Make merry, comrades, eat and drink—
The lights are growing dim.
ADAM LINDSAY GORDON
Sunlight on the Sea (1867)

A man shouldn't send away his plate till he has eaten his fill.
HENRY JAMES
The American (1877)

Part of the secret of success in life is to eat what you like
and let the food fight it out inside.
MARK TWAIN
(1835-1910)

To eat is human
To digest divine.
MARK TWAIN
(1835-1910)

'Eat, drink, and sport; the rest of life's not worth a fillip,'
    quoth the King;
Methinks the saying saith too much: the swine would say
    the selfsame thing.
SIR RICHARD BURTON
Kasidah (1880)

No gentleman dines before seven.
OSCAR WILDE
The Picture of Dorian Gray (1891)

When I am in trouble, eating is the only thing that
consoles me. Indeed, when I am really in great trouble, as
anyone who knows me intimately will tell you, I refuse
everything except food and drink.
OSCAR WILDE
(1855-1900)

Never speak to a white man till he is fed.
RUDYARD KIPLING
Kim (1901)

Eat: To perform successively (and successfully) the func-
tions of mastication, humectation, and deglutition.
AMBROSE BIERCE
The Devil's Dictionary (1906)

Eat, drink, and be leary.
O. HENRY
The Man Higher Up (1908)

You can't expect a person to dance before he's eaten.
SHOLEM ALEICHEM
Tevye Wins a Fortune (c. 1910)

Eating will never regain its old place at the head of the arts.
H.L. MENCKEN
in the Baltimore Evening Sun (1910)

All eating is a kind of proselytizing—a kind of dogmatiz-
ing—a maintaining that the eater's way of looking at things
is better than the eatee's.
SAMUEL BUTLER
Notebooks (1912)

If there were no such thing as eating, we should have to
invent it to save man from despairing.
DR. WILHELM STEKEL
(1868-1940)

Everybody acts as he feeds.
NORMAN DOUGLAS
Alone (1921)

One cannot think well, love well, sleep well, if one has
not dined well.
VIRGINIA WOOLF
A Room of One's Own (1929)

Beauty is a mystery. You can neither eat it nor make
flannel out if it.
D.H. LAWRENCE
Sex Versus Loveliness (1930)

Keeping time,
Keeping the rhythm in their dancing
As in their living in the living seasons
The time of the seasons and the constellation
The time of milking and the time of harvest
The time of the coupling of man and woman
And that of beasts. Feet rising and falling,
Eating and drinking. Dung and death.
T.S. ELIOT
Four Quartets (1935)

To eat is to appropriate by destruction.
JEAN-PAUL SARTRE
Being and Nothingness (1943)

I never eat when I can dine.
MAURICE CHEVALIER
(1888-1972)

Eating is not merely a material pleasure. Eating well gives a spectacular joy to life and contributes immensely to goodwill and happy companionship. It is of great importance to the morale.
ELSA SCHIAPARELLI
Shocking Life (1954)

Seeing is deceiving. It's eating that's believing.
JAMES THURBER
Further Fables for Our Times (1956)

He didn't care one way or the other . . . 'so long's we can eat, son, y'ear me? I'm hungry, I'm starving, let's eat right now!'—and off we'd rush to eat, whereof, as saith Ecclesiastes, 'It is your portion under the sun.'
JACK KEROUAC
On the Road (1957)

In learning to eat, as in psychoanalysis, the customer, in order to profit, must be sensible of the cost.
A.J. LIEBLING
(1904-1963)

More than once during his life in the camps, Shukhov had recalled the way they used to eat in his village: whole pots full of potatoes, pans of oatmeal, and, in the early days, big chunks of meat. And milk enough to bust their guts. That wasn't the way to eat, he learned in camp. You had to eat with all your mind on the food—like now, nibbling the bread bit by bit, working the crumbs up into a paste with your tongue and sucking it into your cheeks. And how good it tasted—that soggy black bread!
ALEXANDER SOLZHENITSYN
One Day in the Life of Ivan Denisovich (1962)

Eating is the experience out of which our image of the world, and our importance in it, grows.
BRUNO BETTELHEIM
(1903-1990)

When the face is strong, one eats long.
CHINESE PROVERB

The way one eats is the way one works.
CZECH PROVERB

Dine and recline if for two minutes, sup and walk if for two paces.
EGYPTIAN PROVERB

Eat whatever you like, but dress as others do.
EGYPTIAN PROVERB

Eat when you're hungry, and drink when you're dry.
ENGLISH PROVERB

What you have, eat.
HAWAIIAN PROVERB

Eating while seated makes one large of size; eating while standing makes one strong.
INDIAN PROVERB

In eating and in business you should not be modest.
INDIAN PROVERB

God preserve you from one who eats without drinking.
ITALIAN PROVERB

Even though your parents have just died it is still a good thing to rest after eating.
JAPANESE PROVERB

To eat quickly, piss quickly, and count quickly may be regarded as skills.
JAPANESE PROVERB

A man can forget everything—except to eat.
JEWISH PROVERB

What is the proper time to eat? If rich, when you will; if poor, when you can.
JEWISH PROVERB

Eating and paying, that is the way to clear the road.
KENYAN PROVERB

Even a gentleman with a beard three feet long cannot do
without eating.
KOREAN PROVERB

E   G   G   S   You would eat chickens i' the shell.
WILLIAM SHAKESPEARE
Troilus and Cressida (1601-02)

You can't make an omelette without breaking eggs.
MAXIMILIEN ROBESPIERRE
(1758-1794)

The vulgar boil, the learned roast an egg.
ALEXANDER POPE
Epistles to Several Persons (1734)

Eggs beaten once are stiff, eggs beaten a thousand times
are soft.
YUAN MEI
The Menu (1797)

Who can help love the land that has taught us
Six hundred and eighty-five ways to dress eggs.
THOMAS MOORE
The Fudge Family in Paris (1818)

To guess (I do not say determine) whether an egg is good,
shut one eye; frame the egg in the hollow of the hand,
telescope-wise, and look at the sun through it with the
open eye. If you can distinctly trace the yolk and the white
looks clear around it, the chances are in favor of the egg
and the buyer. Or, shake it gently at your ear. If addled, it
will gurgle like water; if there is a chicken inside, you
may distinguish a slight 'thud' against the sides of the egg.
MARION HARLAND
Common Sense in the Household (1893)

An egg is always an adventure: it may be different.
OSCAR WILDE
(1855-1900)

Be content to remember that those who can make omelettes properly can do nothing else.
HILAIRE BELLOC
(1870-1953)

If I were given my choice between an egg and ambrosia for breakfast, I should choose an egg.
ROBERT LYND
(1879-1949)

Nothing stimulates the practiced cook's imagination like an egg.
IRMA ROMBAUER AND MARION ROMBAUER BECKER
The Joy of Cooking (1931)

An omelette so light we had to lay our knives across it and even then it struggled.
MARGARET HALSEY
With Malice Toward Some (1938)

'What'll youse 'ave,' said the waiter,
Reflectively pickin' 'is nose.
'I'll 'ave two boiled eggs, you bastard,
You can't get yer fingers in those.'
GEORGE WALLACE
(1894-1960)

Say!
I like green eggs and ham!
I do! I like them Sam-I-am!
And I would eat them in a boat.
And I would eat them with a goat . . .
And I will eat them in the rain.
And in the dark. And on a train.
And in a car. And in a tree.
They are so good, so good, you see!
THEODOR SEUSS GEISEL
Green Eggs and Ham (1960)

I'm frightened of eggs. Worse than frightened, they revolt me. That white round thing without any hole . . . have you ever seen anything more revolting than an egg yolk breaking and spilling its yellow liquid? Blood is jolly, red. But egg is yellow, revolting. I've never tasted it.
ALFRED HITCHCOCK
(1963)

There is no such thing as a pretty good omelette.
FRENCH PROVERB

The more the eggs, the thicker the soup.
SERBIAN PROVERB

E M E S I S

If thou hast been forced to eat much, arise, go out, and vomit; and it shall refresh thee, and thou shalt not bring sickness upon thy body.
ECCLESIASTICUS 31:25
(c. 180 B.C.)

E U R O P E

For king-like rolls the Rhine,
And the scenery's divine,
And the victuals and the wine
Rather good.
C.S. CALVERLEY
Dover to Munich (1860)

German cookery is an education for the sentiment of hogs.
GEORGE MEREDITH
Sandra Belloni (1864)

German cooking, above all!—how much it has upon its conscience! Soup before the meal, meats cooked to death, fat and mealy vegetables.
FRIEDRICH NIETZSCHE
Ecce Homo (1888)

Italy is so tender—like cooked macaroni—yards and yards of soft tenderness ravelled round everything.

D.H. LAWRENCE
(1885-1930)

It has always been my contention that the people of the Western European countries ate pretty dull food until the discovery of America.

JAMES BEARD
Delights and Prejudices (1964)

In the Puszta (Great Plains) of Bugac, as the local saying goes, the breakfast consists of bread with bacon, the lunch is bacon with bread, and the dinner is a combination of the two.

GEORGE LANG
The Cuisine of Hungary (1971)

The food in Yugoslavia is either very good or very bad. One day they served us fried chains.

MEL BROOKS
(1926 -)

EXERCISE

That old English saying: After dinner sit a while, and after supper walk a mile.

THOMAS COGAN
Haven of Health (1588)

Exercise is a modern superstition, invented by people who ate too much, and had nothing to think about.

GEORGE SANTAYANA
(1863-1952)

Exercise is the most awful illusion. The secret is a lot of aspirin and marrons glaces.

NOEL COWARD
(1899-1973)

Walk 300 paces after meals and you'll keep the doctor away.

CHINESE PROVERB

F A M I L Y   The family that dines the latest
Is in our street esteemed the greatest.
HENRY FIELDING
Letter to Robert Walpole (1743)

Blest be those feasts, with simple plenty crowned, with all
the ruddy family around.
OLIVER GOLDSMITH
The Traveller (1764)

Happy is said to be the family which can eat onions
together. They are, for the time being, separate from the
world, and have a harmony of aspiration.
CHARLES DUDLEY WARNER
My Summer in a Garden (1870)

After a good dinner, one can forgive anybody, even one's
own relations.
OSCAR WILDE
A Woman of No Importance (1893)

It's enormously important that families eat together. One
of the things that's wrong with us is the damn microwave.
Kids come in one by one and fix themselves something to
eat, and the family never sits down together.
SHELBY FOOTE
in Bon Appetit (1993)

Kinfolk under one roof
Look daggers at each other.
Comes the cousin, long absent—
For him, kill the chicken, prepare the feast!
CHINESE PROVERB

Eat a family's food but do not tell its secrets.
JAMAICAN PROVERB

That which is eaten in the parents' house lasts three days.
JAPANESE PROVERB

When there is no bread at home everyone grumbles and
no one is right.
PORTUGUESE PROVERB

Rice and fish are as inseparable as mother and child.
VIETNAMESE PROVERB

F A M I N E

Famine is in thy cheeks,
Need and oppression starveth in thine eyes,
Contempt and beggary hangs upon thy back.
WILLIAM SHAKESPEARE
Romeo and Juliet (1594-95)

They that die by famine die by inches.
MATTHEW HENRY
Commentary on the Bible (1710)

All's good in a famine.
THOMAS FULLER
Gnomologia (1732)

Our stern foe
Had made a league with Famine.
ROBERT SOUTHEY
Joan of Arc (1796)

Famine seems to be the last, the most dreadful resource
of nature.
THOMAS MALTHUS
Essay on the Principle of Population (1798)

F A S T
F O O D

Snatch and eat, snatch and drink, for this world is like a
wedding.
TALMUD: ERUBIN
(c. 200 A.D.)

Quick at meals, quick at work, is a saying as old as the hills.
WILLIAM COBBETT
Advice to Young Men (1829)

'Here, dearest Eve,' he exclaims, 'here is food.' 'Well,' answers she, with the germ of a housewife stirring within her, 'we have been so busy to-day that a picked-up dinner must serve.'
NATHANIEL HAWTHORNE
Mosses from an Old Manse (1846)

We have to get away from the 'bolt it and beat it' idea of eating.
DUNCAN HINES
Adventures in Good Eating (1936)

A McDonald's hamburger patty is a piece of meat with character. Now consider the hamburger bun, it requires a certain type of mind to see the beauty in a hamburger bun. Yet, is it any more unusual to find grace in the curved silhouette of a bun . . . than in the arrangement of textures and colors in a butterfly's wing? Not if you view the bun as an essential material in the art of serving a great many meals fast . . .
RAY KROC
Grinding It Out (1977)

McDonald's is a reductive kitchen for a classless culture that hasn't time to dally on its way to the next rainbow's end.
TOM ROBBINS
in Esquire (1983)

F A S T I N G   Feast today makes fast tomorrow.
PLAUTUS
(254-184 B.C.)

Is this a cause why one should not dine?
PERSIUS
Satires (c. 60 A.D.)

When ye fast, be not, as the hypocrites, of a sad countenance.
MATTHEW 6:16
(c. 75 A.D.)

Fasting is better than prayer.
SAINT CLEMENT
Second Epistle to the Corinthians (c. 150 A.D.)

Fasting is a medicine.
SAINT JOHN CHRYSOSTOM
Homilies (c. 388 A.D.)

When the stomach is full it is easy to talk of fasting.
SAINT JEROME
Letters (c. 400 A.D.)

Fast so that you may condemn excess. Do not believe that
much eating and drinking make the body grow, or enlarge
the understanding; the reverse is true.
MAIMONIDES
Responsa Medica (c. 1200)

When war, pestilence or famine begins to rage, or any
other calamity threatens a country and people, it is the
duty of pastors to exhort the church to fasting, that they
may deprecate the wrath of the Lord.
JOHN CALVIN
Institutes of the Christian Religion (1536)

The popish fasting is murder, whereby many people have
been destroyed, observing the fasts strictly, and, chiefly, by
eating one sort of food, so that nature's strength is thereby
weakened.
MARTIN LUTHER
Table-Talk (1569)

Q. If a man cannot sleep without taking supper, is he
    bound to fast?

A. By no means.
ANTONIO ESCOBAR
Summula casuum conscientiae (1627)

Though a man eat fish till his guts crack, yet if he eat no
flesh he fasts.
JOHN TAYLOR
Jack-a-Lent (1630)

If thou wouldst preserve a sound body, use fasting and walking; if a healthful soul, fasting and praying; walking exercises the body, praying exercises the soul, fasting cleanses both.
FRANCIS QUARLES
(1592-1644)

He who fasteth and doeth no good, saveth his bread, but loseth his soul.
H.G. BOHN
Handbook of Proverbs (1855)

I try now not to eat,
If I owe a beggar crumbs.
JOHN BLIGHT
Bee's Sting (c. 1970)

If a fly gets into the throat of one who is fasting, it is not necessary to pull it out.
AYATOLLAH KHOMEINI
(1900-1989)

Feast, and your halls are crowded; fast and the world goes by.
CHINESE PROVERB

He whose belly is full believes not him who is fasting.
CHINESE PROVERB

It is good fasting when the table is covered with fish.
DANISH PROVERB

Who goes fasting to bed will sleep but lightly.
DUTCH PROVERB

A fast is better than a bad meal.
IRISH PROVERB

He who would enjoy the feast should fast on the eve.
ITALIAN PROVERB

One good deed is better than three days of fasting.
JAPANESE PROVERB

Wherefore do ye spend money for that which is not bread? and your labour for that which satisfieth not? hearken diligently unto me, and eat ye that which is good, and let your soul delight itself in fatness.
ISAIAH 55:2
(c. 700 B.C.)

Fat paunches have lean pates, and dainty bits
Make rich the ribs, but bankrupt quite the wits.
WILLIAM SHAKESPEARE
Love's Labour's Lost (1594-95)

Let me have men about me that are fat;
Sleek-headed men, and such as sleep o' nights.
Yond Cassius has a lean and hungry look;
He thinks too much: such men are dangerous.
WILLIAM SHAKESPEARE
Julius Caesar (1599-1600)

Jack will eat no fat, and Jill doth love no leane.
Yet betwixt them both they lick the dishes cleane.
JOHN CLARKE
Paroemiologia Anglo-Latina (1639)

I am resolved to grow fat, and look young till forty.
JOHN DRYDEN
Secret Love (1668)

Often and little eating makes a man fat.
JOHN RAY
English Proverbs (1670)

Lord, Madame, I have fed like a farmer; I shall grow as fat as a porpoise.
JONATHAN SWIFT
Polite and Ingenious Conversation (1738)

Fat men are the salt and savor of the earth.
HERMAN MELVILLE
Mardi (1849)

Everything I want is either illegal, immoral, or fattening.
ALEXANDER WOOLLCOTT
(1887-1943)

It is better to be plump than to live on baker's bread.
MARJORIE KINNAN RAWLINGS
Cross Creek Cookery (1942)

The whole anti-fat movement astonishes me. We read things written about lard that treat it as the moral equivalent of crack. The upshot of all this hysteria is going to be a generation of teenagers who will be sneaking out to the back shed to smoke not dope but beef brisket. And grandpa is going to slip out after them.
JOHN THORNE
Outlaw Cook (1992)

A fat man has a thin soul.
WELSH PROVERB

F E A S T

The first in banquets, but the last in fight.
HOMER
Iliad (c. 800 B.C.)

And in this mountain shall the Lord of hosts make unto all people a feast of fat things, a feast of wines on the lees, of fat things full of marrow, of wines on the lees well refined.
ISAIAH 25:6
(c. 700 B.C.)

Before the fires reverent stand;
Some take the mighty trays in hand;
Those with the roasted flesh they fill,
Those with the livers broiled. Then still
And reverent, the queen presides,
And every smaller dish provides,
The pious feast to grace.

The guests and visitors draw near.
Divined for, now they all appear,
And take an honoured place.
ANONYMOUS (EDITED BY CONFUCIUS)
Book of Poetry (c. 500 B.C.)

The court sends forth its many lords,
To taste the cheer the king affords,
An hundred vases stand around,
All with choicest spirits crowned.
The mats roast turtle and fresh fish
Present, and many a lordly dish.
And bamboo sprouts, and tender shoots,
And sauces fine, and fragrant fruits,
With their rich perfume fill the air.
Oh! but it was a banquet rare!
ANONYMOUS (EDITED BY CONFUCIUS)
Book of Poetry (c. 500 B.C.)

He that is of a merry heart hath a continual feast.
PROVERBS 15:15
(c. 350 B.C.)

O Soul come back to joys beyond all telling!
Where thirty cubits high at harvest time
The corn is stacked;
Where pies are cooked of millet and bearded maize.
Guests watch the steaming bowls
And sniff the pungency of peppered herbs.
The cunning cook adds slices of bird flesh,
Pigeon and yellow heron and black crane.
They taste the badger stew.
O Soul come back to feed on foods you love!
CHU YUAN
The Great Summons (c. 250 B.C.)

A feast is made for laughter, and wine maketh merry.
ECCLESIASTES 10:19
(c. 200 B.C.)

They are at ease in the Inner Court,
With ivory sticks gold-tipped,
Pick at the fish on a crystal plate, at camel hump.
When bored they drink.

In endless courses serve the Royal Table,
With food like loops and skeins of silk entangled.
Eunuchs stand at the palace gate:
Piebald horses, reined, fret and wait.
TU FU
The Parade of the Beauties (c. 750 A.D.)

Enough is as good as a feast.
JOHN HEYWOOD
Proverbs (1546)

Who riseth from a feast
With that keen appetite that he sits down?
WILLIAM SHAKESPEARE
The Merchant of Venice (1596-97)

The latter end of a fray, and the beginning of a feast,
Fits a dull fighter, and a keen guest.
WILLIAM SHAKESPEARE
1 Henry IV (1597-98)

Our feasts
In every mess have folly,
And the feeders
Digest with it a custom,
I should blush
To see you so attired.
WILLIAM SHAKESPEARE
The Winter's Tale (1610-11)

Yet shall you have to rectify your palate,
An olive, capers, or some better salad
Ushering the mutton; with a short-legged hen,
If we can get her, full of eggs, and then,
Limons, and wine for sauce: to these a coney

Is not to be despaired of for our money;
And though fowl now be scarce, yet there are clerks,
The sky not falling, think we may have larks.

BEN JONSON
Epigrams (1616)

Go to your banquet then, but use delight
So as to rise still with an appetite.

ROBERT HERRICK
Hesperides (1648)

It is not the quantity of the meat, but the cheerfulness of
the guests, which makes the feast; at the feast of the Cen-
taurs they ate with one hand, and had their drawn swords
in the other; where there is no peace, there can be no feast.

EARL OF CLARENDON
History of the Rebellion (1702)

Fools make feasts, and wise men eat them.

BENJAMIN FRANKLIN
Poor Richard's Almanac (1733)

Though you expected nought to eat,
We could have given you some Meat,
Veal that had sucked two well-fed Cows,
Lamb that was fattened in a House,
Bacon well-fed on Indian Corn,
And Chicken crammed both Night & Morn,
Sturgeon likewise adorned the Board,
Of Pears we had a monstrous Hoard.
Half ate, and half untouched remained
For scanty messes we disdained.
Next Strawberries in View appear,
And Apple Tarts bring up the Rear.
These Dainties too were one half left.
Madeira filled each Chink & Cleft.
We ate, we drank, we went to Bed,
And slept as though we all were Dead.

SIR GEORGE TUCKER
Williamsburg, Virginia (1781)

'Twas a public feast and public day—
Quite full, right dull, guests hot, and dishes cold,
Great plenty, much formality, small cheer,
And everybody out of their own sphere.
LORD BYRON
(1788-1824)

And nearer as they came, a genial savour
Of certain stews, and roast-meats, and pilaus,
Things which in hungry mortals' eyes find favour.
LORD BYRON
Don Juan (1823)

The pet of the harem, Rose-in-Bloom,
Orders a feast in his favorite room—
Glittering squares of colored ice,
Sweetened with syrup, tinctured with spice,
Creams, and cordials, and sugared dates,
Syrian apples, Othmanee quinces,
Limes and citrons and apricots,
And wines that are known to Eastern princes.
THOMAS BAILEY ALDRICH
When the Sultan Goes to Ispahan (1859)

And they brought an Owl, and a useful Cart,
And a pound of Rice, and a Cranberry Tart,
And a hive of silvery Bees.
And they brought a Pig, and some green Jack-daws,
And a lovely monkey with lollipop paws,
And forty bottles of Ring-Bo-Ree,
And no end of Stilton Cheese.
EDWARD LEAR
The Jumblies (1871)

And she made him a feast at his earnest wish
Of eggs and buttercups fried with fish;
And she said, 'It's a fact the whole world knows,
That Pobbles are happier without their toes.'
EDWARD LEAR
The Pobble Who Has No Toes (1871)

Now to the banquet we press;
Now for the eggs, the ham,
Now for the mustard and cress,
Now for the strawberry jam!
Now for the tea of our host,
Now for the rollicking bun,
Now for the muffin and toast,
Now for the gay Sally Lunn!

W.S. GILBERT
The Sorcerer (1877)

In the morning they rose in a house pungent with breakfast cookery and they sat at a smoking table loaded with
brains and eggs, ham, hot biscuits, fried apples seething in
their gummed syrups, honey, golden butter, fried steaks,
scalding coffee. Or there were stacked butter-cakes, rum-
colored molasses, fragrant brown sausages, a bowl of wet
cherries, plums, fat, juicy bacon, jam. At the midday meal
they ate heavily: a huge, hot roast of beef, fat, buttered
lima beans, tender corn smoking on the cob, thick red
slabs of sliced tomatoes, rough savory spinach, hot yellow
corn bread, flaky biscuits, deep-dished peach and apple
cobbler spiced with cinnamon, tender cabbage, deep glass
dishes piled with preserved fruits—cherries, pears, peaches.
At night they might eat fried steak, hot squares of grits
fried in egg and butter, pork chops, fish, young fried
chicken.

THOMAS WOLFE
Look Homeward, Angel (1929)

Obeierika's compound was as busy as an anthill. Tempo-
rary cooking tripods were erected on every available space
by bringing together three blocks of sun-dried earth and
making a fire in their midst. Cooking pots went up and
down the tripods, and foo-foo was pounded in a hundred
wooden mortars. Some of the women cooked the yams and
the cassava, and others prepared vegetable soup. Young men

pounded the foo-foo or split firewood. The children made endless trips to the stream.
Chinua Achebe
Things Fall Apart (1958)

On the kitchen table Zina had laid out a feast, even some food he had never seen before. There were stuffed cucumbers, raw Danube herring, fat sausages, pickled sturgeon with mushrooms, assorted meats, wine, cakes and cherry brandy. The fixer, overwhelmed by the spread, felt at first self-conscious. . . . But he swept that aside and ate hungrily those things he had eaten before. He sucked the red wine through delicious chunks of white bread.
Bernard Malamud
The Fixer (1966)

Every great feast has its last course.
Chinese proverb

F   I   S   H

He said unto them: Have ye here any meat? And they gave him a piece of a broiled fish, and of a honeycomb.
Luke 24:42
(c. 75 A.D.)

However wide the dish that bears the turbot, yet the turbot is wider than the dish.
Martial
Epigrams (c. 95 A.D.)

Out in the garden in the moonlight, our servant is scraping a golden carp with so much vigor that the scales fly in every direction—perhaps they go as high as heaven. Those beautiful stars up there might be the scales of our fish.
Anonymous
Before the Repast (c. 800 A.D.)

A man may fish with the worm that hath eat of a king, and eat of the fish that hath fed of that worm.
William Shakespeare
Hamlet (1600-01)

What an idiot is man to believe that abstaining from flesh, and eating fish, which is so much more delicate and delicious, constitutes fasting.

NAPOLEON BONAPARTE
To Barry E. O'Meara at Saint Helena (1817)

They broke the ice and snared a lot of trout. In their cellar they had a barrel of trout prepared exactly like mackerel, and they were more delicious than mackerel because they were finer-grained.

JAMES FENIMORE COOPER
The Pathfinder (1840)

Fishiest of all fishy places was the Try Pots, which well deserved its name; for the pots there were always boiling chowders. Chowder for breakfast, and chowder for dinner, and chowder for supper, till you began to look for fish bones coming through your clothes.

HERMAN MELVILLE
Moby Dick (1851)

Fish is eaten with an ordinary fork, with as much dexterity in the evasion of bones as can be commanded with such an inadequate instrument, and a bit of bread as an aid.

FREDERICK A. STOKES
Good Form: Dinners Ceremonious and Unceremonious (1890)

If I were a jolly archbishop
On Fridays I'd eat all the fish up—
Salmon and flounder and smelts;
On other days everything else.

AMBROSE BIERCE
The Devil's Dictionary (1906)

Once they discovered that the smelt was delicious the Puritan lawmakers, of course, launched upon it their major excommunication. According to the Hon. Henry Cabot Lodge and other New England historians, the penalty for eating a smelt in the year 1862, was a fine of 100 shillings and 10 strokes of the bastinado.

H.L. MENCKEN
in the Baltimore Evening Sun (1910)

Some things can't be ravished. You can't ravish a tin of sardines.
D.H. LAWRENCE
Lady Chatterley's Lover (1928)

Until prohibited by law—and even yet on dark nights—the crackers have had their own ways of obtaining abundant supplies of fresh-water fish—by dynamiting, seining, and toxic stupefaction with sawdust or berries. Their ancestors learned the berry trick from the Indians.
STETSON KENNEDY
Palmetto Country (1942)

A man who has spent much time and money in dreary restaurants moodily chewing filet of sole on the special luncheon is bound to become unmanageable when he discovers that he can produce the main fish course directly, at the edge of his own pasture, by a bit of trickery on a fine morning.
E.B. WHITE
One Man's Meat (1942)

In the selection of seafood you won't go wrong if you stick to things the other fish won't eat.
CHARLES MERRILL SMITH
Instant Status (1972)

They used to have a fish on the menu . . . that was smoked, grilled and peppered. . . . They did everything to this fish but pistol-whip it and dress it in Bermuda shorts.
WILLIAM E. GEIST
in the New York Times (1987)

Eating an anchovy is like eating an eyebrow.
ANONYMOUS

Eat of the fish belly and you will be satisfied.
HAWAIIAN PROVERB

To eat fish one has to go angling.
VIETNAMESE PROVERB

F L A V O R

The flavors are only five in number but their blends are so various that one cannot taste them all.
SUN-TZU
The Art of War (c. 350 B.C.)

The fat in meat, fish, ducks and chicken must be kept in the meat and not allowed to run out, else the flavor is all in the juices.
YUAN MEI
The Menu (1797)

Those who like greasy food might just as well dine on lard. When some dish is hsien, its true flavor is present. Not the least particle of error can be tolerated or you will have missed the mark.
YUAN MEI
The Menu (1797)

Things taste better in small houses.
QUEEN VICTORIA OF ENGLAND
(1819-1901)

The flavor of food should not be apparent immediately but come to you in a matter of moments. The enjoyment of food requires time.
HSIANG JU LIN AND TSUIFENG LIN
Chinese Gastronomy (1969)

When the taste changes with every bite and the last bite is as good as the first, that's Cajun.
PAUL PRUDHOMME
in Cook's Magazine (1985)

If it tastes good, it's trying to kill you.
ROY QUALLEY
quoted in Cyra McFadden's Rain or Shine (1986)

Sour, sweet, bitter, pungent—all must be tasted.
CHINESE PROVERB

F   O   O   D   The asses be for the king's household to ride on; and the
bread and summer fruit for the young men to eat; and the
wine, that such as be faint in the wilderness may drink.
II SAMUEL 16:2
(c. 500 B.C.)

What is food to one man may be sharp poison to others.
LUCRETIUS
On the Nature of Things (c. 60 B.C.)

Food is heaven to the vulgar masses.
ANONYMOUS
Book of Han (c. 100 A.D.)

Food is better than drink up to the age of forty; after forty,
drink is better.
TALMUD: SHABBATH
(c. 200 A.D.)

Food to a man is like oil to a lamp: if it has much, it
shines, if too little, it is quenched; yet a lamp is sooner
extinguished by too much oil than by too little.
JUDAH BEN ASHER
(1270-1349)

Chewing the food of sweet and bitter fancy.
WILLIAM SHAKESPEARE
As You Like It (1599-1600)

Who doth ambition shun,
And loves to live in the sun,
Seeking the food he eats,
And pleased with what he gets.
WILLIAM SHAKESPEARE
As You Like It (1599-1600)

The food that to him now is as luscious as locusts, shall be
to him shortly as bitter as coloquintida.
WILLIAM SHAKESPEARE
Othello (1604-05)

It is the mark of a mean, vulgar and ignoble spirit to dwell
on the though of food before meal times or worse to dwell
on it afterwards, to discuss it and wallow in the remem-
bered pleasures of every mouthful. Those whose minds
dwell before dinner on the spit, and after on the dishes,
are fit only to be scullions.
SAINT FRANCIS DE SALES
Introduction to the Devout Life (1609)

He bringeth forth grass for the cattle: and green herb for
the service of men; that he may bring food out of the
earth, and wine that maketh glad the heart of man: and
oil to make him a cheerful countenance, and bread to
strengthen man's heart.
THE BOOK OF COMMON PRAYER 104:14
(1662)

It's good food and not fine words that keeps me alive.
MOLIERE
The Wise Women (1672)

When food is scarce, and when food is plenty, a wolf
grows bold.
JAMES FENIMORE COOPER
The Last of the Mohicans (1826)

The body craves food only that the mind may think.
WILLIAM GILMORE SIMMS
The Partisan (1835)

As particular food begets particular dreams, so particular
experiences or books particular feelings or beliefs.
HERMAN MELVILLE
The Confidence Man (1857)

The most interesting thing in the world is to find out
how the next man gets his vittles.
RUDYARD KIPLING
Captains Courageous (1897)

Food is a weapon.
MAXIM LITVINOV
in a statement to Herbert Hoover (1922)

Strange how one's thoughts turn to food when there is nothing else to think of.
JOHN COLTON AND CLEMENCE RANDOLPH
Rain (1923)

Grub first, then ethics.
BERTOLT BRECHT
Threepenny Opera (1928)

Another sad comestive truth is that the best foods are the products of infinite and wearying trouble. The trouble need not be taken by the consumer, but someone, ever since the Fall, has had to take it.
ROSE MACAULAY
Personal Pleasures (1936)

If a man will be sensible and one fine morning, while he is lying in bed, count at the tips of his fingers how many things in this life truly give him pleasure, invariably he will find food is the first one.
LIN YUTANG
The Importance of Living (1937)

Sharing food with another human being is an intimate act that should not be indulged in lightly.
M.F.K. FISHER
An Alphabet for Gourmets (1949)

Offerings of food have been breaking down barriers for centuries.
ESTEE LAUDER
(1908 -)

There's something I've noticed about food: whenever there's a crisis if you can get people to eating normally things get better.
MADELEINE L'ENGLE
The Moon by Night (1963)

I eat merely to put food out of my mind.
N.F. SIMPSON
The Hole (1964)

Food for all is a necessity. Food should not be a merchandise, to be bought and sold by those who have the money to buy. Food is a human necessity, like water and air, and it should be available.
PEARL BUCK
To My Daughters, with Love (1967)

With the exception of black bottom pie and niggertoes, there is no reference to black people's contribution to the culinary arts. White folks act like they invented food and like there is some weird mystique surrounding it. . . . There is no mystique. Food is food.
VERTAMAE GROSVENOR
Vibration Cooking (1970)

Food is the most primitive form of comfort.
SHEILAH GRAHAM
A State of Heat (1972)

Food is our common ground, a universal experience.
JAMES BEARD
Beard on Food (1974)

Food is an important part of a balanced diet.
FRAN LEBOWITZ
Metropolitan Life (1978)

There are only two questions to ask about food. Is it good? And is it authentic? We are open ⌈to⌉ new ideas, but not if it means destroying our history. And food is history.
GIULIANO BUGIALLI
New York Times (1984)

Food is never just something to eat.
MARGARET VISSER
Much Depends on Dinner (1986)

Young people relish fine clothes; old people prefer food.
CHINESE PROVERB

No food was ever cooked by gay clothes and frivolity.
FIJIAN PROVERB

He who has good food has heaps of difficulties.
INDIAN PROVERB

There is no enemy like food.
INDIAN PROVERB

Food without hospitality is medicine.
INDIAN PROVERB

Food given by another person is only a throat tickler, but food gained by the labor of one's own hand is the food which satisfies.
MAORI PROVERB

Whoever cooks the food of malice, remnants will stick to his pot.
NIGERIAN PROVERB

F O O D
S N O B S

Only a stomach that rarely feels hungry scorns common food.
HORACE
Satires (c. 30 B.C.)

Food snobs are merely those people who covet expensive things. Their tastes are influenced by hearsay, not by their own judgment. They do not know that bean curd tastes better than bird's nest, and seaweed, unless it is of the best quality, does not compare with bamboo shoots.
YUAN MEI
The Menu (1797)

The man who bites his bread, or eats peas with a knife, I look upon as a lost creature.
W.S. GILBERT
Ruddigore (1887)

Shall we never learn the worthlessness of other people's views of food? There is no authoritative body of comment on food. Like all the deeper personal problems of life, you must face it alone.

FRANK MOORE COLBY
(1865-1925)

The early Puritans, even when they made a feast, feasted upon unappetizing and indigestible food—parched corn, dried beans, codfish, chicory coffee, blackstrap molasses, soggy pies, fresh game, clams without butter, hard bread. Their chief delicacy, after venison, was turkey, and they invented the atrocity of roasting it. To this day that atrocity disfigures American cookery.

H.L. MENCKEN
in Smart Set (1919)

There are a lot of people who must have the table laid in the usual fashion or they will not enjoy the dinner.

CHRISTOPHER MORLEY
Inward Ho (1923)

there is some shit I will not eat

E.E. CUMMINGS
i sing of Olaf glad and big (1931)

The real native South Seas food is lousy. You can't eat it.

VICTOR "TRADER VIC" BERGERON
in Newsweek (1958)

Some people like to eat octopus. Liberals, mostly.

RUSSELL BAKER
(1925 -)

As long as I have fat turtle-doves, a fig for your lettuce, my friend, and you may keep your shellfish to yourself. I have no wish to waste my appetite.

MARTIAL
Epigrams (c. 95 A.D.)

F   O   W   L

Let a duck certainly be served up whole; but it is tasty only in the breast and neck: the rest return to the cook.

MARTIAL
Epigrams (c. 95 A.D.)

Whether woodcock or partridge, what does it matter, if the flavor be the same? A partridge is dearer, and thus has better flavor.
MARTIAL
Epigrams (c. 95 A.D.)

Wood-pigeons check and blunt the manly powers: let him not eat this bird who wishes to be amorous.
MARTIAL
Epigrams (c. 95 A.D.)

Pheasant exceedeth all fowls in sweetness and wholesomeness, and is equal to capon in nourishment.
SIR THOMAS ELYOT
The Castle of Helth (1530)

If God grants me the usual length of life, I hope to make France so prosperous that every peasant will have a chicken in his pot on Sunday.
HENRY IV OF FRANCE
(1553-1610)

Some pigeons, Davy
A couple of short-legged hens,
A joint of mutton,
And any pretty little tiny kickshaws,
tell William cook.
WILLIAM SHAKESPEARE
2 Henry IV (1597-98)

An honest fellow enough, and one that loves quails.
WILLIAM SHAKESPEARE
Troilus and Cressida (1601-02)

Poultry is for the cook what canvas is for the painter.
ANTHELME BRILLAT-SAVARIN
The Physiology of Taste (1825)

When I demanded of my friend what viands he preferred
He quoth: 'A large cold bottle, and a small hot bird!'
EUGENE FIELD
The Bottle and the Bird (1889)

The greatest of all chicken dishes, of course, is . . . the chicken pot pie, an English invention . . . . Like the mazurkas of Chopin, it leaves room for the self expression of the artist.

H.L. Mencken
in the Baltimore Evening Sun (1910)

To get a better piece of chicken, you'd have to be a rooster.

slogan for Mickey Mantle's Country Cookin'
(c. 1975)

I wouldn't dream of cooking a fowl of any kind without rubbing it first with half a lemon, then with frayed garlic, then a little salt, then lots of either butter or bacon fat or olive oil.

Eugene Walter
Hints and Pinches (1991)

Lunch kills half of Paris, supper the other half.

F R E N C H

Montesquieu
(1689-1755)

If a lump of soot falls into the soup, and you cannot conveniently get it out, stir it well in, and it will give the soup a high French taste.

Jonathan Swift
Directions to Servants (1745)

A true German can't endure a Frenchman, but he likes French wine.

Johann Wolfgang von Goethe
Faust, Part I (1808)

Few things bought with money are more delightful than a French breakfast . . . [it] costs about one-third as much as the beefsteaks and coffee in America.

N.P. Willis
Pencillings by the Way (1835)

She had been in France, and loved, ever after, French novels, French cookery, and French wines.
WILLIAM MAKEPEACE THACKERAY
Vanity Fair (1847-48)

The French would be the best cooks in Europe if they had got any butcher's meat.
WALTER BAGEHOT
Biographical Studies (1880)

Mayonnaise: One of the sauces which serve the French in place of a state religion.
AMBROSE BIERCE
The Devil's Dictionary (1906)

Bouillabaisse is only good because it is cooked by the French, who if they cared to try, would produce an excellent and nutritious substitute out of cigar stumps and empty matchboxes.
NORMAN DOUGLAS
(1868-1952)

French cuisine is so delicious that it's a tribute to Gallic willpower that Frenchmen ever leave the dinner table and attend to business.
HENRY O. DORMANN
A Millionaire's Guide to Europe (1945)

Three million frogs' legs are served in Paris—daily. Nobody knows what became of the rest of the frogs.
FRED ALLEN
(1894-1956)

Everything ends this way in France—everything. Weddings, christenings, duels, burials, swindlings, diplomatic affairs—everything is a pretext for a good dinner.
JEAN ANOUILH
(1910-1987)

Never underestimate the place of food in the life of the French; when a couple, whether married or not, no longer

has any desire for each other, the table remains a far
stronger bond than the bed.
PHILLIPPE JULLIAN
in Town & Country (c. 1975)

Americans are just beginning to regard food the way the
French always have. Dinner is not what you do in the
evening before something else. Dinner is the evening.
ART BUCHWALD
(1925 -)

The friendship of the French is like their wine: it is
pleasant but it does not last long.
GERMAN PROVERB

As soon as they tasted that honey-sweet fruit, they thought   F   R   U   I   T
no more of coming back to us with news, but chose rather
to stay there with the lotus-eating natives, and chew their
lotus, and goodbye to home.
HOMER
Odyssey (c. 800 B.C.)

And they shall build houses, and inhabit them; and they
shall plant vineyards, and eat the fruit of them. They
shall not build, and another inhabit; they shall not plant,
and another eat.
ISAIAH 65:21-22
(c. 700 B.C.)

By their fruits ye shall know them.
MATTHEW 7:20
(c. 75 A.D.)

The savoury pulp they chew, and in the rind
Still as they thirsted scooped the brimming stream.
JOHN MILTON
Paradise Lost (1667)

The green limes that I gathered were not only pleasant to
eat but very wholesome; and I mixed their juice afterwards

with water, which made it very wholesome and very cool and refreshing.
DANIEL DEFOE
Robinson Crusoe (1719)

I'll be with you in the squeezing of a lemon.
OLIVER GOLDSMITH
She Stoops to Conquer (1773)

In an orchard there should be enough to eat, enough to lay up, enough to be stolen, and enough to rot upon the ground.
SAMUEL MADDEN
Boswell's Life of Johnson (1783)

This lemonade is as insipid as your soul—try it.
J.C.F. SCHILLER
Conspiracy and Love (1784)

Talking of Pleasure, this moment I was writing with one hand and with the other holding to my Mouth a Nectarine—good God how fine. It went down soft, pulpy, slushy, oozy—all its delicious embodiment melted down my throat like a large Beautiful strawberry. I shall certainly breed.
JOHN KEATS
in a letter (c. 1820)

Orange-peel will be my death, or I'll be content to eat my own head.
CHARLES DICKENS
Oliver Twist (1837-38)

The apple is our national fruit, and I like to see that the soil yields it; I judge of the country so. The American sun paints himself in these glowing balls amid the green leaves. Man would be more solitary, less friended, less supported, if the land yielded only the useful maize and potato, and withheld this ornamental and social fruit.
RALPH WALDO EMERSON
Journals (1820-1876)

What beautiful fruit! I love fruit when it's expensive.
SIR ARTHUR WING PINERO
The Second Mrs. Tanqueray (1893)

The true Southern watermelon is a boon apart, and not to be mentioned with commoner things.
MARK TWAIN
Pudd'nhead Wilson (1894)

When one has tasted watermelons, he knows what angels eat. It was not a Southern watermelon that Eve took; we know it because she repented.
MARK TWAIN
Pudd'nhead Wilson (1894)

Do I dare to eat a peach?
T.S. ELIOT
The Love Song of J. Alfred Prufrock (1915)

Watermelon—it's a good fruit. You eat, you drink, you wash your face.
ENRICO CARUSO
(1873-1921)

In the fall one walks in the orchards and the ground is hard with the frost underfoot. The apples have been taken from the trees by the pickers. . . . On the trees are only a few gnarled apples that the pickers have rejected. . . . One nibbles at them and they are delicious. Into a little round place at the side of the apple has been gathered all of its sweetness. One runs from tree to tree over the frosted ground picking the gnarled, twisted apples and filling his pockets with them. Only the few know the sweetness of the twisted apples.
SHERWOOD ANDERSON
Winesburg, Ohio (1919)

While forbidden fruit is said to taste sweeter, it usually spoils faster.
ABIGAIL VAN BUREN
(1918 -)

Success to me is having ten honeydew melons and eating only the top half of each one.
BARBRA STREISAND
(1942 -)

If you've got AIDS, you can come into this country. If you've got fruit, you can't.
JACKIE MASON
in The New Yorker (1994)

A grapefruit is a lemon that had a chance and took advantage of it.
ANONYMOUS

Nothing raises false hopes in a human being like one good cantaloupe.
ANONYMOUS

A watermelon will not ripen in your armpit.
ARMENIAN PROVERB

Sweet fruit usually has a bitter rind.
FILIPINO PROVERB

The sweetest grapes hang highest.
GERMAN PROVERB

A thin plantain is better than none at all.
JAMAICAN PROVERB

Eating pears also cleans one's teeth.
KOREAN PROVERB

Every raisin contains a pip.
LIBYAN PROVERB

Gather the most distant breadfruit first.
SAMOAN PROVERB

It will beggar a doctor to live where orchards thrive.
SPANISH PROVERB

FUNGI

[Mushrooms] are not really food, but are relished to bully the sated stomach into further eating.
SENECA
(4 B.C.-65 A.D.)

Few of them ⌈mushrooms⌉ are good and most produce a choking sensation.
ATHENAEUS
The Gastronomers (c. 200 A.D.)

We don't care to eat toadstools that think they are truffles.
MARK TWAIN
Pudd'nhead Wilson (1894)

I am in revolt against the mushroom of Paris, an insipid creature born in the dark and incubated by humidity. I have had enough of it, bathing chopped in all the sauces it thickens. I forbid it to usurp the place of the chanterelle or the truffle; and I command it, together with its fitting companion, canned cocks' combs, never to cross the threshold of my kitchen.
SIDONIE COLETTE
(1873-1954)

Life is too short to stuff a mushroom.
SHIRLEY CONRAN
Superwoman (1975)

A feast is not made of mushrooms only.
ENGLISH PROVERB

Awake, O north wind; and come, thou south; blow upon my garden, that the spices thereof may flow out. Let my beloved come into his garden, and eat his pleasant fruits.
SONG OF SOLOMON 4:16
(c. 200 B.C.)

GARDEN

What can your eye desire to see, your ears to hear, your mouth to take, or your nose to smell that is not to be had in a garden?
WILLIAM LAWSON
A New Orchard and Garden (1648)

The infinite conveniences of what a well-stor'd garden and cellar affords. . . . All so near at hand, readily drest, and of so easie digestion as neither to offend the brain, or dull the senses.

JOHN EVELYN
Acetaria (1699)

For all things produced in a garden, whether of salads or fruits, a poor man will eat better that has one of his own, than a rich man that has none.

J.C. LOUDON
An Encyclopedia of Gardening (1826)

I now begin to think myself happy in my present way of life; I cultivate a few vegetables to support me; and the little well over there is a very clear one.

WILLIAM SHENSTONE
The Hermit (1868)

Our vegetable garden is coming along well, with radishes and beans up, and we are less worried about revolution than we used to be.

E.B. WHITE
One Man's Meat (1942)

People say British food is terrible, but it's not. It's wonderful. We set out to find the wonder. We don't want green and red peppers grown under glass in Holland and packed in plastic containers. We want the gnarled things from our own garden.

KEITH FLOYD
(1939 -)

G A R L I C Well loved he garlic, onions, and eke leeks,
And for to drinken strong wine, red as blood.

GEOFFREY CHAUCER
Canterbury Tales (c. 1395)

It is not really an exaggeration to say that peace and happiness begin, geographically, where garlic is used in cooking.

MARCEL BOULESTIN
(1878-1943)

There are five elements: earth, air, fire, water, and garlic.
LOUIS DIAT
(1885-1957)

The grotesque prudishness and archness with which garlic
is treated in ⌈England⌉ has led to the superstition that
rubbing the bowl with it before putting the salad in gives
sufficient flavor. It rather depends whether you are going
to eat the bowl or the salad.
ELIZABETH DAVID
Summer Cooking (1955)

Tomatoes and oregano make it Italian; wine and tarragon
make it French. Sour cream makes it Russian; lemon and
cinnamon makes it Greek. Soy sauce makes it Chinese;
garlic makes it good.
ALICE MAY BROCK
Alice's Restaurant Cookbook (1969)

There is no such thing as a little garlic.
ANONYMOUS

Garlic makes a man wink, drink, and stink.
ENGLISH PROVERB

Garlic is as good as ten mothers.
INDIAN PROVERB

He who does not eat garlic does not smell of garlic.
LEBANESE PROVERB

The drunkard and the glutton shall come to poverty; and
drowsiness shall clothe a man with rags.
PROVERBS 23:21
(c. 350 B.C.)

Gluttony and drunkenness have two evils attendant upon
them; they make the carcass smart, as well as the pocket.
MARCUS ANTONINUS
(82-30 B.C.)

GLUTTONY

Let him herd with the dumb brutes—an animal whose
delight is in fodder.
SENECA
Moral Letters (c. 63 A.D.)

The Son of man came eating and drinking, and they say,
Behold a man gluttonous, and a winebibber, a friend of
publicans and sinners.
MATTHEW 11:19
(c. 75 A.D.)

Ingenious is gluttony.
MARTIAL
Epigrams (c. 95 A.D.)

O what gluttony is his who has whole boars served up for
himself, an animal born for banquets.
JUVENAL
Satires (c. 120 A.D.)

Gluttony hinders chastity.
POPE SIXTUS I
The Ring (c. 150 A.D.)

For two nights the glutton cannot sleep for thinking, first
on an empty, and next on a sated stomach.
SA'DI
Golestan (1258)

Afterward he wisheth that he had neck of crane and belly
of cow, that the morsels might remain longer in the throat
and be digested more.
BROTHER LORENS
The Sum of the Vices and the Virtues (1279)

Heavy eating is worse than daggers.
JUDAH BEN ASHER
(1270-1349)

To kindle and blow the fire of lechery
That is annexed unto gluttony.
GEOFFREY CHAUCER
Canterbury Tales (c. 1395)

Many more people by gluttony are slain
Than in battle or in fight, or with other pain.
ANONYMOUS
The Dialoges of Creatures Moralysed (c. 1535)

None is happy but a glutton.
JOHN LYLY
A Serving Men's Song (1584)

With eager feeding, food doth choke the feeder.
WILLIAM SHAKESPEARE
Richard II (1595-96)

He hath eaten me out of house and home.
WILLIAM SHAKESPEARE
2 Henry IV (1597-98)

What is a man
If his chief good and market of his time
Be but to sleep and feed?
A beast, no more.
WILLIAM SHAKESPEARE
Hamlet (1600-01)

I am Gluttony. My parents are all dead, and the devil a
penny they have left me, but a bare pension, and that is
thirty meals a day—a small trifle to suffice nature. I come
of a royal parentage! My grandfather was a gammon of
bacon, my grandmother a hogshead of claret wine.
CHRISTOPHER MARLOWE
Dr. Faustus (1604)

I will eat exceedingly, and prophesy.
BEN JONSON
Bartholomew Fair (1614)

Swinish gluttony
Ne'er looks to heav'n amidst his gorgeous feast,
But with besotted base ingratitude
Crams, and blasphemes his feeder.
JOHN MILTON
Comus (1637)

Gluttony is the sin of England.

THOMAS FULLER
Sermons (1640)

Who hastens a glutton, chokes him.

GEORGE HERBERT
Outlandish Proverbs (1640)

A fully gorged belly never produced a sprightly mind.

JEREMY TAYLOR
Twenty-seven Sermons (1651)

Formidable is the state of an intemperate man whose employment is the same as the work of the sheep or the calf—always to eat.

JEREMY TAYLOR
Twenty-seven Sermons (1651)

Gluttony is no sin if it doesn't injure health.

ANONYMOUS
doctrine condemned by Pope Alexander VII (1665)

He needs no more than birds and beasts to think,
All his occasions are to eat and drink.

JOHN DRYDEN
Absalom and Achitophel (1681)

He will never have enough till his mouth is full of mould.

THOMAS FULLER
Gnomologia (1732)

What slaughter'd hecatombs, what floods of wine
Fill the capacious squire and deep divine.

ALEXANDER POPE
Moral Essays (1733)

They were at once dainty and voracious, understood the right and the wrong of every dish, and alike emptied the one and the other.

FRANCES BURNEY
Evelina (1778)

Why so many different dishes? Man sinks almost to the
level of an animal when eating becomes his chief pleasure.
LUDWIG VON BEETHOVEN
(1770-1827)

Gluttony is mankind's exclusive prerogative.
ANTHELME BRILLAT-SAVARIN
The Physiology of Taste (1825)

He who eats too much knows not how to eat.
ANTHELME BRILLAT-SAVARIN
The Physiology of Taste (1825)

He who distinguishes the true savor of his food can never
be a glutton; he who does not cannot be otherwise.
HENRY DAVID THOREAU
(1817-1862)

All day long they ate with the resolute greed of brutes.
ROBERT LOUIS STEVENSON
The Song of Rahero (1890)

They consumed the whole animal kingdom at each meal.
GEORGE BERNARD SHAW
(1856-1950)

Eat slowly; only men in rags
And gluttons old in sin
Mistake themselves for carpet-bags
And tumble victuals in.
SIR WALTER RALEIGH
Stans Puer ad Mensam (1923)

Not for renewal, but for eating's sake,
They stuff their bellies with to-morrows ache.
EDMUND VANCE COOKE
From the Book of Extenuations (1927)

A big man is always accused of gluttony, whereas a
wizened or osseous man can eat like a refugee at every
meal, and no one ever notices his greed.
ROBERTSON DAVIES
The Table Talk of Samuel Marchbanks (1949)

Gluttony is an emotional escape, a sign something is eating us.

PETER DE VRIES
Comfort Me with Apples (1956)

Gluttony is not a secret vice.

ORSON WELLES
(1915-1985)

I am not a glutton—I am an explorer of food.

ERMA BOMBECK
(1927 -)

An immense woman with a glossy picture of a hooked bass leaping the front of her shirt said, 'I'm gonna be sick from how much I've ate.'

WILLIAM LEAST HEAT-MOON
Blue Highways (1982)

Eat standing, eat walking.

HAWAIIAN PROVERB

Eat until the lips protrude.

HAWAIIAN PROVERB

Before good food goes to waste, one should overeat.

JAMAICAN PROVERB

One man can't eat with two mouths.

JEWISH PROVERB

The glutton for cake often loses the bread.

JEWISH PROVERB

GOURMETS,
GOURMANDS
&
EPICURES

If my opinion is of any worth, the fieldfare is the greatest delicacy among birds, the hare among quadrupeds.

MARTIAL
Epigrams (c. 95 A.D.)

Make less thy body hence, and more thy grace;
Leave gormandizing.

WILLIAM SHAKESPEARE
2 Henry IV (1597-98)

Epicurean cooks
Sharpen with cloyless sauce his appetite.
WILLIAM SHAKESPEARE
Antony and Cleopatra (1606-07)

A fair sepulchre in the grateful stomach of the judicious
epicure.
CHARLES LAMB
Essays of Elia (1823)

I have been a great observer and I can truly say that I
have never known a man 'fond of good eating and drinking,' as it is called; that I have never known such a man
(and hundreds I have known) who was not worthy of
respect.
WILLIAM COBBETT
Advice to Young Men (1829)

Serenely full, the epicure would say,
Fate cannot harm me—I have dined today.
SYDNEY SMITH
quoted in Lady Holland's Memoir (1855)

A true gastronome should always be ready to eat, just as a
soldier should always be ready to fight.
CHARLES MONSELET
(1825-1888)

Nine-tenths of the current writers upon the topic ⌈of
cookery⌉ in America are female professors of what is
called domestic science; that is to say, they know a great
deal about calories and vitamins, but nothing whatever
about civilized dining. The meals they advocate are excellent for diabetics, but fatal to epicures.
H.L. MENCKEN
in American Mercury (1925)

The ⌈cooking-school⌉ ma'am is primarily a cook, not an
epicure. She is interested in materials and processes, not in
gustatory effects.
H.L. MENCKEN
in the Chicago Tribune (1926)

A gourmet can tell from the flavor whether a woodcock's leg is the one on which the bird is accustomed to roost.
LUCIUS BEEBE
(1902-1966)

A gourmet is just a glutton with brains.
PHILLIP W. HABERMAN, JR.
in Vogue (1961)

The true gourmet, like the true artist, is one of the unhappiest creatures existent. His trouble comes from so seldom finding what he constantly seeks: perfection.
LUDWIG BEMELMANS
recalled on his death (1962)

There is a difference between the savage gnawing at a bone, and the civilized eating of tiny parts.
HSIANG JU LIN AND TSUIFENG LIN
Chinese Gastronomy (1969)

A gourmet who thinks of calories is like a tart who looks at her watch.
JAMES BEARD
(1903-1985)

After eating, an epicure gives a thin smile of satisfaction; a gastronome, burping into his napkin praises the food in a magazine; a gourmet, repressing his burp, criticizes the food in the same magazine; a gourmand belches happily and tells everybody where he ate; a glutton embraces the white porcelain altar, or, more plainly, he barfs.
WILLIAM SAFIRE
in the New York Times (1985)

In the lexicon of lip-smacking, an epicure is fastidious in his choice and enjoyment of food, just a soupcon more expert than a gastronome; a gourmet is a connoisseur of the exotic, taste buds attuned to the calibrations of deliciousness, who savors the masterly techniques of great chefs; a gourmand is a hearty bon vivant who enjoys food

without truffles and flourishes; a glutton overindulges
greedily, the word rooted in the Latin for 'one who
devours.'
WILLIAM SAFIRE
in the New York Times (1985)

The gourmand puts his purse into his belly; and the miser
his belly into his purse.
ANONYMOUS

Gourmands make their grave with their teeth.
FRENCH PROVERB

Ruling a big country is like cooking a small fish.
LAO-TZU
(604-531 B.C.)

GOVERNMENT

Good dyet is a perfect way of curing:
And worthy much regard and health assuring.
A King that cannot rule him in his dyet,
Will hardly rule his Realme in peace and quiet.
MAIMONIDES
Regimen Sanitatis (c. 1200)

So long as people, being ill-governed, suffer from hunger,
criminals will never disappear.
KENKO HOSHI
The Harvest of Leisure (c. 1330)

Dinners have become a means of government, and the
fates of peoples are decided at a banquet. This is neither a
paradox nor even a novelty, but a simple observation of
facts. If we look at any historian, from the time of
Herodotus to the present, it will seem that, without even
excepting conspiracies, no great event ever took place that
was not previously concocted, planned, and determined at
a banquet.
ANTHELME BRILLAT-SAVARIN
The Physiology of Taste (1825)

Every cook has to learn how to govern the state.
VLADIMIR LENIN
Will The Bolsheviks Retain Government Power? (1917)

No amount of political freedom will satisfy the hungry masses.
VLADIMIR LENIN
(1870-1924)

An empty stomach is not a good political advisor.
ALBERT EINSTEIN
Cosmic Religion (1931)

True individual freedom cannot exist without economic
security and independence. People who are hungry and out
of a job are the stuff of which dictatorships are made.
FRANKLIN DELANO ROOSEVELT
(1882-1945)

There is no such thing as the State
And no one exists alone;
Hunger allows no choice
To the citizen or the police;
We must love one another or die.
W.H. AUDEN
September 1, 1939 (1939)

Undoubtedly the desire for food has been, and still is, one
of the main causes of great political events.
BERTRAND RUSSELL
(1872-1970)

All forms of government fall when it comes up to the
question of bread—bread for the family, something to eat.
Bread to a man with a hungry family comes first—before
his union, before his citizenship, before his church affilia-
tion. Bread!
JOHN L. LEWIS
(1880-1969)

Hunger and self-government are incompatible.
ALDOUS HUXLEY
Brave New World Revisited (1958)

Madam, I have been looking for a person who disliked gravy all my life; let us swear eternal friendship.
SYDNEY SMITH
quoted in Lady Holland's Memoir (1855)

G R A V Y

I come from a home where gravy is a beverage.
ERMA BOMBECK
(1927 -)

First, there will be given you lettuce, useful for releasing the bowels.
MARTIAL
Epigrams (c. 95 A.D.)

G R E E N S

Tell me why is it that lettuce, which used to end our grandsires' dinners, ushers in our banquets?
MARTIAL
Epigrams (c. 95 A.D.)

Eat well of the cresses.
JOHN GRANGE
The Golden Aphroditis (1577)

[Lettuce] is, of all herbs, the best and wholesomest for hot seasons, for young men, and them that abound with choler, and also for the sanguine, and such as have hot stomachs.
TOBIAS VENNER
Via recta (1620)

Lettuce is like conversation: it must be fresh and crisp, and so sparkling that you scarcely notice the bitter in it.
CHARLES DUDLEY WARNER
My Summer in a Garden (1870)

The effect of eating too much lettuce is 'soporific.'
BEATRIX POTTER
The Tale of the Flopsy Bunnies (1909)

I've heard my neighbor Johnson say
His choice was chicken pie;
And Perkins 'lows he likes to stay
His stomach with a fry;
And Jones, he says, says he, 'I think
Good old Kentucky rye
Suits me the best; give me a drink,
Whenever I am dry.'
But I have never tasted meat,
Nor cabbage, corn nor beans,
Nor fluid food one half as sweet
As that first mess of greens.

COTTON NOE
The Loom of Life (1912)

'Collard greens!' she said, spitting the word from her mouth
this time as if it were a poisonous seed.

FLANNERY O' CONNOR
A Stroke of Good Fortune (1949)

Spinach is the broom of the stomach.

FRENCH PROVERB

A little taro green is delicious when love is present.

HAWAIIAN PROVERB

H E A L T H   Seest thou how pale the sated guest rises from supper,
where the appetite is puzzled with varieties? The body,
too, burdened with yesterday's excess, weighs down the
soul, and fixes to the earth this particle of the divine
essence.

HORACE
Satires (c. 30 B.C.)

Too much good food does more harm than too little
bad food.

SHEM-TOV FALAQUERA
Book of the Seeker (c. 1275)

For the sake of health, medicines are taken by weight and measure; so ought food to be, or by some similar rule.
JOHN SKELTON
(1460-1529)

Food by measure, and defy the physician.
JOHN HEYWOOD
Proverbs (1546)

Make hunger thy sauce as a medicine for health.
THOMAS TUSSER
Five Hundred Points of Good Husbandry (1557)

Many dishes make many diseases.
THOMAS MOFFETT
Health's Improvement (1590)

They are as sick that surfeit with too much,
as they that starve with nothing.
WILLIAM SHAKESPEARE
The Merchant of Venice (1596-97)

Declare unto me a dayly dyet, whereby I may live in health, and not trouble my selfe in Physicke.
WILLIAM VAUGHAN
Naturall and Artificial Directions for Health (1602)

Now good digestion wait on appetite, and health on both!
WILLIAM SHAKESPEARE
Macbeth (1605-06)

Use three physicians still: Dr. Quiet, then Dr. Merry, and lastly, Dr. Diet.
JOHN HARINGTON
The Englishman's Doctor (1608)

The spirit cannot endure the body when overfed, but, if underfed, the body cannot endure the spirit.
SAINT FRANCIS DE SALES
Introduction to the Devout Life (1609)

Our apothecary's shop is our garden full of pot-herbs, and our doctor is a clove of garlic.
ANONYMOUS
A Deep Snow (1615)

Whatsoever was the father of a disease, ill diet was the mother.
GEORGE HERBERT
Jacula Prudentum (1651)

An apple, an egg and a nut
You may eat after a slut.
JOHN RAY
English Proverbs (1670)

Preserve a good constitution of body and mind. To this a spare diet contributes much. Have wholesome, but no costly food.
WILLIAM PENN
Fruits of Solitude (1693)

Much meat, much malady.
THOMAS FULLER
Gnomologia (1732)

If, after exercise, we feed sparingly, the digestion will be easy and good, the body lightsome, the temper cheerful, and all the animal functions performed agreeably.
BENJAMIN FRANKLIN
The Art of Procuring Pleasant Dreams (1772)

To rise at six, sup at ten,
To sup at six, to sleep at ten,
Makes a man live for ten times ten.
VICTOR HUGO
inscription over his study door (c. 1860)

Ministers are tempted to eat too much. . . . The people should have too much true kindness to press such an alternative upon him. They err when they tempt the minister with unhealthful food.
ELLEN G. WHITE
Counsels on Diet and Food (1870)

Everything I eat has been proved by some doctor or other to be a deadly poison, and everything I don't eat has been proved to be indispensable to life. . . . But I go marching on.
GEORGE BERNARD SHAW
(1856-1950)

There is something in the freshness of food, especially vegetable food—some form of energy perhaps; it may be certain rays of light or electrical property—which gives to it a health-promoting influence.
SIR ROBERT MCCARRISON
Nutrition and National Health (1944)

Wholesome food and drink are cheaper than doctors and hospitals.
DR. CARL C. WAHL
Essential Health Knowledge (1966)

I refuse to spend my life worrying about what I eat. There is no pleasure worth foregoing just for an extra three years in the geriatric ward.
JOHN MORTIMER
(1923 -)

I can sing much better after shooting smack in both arms than after eating too much.
LINDA RONSTADT
(1942 -)

Six Don'ts for 24 Hours:
1. No hot/spicy foods
2. No sour foods
3. No cold drinks
4. No alcohol
5. No sex
6. No duck
Post-treatment guidelines from a Honolulu acupuncture clinic (1994)

He that takes medicine and neglects diet, wastes the skill of the physician.
CHINESE PROVERB

He who eats garlic and butter need fear no poison.
CZECH PROVERB

A land with lots of herring can get along with few doctors.
DUTCH PROVERB

The nurse's bread is sweeter than the mother's cake.
DUTCH PROVERB

Diet cures more than doctors.
ENGLISH PROVERB

Eat an apple on going to bed, and you'll keep the doctor from earning his bread.
ENGLISH PROVERB

Bread and cheese are medicine for the well.
FRENCH PROVERB

Fasting is the best medicine.
INDIAN PROVERB

If in excess even nectar is poison.
INDIAN PROVERB

When a severe illness comes, eat bread and onions.
INDIAN PROVERB

He that eats till he is sick must fast till he is well.
JEWISH PROVERB

Drink a glass of wine after your soup, and you steal a ruble from the doctor.
RUSSIAN PROVERB

What the sick man likes to eat is his medicine.
RUSSIAN PROVERB

H E A L T H
F O O D

I want nothing to do with natural foods. At my age I need all the preservatives I can get.
GEORGE BURNS
(1896 -)

Health food may be good for the conscience, but Oreos taste a hell of a lot better.
ROBERT REDFORD
in the Chicago Tribune (1978)

We load up on oat bran in the morning so we'll live forever. Then we spend the rest of the day living like there's no tomorrow.
LEE IACOCCA
(1924 -)

Better is a dinner of herbs where love is, than a fatted ox in the midst of hatred.
PROVERBS 15:17
(c. 350 B.C.)

Tarragon is not to be eaten alone in sallades, but joyned with other herbes, as Lettuce, Purslain, and such like, that it may also temper the coldnesse of them, like as Rockets doth, neither do we know what other use this herbe hath.
JOHN GERARD
Gerard's Herball (1597)

To take parsley away from the cook would make it almost impossible for him to exercise his art.
LOUIS AUGUSTIN GUILLAUME BOSC D'ANTIC
(c. 1895)

The odor of saffron is extremely penetrating. . . . It can cause violent headaches and even death.
ALEXANDRE DUMAS
The Dictionary of Cuisine (c. 1900)

Parsley
Is gharsley.
OGDEN NASH
Further Reflection on Parsley (1942)

It is the destiny of mint to be crushed.
WAVERLEY ROOT
Food (1980)

Parsley must be sown nine times, for the Devil takes all but the last.
ENGLISH PROVERB

171

H O M E
C O O K I N G

The yoongest ladies of the court, when they be at home,
can helpe to supplie the ordinarie want of the kitchen
with a number of delicat dishes of their own devising.
RAPHAEL HOLINSHED
The Chronicles of England, Scotlande and Irelande (1577)

If you like good food, cook it yourself.
LI LIWENG
(1611-1676)

Cornwall squab-pie, and Devon white-pot brings;
And Leicester beans and bacon, food of kings.
WILLIAM KING
The Art of Cookery (1708)

Homeward he hies, enjoys that clean coarse food
Which, season'd with good humour, his fond bride
'Gainst his return is happy to provide.
Short are his meals, and homely is his fare;
His thirst he slakes at some pure neighborhood brook,
Nor asks for sauce where appetite stands cook.
CHARLES CHURCHILL
The Villager (1760)

I wonder, now and then, if the prevalence of divorce has
any connection to the decline of home cooking?
MARTHA McCULLOCH-WILLIAMS
Dishes and Beverages of the Old South (1913)

Talk of joy: there may be things better than beef stew and
baked potatoes and homemade bread—there may be.
DAVID GRAYSON
(1870-1946)

There is even in so clean a household as this an odor of
pork, of sweat, so subtle it seems to get into the very
metal of the cooking-pans . . . yet this is the odor and
consistency and temper and these are the true tastes of
home; I know this even of myself; much as my reflexes

are twitching in refusal of each mouthful, a true homesick and simple fondness for it has so strong hold of me that in fact there is no fight to speak of and no faking of enjoyment at all.

JAMES AGEE
Let Us Now Praise Famous Men (1939)

'How much are your yams?' I said, suddenly hungry. 'They ten cents and they sweet,' he said, his voice quavering with age. . . . I took a bite, finding it as sweet and hot as any I'd ever had, and was overcome with such a surge of homesickness that I turned away to keep my control.

RALPH ELLISON
Invisible Man (1947)

Close to noon on Christmas day we saw them coming down the road: forty-eight men in stripes, with their guards. They came up the hill and headed for the house, a few laughing, talking, others grim and suspicious. All had come, white and Negro. We had helped Mother make two caramel cakes and twelve sweet potato pies and a wonderful backbone-and-rice dish (which Mother, born on the coast, called pilau); and there were hot rolls and Brunswick stew, and a washtub full of apples which our father had polished in front of the fire on Christmas Eve. It would be a splendid dinner . . .

LILLIAN SMITH
Memory of a Large Christmas (1961)

When I come home to my kitchen, I realize it is there that I can best satisfy the eccentricities of my own palate.

JAMES BEARD
Delights and Prejudices (1964)

I never see any home cooking. All I get is fancy stuff.

PRINCE PHILIP
Duke of Edinburgh (1921 -)

I hoped to find down the county roads Ma in her beanery and Pap over his barbecue pit, both still serving slow food

from the same place they did thirty years ago. Where-you-from-buddy restaurants.
WILLIAM LEAST HEAT-MOON
Blue Highways (1982)

There is . . . something about the foodways of the mountains . . . that is undeniably compelling, even graceful.
ELIOT WIGGINGTON
The Foxfire Book of Appalachian Cookery (1984)

HONEY

What is sweeter than honey?
JUDGES 14:18
(c. 500 B.C.)

I did but taste a little honey with the end of the rod that was in mine hand, and lo, I must die.
I SAMUEL 14:43
(c. 500 B.C.)

My son, eat this honey, because it is good.
PROVERBS 24:13
(c. 350 B.C.)

John had his raiment of camel's hair, and a leathern girdle about his loins; and his meat was locusts and wild honey.
MATTHEW 3:4
(c. 75 A.D.)

Dear is bought the honey that is licked of the thorn.
ANONYMOUS
The Proverbs of Hendyng (c. 1300)

A kiss is but a kiss now! and no wave
Of a great flood that whirls me to the sea.
But, as you will! we'll sit contentedly,
And eat our pot of honey on the grave.
GEORGE MEREDITH
Modern Love (1862)

Honey is not for asses.
FRENCH PROVERB

Make yourself all honey, and the flies will eat you.
ITALIAN PROVERB

To a sick man even honey tastes bitter.
RUSSIAN PROVERB

HUMANKIND

Not on the store of sprightly wine, nor plenty of delicious
    meats,
Though generous Nature did design to court us with
    perpetual treats—
'Tis not on these we for content depend, so much as on
    the shadow of a Friend.
MENANDER
Of Brotherly Love (c. 300 B.C.)

You cannot pursue knowledge without eating and drinking;
if men engaged only in the pursuit of knowledge, the
human species would die out.
SAADIA BEN JOSEPH
(892-942 A.D.)

Man and the animals are merely a passage and channel
for food, a tomb for other animals, a haven for the dead,
giving life by the death of others, a coffer full of
corruption.
LEONARDO DA VINCI
The Notebooks (1508-18)

In general, mankind, since the improvement of cookery, eat
twice as much as nature requires.
BENJAMIN FRANKLIN
(1706-1790)

Drinking when we are not thirsty and making love at any
time madame: that is all there is to distinguish us from
the animals.
PIERRE AGUSTIN DE BEAUMARCHAIS
(1732-1799)

Man is a cooking animal. The beasts have memory, judgment, and all the faculties and passions of our mind, in a certain degree; but no beast is a cook.
JAMES BOSWELL
Boswell's Tour of the Hebrides (1785)

Let there be no other difference between human beings than those of age and sex. Since all have the same needs and the same faculties, let there be one education for all, one food for all.
FRANCOIS NOEL BABEUF
Manifesto of the Equals (1795)

Animals feed, man eats; the man of intellect alone knows how to eat.
ANTHELME BRILLAT-SAVARIN
The Physiology of Taste (1825)

The destiny of nations depends upon the manner in which they feed themselves.
ANTHELME BRILLAT-SAVARIN
The Physiology of Taste (1825)

The discovery of a new dish does more for the happiness of a man than the discovery of a star.
ANTHELME BRILLAT-SAVARIN
The Physiology of Taste (1825)

I have come to the conclusion that mankind consume twice too much food.
SYDNEY SMITH
(1771-1845)

Scanty food and hard labor are in their way, if not exactly moralists, a tolerably good police.
BENJAMIN DISRAELI
Sybil (1845)

There is a savor of life and immortality in substantial fare. Like balloons, we are nothing till filled.
HERMAN MELVILLE
Mardi (1849)

When the parlor fire gets low, put coals on the kitchen fire. Such is man: no use in having their hearts, if ye don't have their stomachs.

GEORGE MEREDITH
The Ordeal of Richard Feverel (1859)

We mortals, men and women, devour many a disappointment between breakfast and dinnertime.

GEORGE ELIOT
Middlemarch (1872)

Bad cooks—and the utter lack of reason in the kitchen—have delayed human development longest and impaired it most.

FRIEDRICH NIETZSCHE
Beyond Good and Evil (1886)

Hunger and love are the pivots on which the world turns. Mankind is entirely determined by love and hunger.

ANATOLE FRANCE
The Literary Life (1888)

Man is the only animal that can remain on friendly terms with victims he intends to eat until he eats them.

SAMUEL BUTLER
(1835-1902)

Every man, of course, works out, in the course of years, a diet that seems to meet the demands of his being, but that process is slow and inaccurate. It leads to all sorts of false reasoning; it is the father and mother of prejudices; it engenders that finicky fear of certain dishes, that absurd victualaphobia which curses so many folk.

H.L. MENCKEN
in the Baltimore Evening Sun (1910)

Man is the only animal, I believe, who pretends he is thinking of other things while he is eating.

ROBERT LYND
(1879-1949)

The boa constrictor, when he has had an adequate meal, goes to sleep, and does not wake until he needs another meal. Human beings, for the most part, are not like this.
BERTRAND RUSSELL
(1872-1970)

i have noticed that when chickens quit quarreling over their food they often find that there is enough for all of them i wonder if it might not be the same with the human race.
DONALD ROBERT PERRY MARQUIS
archy's life of mehitabel (1933)

There are people who eat the earth and eat all the people on it like in the Bible with the locusts. And other people who stand around and watch them eat it.
LILLIAN HELLMAN
The Little Foxes (1939)

It is not a meaningless custom that we honor distinguished persons by dining them. By so doing we create a situation in which there is no superiority and in which we feel ourselves at one with the great man and on a level with him.
DR. WILHELM STEKEL
(1868-1940)

We are all intrinsically drawn toward our nourishment.
CHARLES JAMES
(1964)

Man is born to eat.
CRAIG CLAIBORNE
Craig Claiborne's Kitchen Primer (1969)

People are the only animals who eat themselves to death.
AMERICAN MEDICAL ASSOCIATION ADVERTISEMENT
(1971)

Food is a celebration of life. It's a universal thing: shared needs and shared experiences. It keeps us alive, it affects our attitudes, it's a social experience.
PAUL PRUDHOMME
(1984)

A hungry stomach will not allow its owner to forget it, whatever his cares and sorrows.
HOMER
Odyssey (c. 800 B.C.)

Hunger is insolent, and will be fed.
HOMER
Odyssey (c. 800 B.C.)

Hunger is the faithful comrade of the idle.
HESIOD
Works and Days (c. 700 B.C.)

Once a man be done with hunger, rich and poor are all as one.
EURIPIDES
Electra (c. 413 B.C.)

Hunger makes everything sweet except itself, for want is the teacher of habits.
ANTIPHANES
(c. 380 B.C.)

Men do not despise a thief if he steal to satisfy his soul when he is hungry.
PROVERBS 6:30
(c. 350 B.C.)

To the hungry soul every bitter thing is sweet.
PROVERBS 27:7
(c. 350 B.C.)

If only it was as easy to banish hunger by rubbing the belly as it is to masturbate.
DIOGENES THE CYNIC
(c. 390-320 B.C.)

Is it only the mouth and belly which are injured by hunger and thirst? Men's minds are also injured by them.
MENCIUS
Book of Mencius (c. 320 B.C.)

There is no word with which to answer hunger.
MENANDER
Monosticha (c. 300 B.C.)

I can fight anyone more easily than hunger.
PLAUTUS
Stichus (c. 200 B.C.)

I suspect that hunger was my mother.
PLAUTUS
Stichus (c. 200 B.C.)

When thou hast enough, remember the time of hunger.
ECCLESIASTICUS 18:25
(c. 180 B.C.)

It is not these well-fed long-haired men that I fear, but the pale and the hungry-looking.
JULIUS CAESAR
(100-44 B.C.)

Hunger is the best sauce.
CICERO
On Ethics (43 B.C.)

Hunger persuades to evil.
VIRGIL
The Aeneid (c. 19 B.C.)

Hunger is the teacher of the arts and bestower of invention.
PERSIUS
Satires (c. 60 A.D.)

He would fain have filled his belly with the husks that the swine did eat: and no man gave unto him. And when he came to himself, he said, How many hired servants of my father's have bread enough and to spare, and I perish with hunger! I will arise and go to my father, and will say unto him, Father, I have sinned against heaven, and before thee, and am no more worthy to be called thy son: make me as one of thy hired servants.
LUKE 15:16-19
(c. 75 A.D.)

For I was hungered, and ye gave me meat: I was thirsty
and ye gave me drink: I was a stranger, and ye took me in.
MATTHEW 25:35
(c. 75 A.D.)

Mithriades, by frequently drinking poison, rendered it
impossible for any poison to hurt him. You, Cinna, by
always dining on next to nothing, have taken due precaution against ever perishing from hunger.
MARTIAL
Epigrams (c. 95 A.D.)

They shall hunger no more, neither thirst any more;
neither shall the sun light on them, nor any heat.
REVELATION 7:16
(c. 95 A.D.)

Of all diseases, hunger is the worst.
ANONYMOUS
The Dhammapada (c. 100 A.D.)

All arts his own, the hungry Greekling counts;
And bid him mount the skies, the skies he mounts.
JUVENAL
Satires (c. 120 A.D.)

Hunger is a cloud out of which falls a rain of eloquence
and knowledge; when the belly is empty, the body becomes
spirit; when it is full, the spirit becomes body.
SA'DI
Golestan (1258)

If hunger makes you irritable, better eat and be pleasant.
ANONYMOUS
Book of the Pious (c. 1300)

I am more hungry than any wolf.
JOHN PALSGRAVE
Alcolastus (1540)

I am so sore forhungered that my belly weeneth my throat
is cut.
JOHN PALSGRAVE
Alcolastus (1540)

Hunger makes hard beans sweet.

JOHN HEYWOOD
Proverbs (1546)

Hunger pierceth stone walls.

JOHN HEYWOOD
Proverbs (1546)

Hunger is sharper than thorn.

THOMAS BECON
Catechism (c. 1560)

Hunger forceth the wolf out of her den.

WILLIAM PAINTER
Palace of Pleasure (1567)

Empty platters make greedy stomachs, and where scarcity
is kept, hunger is nourished.

THOMAS DELONEY
Jack of Newbury (1597)

Oppressed by two weak evils, age and hunger.

WILLIAM SHAKESPEARE
As You Like It (1599-1600)

A murrain on all proverbs. They say hunger breaks
through stone walls; but I am as gaunt as lean-ribbed
famine, yet I can burst through no stone walls.

JOHN MARSTON
Antonio's Revenge (1602)

I am Envy. . . . I am leane with seeing others eate.

CHRISTOPHER MARLOWE
Dr. Faustus (1604)

They said they were an-hungry; sigh'd forth proverbs,
That hunger broke stone walls, that dogs must eat,
That meat was made for mouths, that the gods sent not
Corn for the rich men only: with these shreds
They vented their complainings.

WILLIAM SHAKESPEARE
Coriolanus (1607-08)

I'm not voracious; only peckish.

MIGUEL DE CERVANTES
Don Quixote (1605-15)

Hunger is sharper than the sword.

JOHN FLETCHER
The Honest Man's Fortune (1613)

Hunger is good kitchen meat.

DAVID FERGUSSON
Scottish Proverbs (1641)

I and my men were hungry as hawks.

JOHN TAYLOR
Christmas In and Out (1652)

A hungry man is an angry man.

JAMES HOWELL
Proverbs (1659)

The hungry judges soon the sentence sign,
And wretches hang that jurymen may dine.

ALEXANDER POPE
The Rape of the Lock (1714)

Hunger knows no friend.

DANIEL DEFOE
Robinson Crusoe (1719)

Cruel as death, and hungry as the grave.

JAMES THOMSON
The Seasons: Winter (1726)

A hungry man smells meat afar off.

THOMAS FULLER
Gnomologia (1732)

Hunger is not dainty.

THOMAS FULLER
Gnomologia (1732)

Hungry men think the cook lazy.

THOMAS FULLER
Gnomologia (1732)

Obliged by hunger and request of friends.
ALEXANDER POPE
Epistle to Dr. Arbuthnot (1735)

Hunger is never delicate.
SAMUEL JOHNSON
Boswell's Life of Johnson (1763)

A man, doubtful of his dinner, or trembling at a creditor, is not much disposed to abstracted meditation, or remote enquiries.
SAMUEL JOHNSON
Lives of the English Poets (1779-81)

No man can be a patriot on an empty stomach.
WILLIAM COWPER
(1731-1800)

And homeless near a thousand homes I stood,
And near a thousand tables pined and wanted food.
WILLIAM WORDSWORTH
Guilt and Sorrow (1794)

I came home . . . hungry as a hunter.
CHARLES LAMB
in a letter (1800)

Hunger, by you know whom, 'tis said,
Will break through walls to get its bread.
WILLIAM COMBE
Doctor Syntax in Search of a Wife (1821)

The body craves food only that the mind may think.
WILLIAM GILMORE SIMMS
The Partisan (1835)

Hunger and recent ill-usage are great assistants if you want to cry.
CHARLES DICKENS
Oliver Twist (1837-38)

They that perish by the sword are better than they that perish by hunger.
CHARTIST MOVEMENT SLOGAN
(c. 1840)

He learns the look of things, and none the less
For admonition from the hunger-pinch.
ROBERT BROWNING
Fra Lippo Lippi (1855)

Hunger finds not fault with the cook.
C.H. SPURGEON
John Ploughman's Talk (1869)

Hunger is a slut hound on a fresh track.
JOSH BILLINGS
Josh Billings' Encyclopedia of Wit and Wisdom (1874)

Hungry rooster don't cackle w'en he fine a wum.
JOEL CHANDLER HARRIS
Uncle Remus: Legends of the Old Plantation (1881)

Much had been spoiled off the Cape, and we were on half
allowance of biscuit. . . . We took up another hole in our
belts and went on scraping, polishing, painting the ship
from morning to night. And soon she looked as though
she had come out of a bandbox; but hunger lived on board
of her. Not dead starvation, but steady living hunger that
stalked about the decks, slept in the forecastle; the tormen-
tor of waking moments, the disturber of dreams.
JOSEPH CONRAD
The Nigger of the Narcissus (1897)

No fear can stand up to hunger, no patience can wear it
out, disgust simply does not exist where hunger is; and as
to superstition, beliefs, and what you may call principles,
they are less than chaff in a breeze.
JOSEPH CONRAD
Heart of Darkness (1902)

Hunger can explain many acts. It can be said that all vile
acts are done to satisfy hunger.
MAXIM GORKY
Enemies (1906)

Because of body's hunger are we born,
And by contriving hunger are we fed;

Because of hunger is our work well done,
As so are songs well sung, and things well said.
Desire and longing are the whips of God—
God save us all from death when we are fed.
ANNA WICKHAM
Sehnsucht (1915)

Twelve hours of hunger will reduce any saint, artist, or philosopher to the level of a highwayman.
GEORGE BERNARD SHAW
(1856-1950)

Hunger is the mother of impatience and anger.
ARTHUR ZIMMERMANN
(1864-1940)

As God is my witness, as God is my witness . . . I'm never going to be hungry again. No, nor any of my folks. If I have to steal or kill—as God is my witness, I'm never going to be hungry again.
MARGARET MITCHELL
Gone With the Wind (1936)

Hunger is not debatable.
HARRY HOPKINS
(1890-1946)

The great companies did not know that the line between hunger and anger is a thin line.
JOHN STEINBECK
(1902-1968)

In hunger I am King.
NIKOS KAZANTZAKIS
(1883-1957)

There is poetry in a pork chop to a hungry man.
PHILIP GIBBS
in the New York Times (1951)

A hungry man is not a free man.
ADLAI STEVENSON
in a speech (1952)

It has been well said that a hungry man is more interested
in four sandwiches than four freedoms.
HENRY CABOT LODGE, JR.
in a speech (1955)

I am Goya
of the bare field, by the enemy's beak gouged
till the craters of my eyes gape
I am grief

I am the tongue
of war, the embers of cities
on the snows of the year 1941
I am hunger
ANDREI VOZNESENSKI
I Am Goya (1960)

You've got to stay hungry.
ARNOLD SCHWARZENEGGER
in the film Stay Hungry   (1974)

Eat before shopping. If you go to the store hungry, you are
likely to make unnecessary purchases.
AMERICAN HEART ASSOCIATION COOKBOOK
(1975)

Some people think hunger is necessary for art. It is not.
All that comes from hunger and the lower hardships, is
dullness.
JAMES STEPHENS
(1975)

Nothing changes your attitude like going hungry a couple
of days.
SAM HARRIS
in the film The Great Depression (1993)

Hunger is an infidel.
ARAB PROVERB

Hunger is the first course.
FRENCH PROVERB

Hunger will make a monkey eat pepper.
HAITIAN PROVERB

If you ask the hungry man how much is two and two, he replies four loaves.
INDIAN PROVERB

Even Fuji is without beauty to a hungry man.
JAPANESE PROVERB

When you're hungry nothing is tasteless.
JAPANESE PROVERB

If you go to sleep with an empty stomach, you will count the beams on the ceiling.
JEWISH PROVERB

The hungry man does not hear.
KENYAN PROVERB

Anyone who goes hungry for three days will steal.
KOREAN PROVERB

Hunger teaches you how to chew melon seeds.
NAMIBIAN PROVERB

Hunger is the remedy for poor cooking.
NIGERIAN PROVERB

When hunger gets inside you, nothing else can.
NIGERIAN PROVERB

I C E
C R E A M

A sallow waiter brings me beans and pork . . .
Outside there's fury in the firmament.
Ice-cream, of course, will follow; and I'm content.
O Babylon! O Carthage! O New York!
SIEGFRIED SASSOON
Storm on Fifth Avenue (1923)

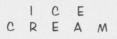

The only emperor is the emperor of ice-cream.
WALLACE STEVENS
The Emperor of Ice-Cream (1923)

You, icy sweetness of strawberry, chocolate or vanilla, melting stickily into your inverted duncecap; ravisher of appetites, leading the younger generation from the straight and narrow paths of spinach; pilferer of the pennies that might go to make a fortune; destroyer of the peace of homes, instrument of bribery and reward of virtue.
H.L. MENCKEN
in the Baltimore Evening Sun (1928)

I doubt the world holds for anyone a more soul-stirring surprise than the first adventure with ice cream.
HEYWOOD BROUN
(1888-1939)

My advice is not to inquire why or whither, but just enjoy your ice cream while it's on your plate.
THORNTON WILDER
(1897-1975)

Isn't there any other part of the matzo you can eat?
MARILYN MONROE
on being served matzo ball soup three meals in a row (c. 1955)

The bagel ⌈is⌉ an unsweetened doughnut with rigor mortis.
BEATRICE AND IRA HENRY FREEMAN
in the New York Times (1960)

It doesn't make sense—prejudice against foods. I mean, I've been eating gefilte fish for years—even before I knew Sammy Davis, Jr.
DICK GREGORY
From the Back of the Bus (1962)

He had visions of Zhitnyak appearing one day with a huge plate of well-seasoned chicken soup, thick with broad

**JEWISH/
YIDDISH**

yellow noodles, a platter of meat kreplach, and half a haleh loaf from which he would tear hunks of sweet foamy bread that melted on the tongue. He dreamed of rice and noodle puddings with raisins and cinnamon . . . and of anything that went with sour cream—blintzes, cheese kreplach, boiled potatoes, radishes scallions, sliced crisp cucumbers.

BERNARD MALAMUD
The Fixer (1966)

Roumanish-Yiddish cooking has killed more Jews than Hitler.

ZERO MOSTEL
(1915-1977)

The egg cream is psychologically the opposite of circumcision—it pleasurably reaffirms your Jewishness.

MEL BROOKS
(1975)

Safety experts agree that it is necessary to wait a week before going into the water after eating a hot knish.

TOM BUCKLEY
in the New York Times (1976)

J U N K
F O O D

I smoked cigarettes and I had affairs with Christians. But I never ate a Baby Ruth or drank a Coca-Cola.

BETTY ROLLIN
(1936 -)

The only way that I could figure they could improve upon Coca-Cola, one of life's most delightful elixirs, which studies prove will heal the sick and occasionally raise the dead, is to put rum or bourbon in it.

LEWIS GRIZZARD
IN THE NEW YORK TIMES (1985)

The Moon Pie is a bedrock of the country store and rural tradition. It is more than a snack. It is a cultural artifact.

WILLIAM FERRIS
in the New York Times (1986)

A good Kitchen is a good Apothicaries shop.
WILLIAM BULLEIN
Bullein's Bulwark of Defense Against All Sickness (1562)

Give me the provisions and whole apparatus of a kitchen,
and I would starve.
MICHEL DE MONTAIGNE
(1533-1592)

I saw him even now going the way of all flesh, that is to
say towards the kitchen.
JOHN WEBSTER
Westward Hoe (1607)

The taste of the kitchen is better than the smell.
THOMAS FULLER
Gnomologia (1732)

Kitchen physic is the best physic.
JONATHAN SWIFT
Polite and Ingenious Conversation (1738)

You better come on in my kitchen
'Cause it's going to be raining outdoors.
ROBERT JOHNSON
Come on in My Kitchen (1936)

Remember you're all alone in the kitchen, and no one can
see you.
JULIA CHILD
(1912 -)

If you can organize your kitchen, you can organize your life.
DR. LOUIS PARRISH
Cooking as Therapy (1975)

It is amazing how serious kitchens are. . . . A kitchen
seems to be a sort of garage for the emotions, a repair
shop. I have, in kitchens, permitted myself to pretend to be
profound. It is in bedrooms that I am laughable.
JOHN LEONARD
in the New York Times (c. 1980)

He who would not lose his appetite should not go into
the kitchen.
GERMAN PROVERB

All that is said in the kitchen should not be heard in
the parlor.
SCOTTISH PROVERB

No kitchen is forsaken where there is cabbage cooking.
SLOVAKIAN PROVERB

LEFTOVERS   When a gentleman makes a present of remains of a
sacrifice, he must first taste it himself.
CONFUCIUS
Analects (c. 500 B.C.)

And they did all eat, and were filled: and they took up of
the fragments that remained twelve baskets full.
MATTHEW 14:20
(c. 75 A.D.)

When they were filled, he said unto his disciples, Gather
up the fragments that remain, that nothing be lost.
JOHN 6:12
(c. 115 A.D.)

Like warmed up cabbage served at each repast,
The repetition kills the wretch at last.
JUVENAL
Satires (c. 120 A.D.)

He that keeps nor crust nor crum,
Weary of all, shall want some.
WILLIAM SHAKESPEARE
King Lear (1605-06)

A warmed-up dinner was never worth much.
NICOLAS BOILEAU
Le Lutrin (1674)

Pray take them, Sir—Enough's a Feast;
Eat some, and pocket up the rest.
ALEXANDER POPE
Imitations of Horace (1733)

Look frequently to the pails, to make sure nothing is
thrown to the pigs which should have been in the
grease-pot.
MRS. LYDIA CHILD
The American Frugal Housewife (1832)

What is left at picnics ought not to be wasted in the
wholesale manner common. I have seen wagon loads of
young people pelting each other with the half-hundred
cream cakes left from lunch. Good taste and thrift forbid
such monkeyish performances.
MRS. S.D. POWER
Anna Maria's House-Keeping (1884)

The most remarkable thing about my mother is that for
thirty years she served the family nothing but leftovers.
The original meal has never been found.
CALVIN TRILLIN
(1935 -)

If there is food left over in the kitchen, there are poor
people in the street.
CHINESE PROVERB

Cabbage twice cooked is death.
GREEK PROVERB

Whatever is eaten and drunk is gained; what remains goes
to the moneylender.
INDIAN PROVERB

Eat some, leave some; remember tomorrow.
JAMAICAN PROVERB

Cabbage is best after it is reheated seven times.
SLOVAKIAN PROVERB

L O V E Don't eat your heart.
PYTHAGORAS
(582-500 B.C.)

Sustain me with raisins, refresh me apples; for I am faint with love.
SONG OF SOLOMON 2:5
(c. 200 B.C.)

Biting poverty and cruel Cupid are my foes. Hunger I can endure; love I cannot.
CLAUDIAN
Carmina minora (c. 400 A.D.)

Let them eat the lie and swallow it with their bread. Whether the two were lovers or no, they'll have accounted to God for it by now. I have my own fish to fry.
MIGUEL DE CERVANTES
Don Quixote (1605-15)

You must sit down, says Love, and taste my meat:
So I did sit and eat.
GEORGE HERBERT
The Temple (1633)

Together let's eat
ears of wheat,
share a grass pillow.
MATSUO BASHO
(1644-1694)

And we meet, with champagne and a chicken, at last.
MARY WORTLEY MONTAGU
The Lover (c. 1747)

Love: A word properly applied to our delight in particular kinds of food; sometimes metaphorically spoken of the favorite objects of all our appetites.
HENRY FIELDING
(1707-1754)

Eat, drink, and love; the rest's not worth a fillip.
LORD BYRON
Sardanapalus (1821)

Ceres presents a plate of vermicelli—
For love must be sustained like flesh and blood—
While Bacchus pours out wine, or hands a jelly:
Eggs, oysters, too, are amatory food.
LORD BYRON
Don Juan (1823)

A Book of Verse underneath the Bough,
A Flask of Wine, a Loaf of Bread—and Thou,
Beside me singing in the Wilderness—
Oh, Wilderness were Paradise enow!
EDWARD FITZGERALD
The Rubaiyat of Omar Khayyam (1859)

It is a wonderful subduer, this need of love—this hunger of
the heart—as peremptory as that other hunger by which
Nature forces us to submit to the yoke, and change the
face of the world.
GEORGE ELIOT
The Mill on the Floss (1860)

A man must live, even though his heart be broken, and
living he must dine.
ANTHONY TROLLOPE
Phineas Finn (1869)

They dined on mince, and slices of quince,
Which they ate with a runcible spoon;
And hand in hand, on the edge of the sand,
They danced by the light of the moon.
EDWARD LEAR
The Owl and the Pussycat (1871)

There is no love sincerer than the love of food.
GEORGE BERNARD SHAW
Man and Superman (1902)

I declare that a meal prepared by a person who loves you will do more good than any average cooking, and on the other side of it a person who dislikes you is bound to get that dislike into your food, without intending to.

LUTHER BURBANK
The Harvest of the Years (1927)

It's no use raising a shout.
No, Honey, you can cut that right out.
I don't want any more hugs;
Make me some fresh tea, fetch me some rugs.
Here am I, here are you:
But what does it mean? What are we going to do?

W.H. AUDEN
It's no use raising a Shout (1929)

For those who love it, cooking is at once child's play and adult joy. And cooking done with care is an act of love.

CRAIG CLAIBORNE
Craig Claiborne's Kitchen Primer (1969)

Casanova's pursuits center entirely on instant gratification and thoughts of the next conquest, but his life seems loveless. By the end of his days, food provided his one remaining pleasure. 'At 73, no longer a god in the garden or a satyr in the forest, he is a wolf at the table,' said one who knew him.

JACQUELINE DEVAL
Reckless Appetites (1993)

The blows of a lover are like the eating of raisins.

EGYPTIAN PROVERB

Without bread, without wine, love is nothing.

FRENCH PROVERB

A lovelorn cook oversalts the porridge.

GERMAN PROVERB

Eating is preferable to amorousness.

JAPANESE PROVERB

No gentleman has soup at luncheon.
LORD GEORGE KEDLESTON
(1859-1925)

A man may be a pessimistic determinist before lunch and
an optimistic believer in the will's freedom after it.
ALDOUS HUXLEY
Do What You Will (1929)

There is no such thing as a free lunch.
MILTON FRIEDMAN
(1912 -)

Ask not what you can do for your country, ask what's
for lunch.
ORSON WELLES
(1915-1985)

Manhattan is a narrow island off the coast of New Jersey
devoted to the pursuit of lunch.
RAYMOND SOKOLOV
in the Wall Street Journal (1984)

MANNERS

At the dinner-table it becomes no one to be bashful.
PLAUTUS
Trinummus (c. 190 B.C.)

Leave off first for manners' sake; and be not unsatiable,
lest thou offend.
ECCLESIASTICUS 31:17
(c. 180 B.C.)

Manners in eating count for something.
OVID
Book of Love (c. 2 B.C.)

Persons of honor never think of eating but at sitting down
at table, and after dinner wash their hands and their

mouths, that they may neither retain the taste nor the scent of what they have been eating.

SAINT FRANCIS DE SALES
Introduction to the Devout Life (1609)

It is impolite to hold the fork, the knife, or the spoon raised in the hand, to make motions with any of those things, to carry a piece of bread to the mouth with the knife, to make use at the same time of the spoon and fork, to wipe them with the tongue, or to thrust them into the mouth. Nothing is more impolite than to lick the fingers.

SAINT JOHN BAPTIST DE LA SALLE
The Rules of Christian Manners and Civility (1695)

Never blow your soup if it is too hot, but wait until it cools. Never raise your plate to your lips, but eat with your spoon.

C.B. HARTLEY
The Gentleman's Book of Etiquette (1873)

To take a soup with a noise, or indeed to make a needless sound with the mouth while eating or drinking anything, is unrefined. To be candid, it is vulgar.

FREDERICK A. STOKES
Good Form: Dinners, Ceremonious and Unceremonious (1903)

Since hunger is the most primitive and permanent of human wants, men always eat, but since their wish not to be a mere animal is also profound, they have always attended with special care to the manners which conceal the fact that at the table we are animals feeding.

JOHN ERSKINE
The Complete Life (1943)

Sufficient food and clothing will produce good manners.

JAPANESE PROVERB

If you have a fine meal, enjoy it in a good light.
TALMUD: YOMAH
(c. 200 A.D.)

Better are meals many than one too merry.
JOHN HEYWOOD
Proverbs (1546)

Two hungry meals make the third a glutton.
JOHN HEYWOOD
Proverbs (1546)

The wholesomest meal is at another man's cost.
JAMES HOWELL
Proverbs (1659)

No prince fares like him; he breaks his fast with Aristotle, dines with Tully, drinks tea at Helicon, sups with Seneca.
COLLEY CIBBER
Love Makes the Man (1701)

He that banquets every day never makes a good meal.
THOMAS FULLER
Gnomologia (1732)

Three good meals a day is bad living.
BENJAMIN FRANKLIN
Poor Richard's Almanac (1744)

So munch on, crunch on, take your nuncheon,
Breakfast, supper, dinner, luncheon.
ROBERT BROWNING
The Pied Piper of Hamelin (1842)

Wine is the intellectual part of a meal while meat is the material.
ALEXANDRE DUMAS
(1802-1870)

I do not want Michael Angelo for breakfast—for luncheon—for dinner—for tea—for supper—for between meals.
MARK TWAIN
The Innocents Abroad (1869)

A choice meal does not necessarily imply great expense, or great skill in preparation. The first requisite for a good dinner is good sense.

WILLIAM JONES
Take My Advice (1872)

'Oh, my friends, be warned by me,
That breakfast, dinner, lunch and tea
Are all the human frame requires . . .'
With that the wretched child expires.

HILAIRE BELLOC
Cautionary Tales (1907)

A good meal makes a man feel more charitable toward the whole world than any sermon.

ARTHUR PENDENYS
(1865-1946)

Nearly everyone wants at least one outstanding meal a day.

DUNCAN HINES
Adventures in Good Eating (1936)

The first of all considerations is that our meals shall be fun as well as fuel.

ANDRE SIMON
(1877-1970)

Eat breakfast like a king, lunch like a prince, and dinner like a pauper.

ADELLE DAVIS
Let's Eat Right to Keep Fit (1954)

She could still taste the plump fine oysters from Zeeland he had ordered for her last meal in the world, the dry sparkle of the vintage Rudesheimer which had cost him the fees of at least five visits to patients, and the ice cream richly sauced with crushed glazed chestnuts which she loved.

KATHRYN HULME
The Nun's Story (1956)

A good meal in troubled times is always that much salvaged from disaster.
A.J. LIEBLING
(1904-1963)

Apart from sleeping, the only time a prisoner lives for himself is ten minutes in the morning at breakfast, five minutes over dinner, and five at supper.
ALEXANDER SOLZHENITSYN
One Day in the Life of Ivan Denisovich (1962)

Long meals, short prayers.
CZECH PROVERB

M E A T

Whatsoever parteth the hoof, and is clovenfooted, and cheweth the cud, among the beasts, that shall ye eat.
LEVITICUS 11:3
(c. 700 B.C.)

I will eat flesh, because thy soul longeth to eat flesh; thou mayest eat flesh, whatsoever thy soul lusteth after.
DEUTERONOMY 12:20
(c. 650 B.C.)

We bend our bows; our shafts we grasp;
There lies the huge behemoth low,
And boars are pierced—spoil for the guests,
At court, when wine-cups overflow.
ANONYMOUS (EDITED BY CONFUCIUS)
Book of Poetry (c. 500 B.C.)

Out of the eater came forth meat, and out of the strong came forth sweetness.
JUDGES 14:14
(c. 500 B.C.)

Strong meat belongeth to them that are of full age.
HEBREWS 5:14
(c. 65 A.D.)

You require flesh if you want to be fat.
MARTIAL
Epigrams (c. 95 A.D.)

Bees are generated from decomposed veal.
SAINT ISIDORE OF SEVILLE
(c. 650 A.D.)

The most nourishing meat is first to be eaten, that ancient proverb ratifieth: Ab ovo ad mala, from the egg to the apples.
THOMAS MOFFETT
Health's Improvement (1590)

It is meat and drink to me.
WILLIAM SHAKESPEARE
As You Like It (1599-1600)

Upon what meat doth this our Caesar feed,
That he is grown so great?
WILLIAM SHAKESPEARE
Julius Caesar (1599-1600)

Come, we have a hot venison pasty to dinner.
WILLIAM SHAKESPEARE
The Merry Wives of Windsor (1600-01)

But mice and rats and such small deer
Have been Tom's food for seven long year.
WILLIAM SHAKESPEARE
King Lear (1605-06)

All flesh is not venison.
GEORGE HERBERT
Outlandish Proverbs (1640)

Out-did the meat, out-did the frolick wine.
ROBERT HERRICK
Hesperides (1648)

This dish of meat is too good for any but anglers, or very honest men.
IZAAK WALTON
The Compleat Angler (1653)

Thou givest them their meat in due season. Thou openest thine hand: and fillest all things living with plenteousness.
THE BOOK OF COMMON PRAYER 145:15
(1662)

Eat thy meat and drink thy drink,
And stand thy ground, old Harry.
JOHN RAY
English Proverbs (1670)

It is good to be merry at meat.
JOHN RAY
English Proverbs (1670)

All courageous animals are carnivorous, and greater courage is to be expected in a people, such as the English, whose food is strong and hearty, than in the half-starved commonalty of other countries.
SIR WILLIAM TEMPLE
Miscellanea (1692)

The flesh is aye fairest that is farthest from the bone.
JAMES KELLY
Complete Collection of Scottish Proverbs (1721)

Catius is ever moral, ever grave,
Thinks who endures a knave, is next a knave,
Save just at dinner—then prefers, no doubt,
A rogue with venison to a saint without.
ALEXANDER POPE
Moral Essays (1733)

It is a fact that great eaters of meat are in general more cruel and ferocious than other men.
JEAN JACQUES ROUSSEAU
Emile (1762)

One cut from venison to the heart can speak
Stronger than ten quotations from the Greek.
PETER PINDAR
Bozzy and Piozzi (1786)

Some hae meat and canna eat,
And some wad eat that want it;
But we hae meat, and we can eat,
and sae the Lord be thankit.
ROBERT BURNS
Grace Before Meat (1795)

It is only by softening and disguising dead flesh by culinary preparation that it is rendered susceptible of
mastication or digestion; and that the sight of its bloody
juices and raw horror does not excite intolerable loathing
and disgust.
PERCY BYSSHE SHELLEY
Queen Mab (1813)

But man is a carnivorous production,
And must have meals, at least one meal a day;
He cannot live, like woodcocks, upon suction,
But, like the shark and tiger, must have prey.
Although his anatomical construction
Bears vegetables, in a grumbling way,
Your laboring people think, beyond all question,
Beef, veal, and mutton better for digestion.
LORD BYRON
Don Juan (1823)

We had venison served in half a dozen different ways. We
had antelope; we had porcupine, or hedgehog, as Pathfinder
called it; and also we had beaver-tail, which he found
toothsome, but which I did not.
JAMES FENIMORE COOPER
The Pathfinder (1840)

A man has often more trouble to digest meat than to
get it.
H.G. BOHN
A Handbook of Proverbs (1855)

He crams with cans of poisoned meat
The subjects of the King

And when they die by thousands
Why, he laughs like anything.
G.K. CHESTERTON
Song Against Grocers (1915)

Avoid fried meats, which angry up the blood.
SATCHEL PAIGE
How to Keep Young (1953)

No butcher ever sold my mother a piece of meat without
holding it up high and twisting it so she could see how fat
it was. You take the meat as it comes today, wrapped in
plastic and half-hidden by cardboard trays out of those
refrigerated boxes in the supermarket. If babies came in
plastic the way our food does, the world would be filled
with waifs.
HARRY GOLDEN
(1903-1981)

We are the knights of Camelot,
We eat ham and jam and Spam-a-lot.
ENSEMBLE CAST
from the film Monty Python and the Holy Grail (1974)

If you buy meat cheap, you will smell what you have saved
when it boils.
ARAB PROVERB

Meat twice cooked and a friend twice reconciled are hardly
ever good.
CZECH PROVERB

Better a mouse in the pot than no flesh at all.
ENGLISH PROVERB

If there is no meat, be content with broth.
FILIPINO PROVERB

Meat, not hay, makes the lion roar.
JEWISH PROVERB

They who eat much meat talk too much.
JEWISH PROVERB

No one will throw away venison for squirrel's flesh.
NIGERIAN PROVERB

Who eats the meat can pick the bone.
SPANISH PROVERB

Locust meat is better than pumpkin relish.
ZIMBABWEAN PROVERB

M E N

Let men take heed how they eate, either of wantonesse, or of appetite.
WILLIAM VAUGHAN
Naturall and Artificial Directions for Health (1602)

Men are all but stomachs, and we all but food;
They eat us hungrily, and when they are full
They belch us.
WILLIAM SHAKESPEARE
Othello (1604-05)

What a relief to the labouring husband to have a warm comfortable meal!
MARIA ELIZA RUNDELL
A New System of Domestic Cookery (1807)

I have heard it remarked by a statesman of high reputation, that most great men have died of over-eating themselves.
HENRY TAYLOR
The Statesman (1836)

Men are . . . conservatives after dinner.
RALPH WALDO EMERSON
Essays: Second Series (1844)

A man is hungry all day long. A man is perpetually eating.
CHARLES DICKENS
David Copperfield (1849-50)

A very man—not one of nature's clods—
With human failings, whether saint or sinner:
Endowed perhaps with genius from the gods
But apt to take his temper from his dinner.
J.G.SAXE
About Husbands (1859)

The way to a man's heart is through his stomach.
FANNY FERN
Willis Parton (c. 1860)

Men don't belong in a kitchen.
LOUISA MAY ALCOTT
An Old-Fashioned Girl (1870)

Men who come courting are just like bad cooks: If you are
kind to them, instead of ascribing it to an exceptional
courtesy on your part, they instantly set it down to their
own marvelous worth.
THOMAS HARDY
The Hand of Ethelberta (1876)

You have to please men with cookery, or they will be
worse than bears with sore heads.
HANNAH WHITALL SMITH
(1832-1911)

After violent emotions most people and all boys demand
food.
RUDYARD KIPLING
Captains Courageous (1897)

Men make better cooks than women because they put so
much more feeling into it.
MYRTLE REED
The Spinster Book (1901)

How to Cook a Husband: A good many husbands are
entirely spoiled by mismanagement in cooking, and so are
not tender and good. Some women keep them too constantly
in hot water; others freeze them; others put them in a
stew; others keep them constantly in a pickle. It cannot be

supposed that any husband will be good and tender if managed in this way. But they are truly delicious if properly treated, agreeing nicely with you, and he will keep as long as you want to have him.

ANONYMOUS
in the Bermuda Royal Gazette (1916)

Out of the ash
I rise with my red hair
And I eat men like air.

SYLVIA PLATH
Lady Lazarus (1966)

I have always believed that among his unalienable rights, a man has a right to cook: especially Sunday breakfast when time is not of the essence. He should be able to cook the things he wants the way he wants them and when he wants them. And I propose that he do it alone. For there's nothing more disturbing to a man in the kitchen than a woman.

WILLIAM C. ROUX
Fried Coffee and Jellied Bourbon (1967)

The first want of man is his dinner, and the second is his girl.

JOHN ADAMS
quoted in James David Barbar's The Presidential Character (1972)

Bigamist—A man who marries a beautiful girl and a good cook.

ANONYMOUS

MODERATION   Be not among winebibbers; among riotous eaters of flesh.

PROVERBS 23:20
(c. 350 B.C.)

If you feel driven to eat, get up in the middle of a meal—and stop.

ECCLESIASTICUS 31:21
(c. 180 B.C.)

Just enough food and drink should be taken to restore our strength, and not to overburden it.
CICERO
On Old Age (c. 78 B.C.)

Stop short of your appetite; eat less than you are able.
OVID
Book of Love (c. 2 B.C.)

Eat a third, drink a third, and leave a third of your stomach empty; then, should anger seize you, there will be room for its rage.
TALMUD: GITTIN
(c. 200 A.D.)

There are eight things of which little is good and much is bad: travel, mating, wealth, work, wine, sleep, spiced drinks, and medicine.
TALMUD: GITTIN
(c. 200 A.D.)

Work before eating, rest after eating. Eat not ravenously, filling the mouth gulp after gulp without breathing space.
MAIMONIDES
Responsa Medica (c. 1200)

Eat without surfeit: drink without drunkenness.
JOHN RUSSELL
Boke of Nurture (c. 1460)

Unhappy are they which have more appetite than their stomake.
SIR THOMAS ELYOT
The Bankette of Sapience (1545)

Leave with an appetite.
WILLIAM BULLEIN
The Government of Health (1558)

Food, improperly taken, not only produces original diseases, but affords those that are already engendered both matter and sustenance; so that, let the father of disease be what it may, Intemperance is certainly its mother.
ROBERT BURTON
The Anatomy of Melancholy (1651)

Eat less and drink less,
And buy a knife at Michaelmas.
JAMES HOWELL
Proverbs (1659)

Eat at pleasure, drink by measure.
JOHN RAY
English Proverbs (1670)

To lengthen thy life, lessen thy meals.
BENJAMIN FRANKLIN
Poor Richard's Almanac (1733)

Quantity in food is more to be regarded than quality: a full meal is the great enemy both to study and industry.
SAMUEL RICHARDSON
Clarissa (1747-48)

Eat not to dullness; drink not to elevation.
BENJAMIN FRANKLIN
Autobiography (1759)

A good cook is a certain slow poisoner, if you are not temperate.
VOLTAIRE
Philosophical Dictionary (1764)

We never repent of having eaten too little.
THOMAS JEFFERSON
(1743-1826)

He who restrains his appetite avoids debt.
CHINESE PROVERB

Light suppers make clean sheets.
ENGLISH PROVERB

When the food tastes best, stop eating.
SLOVAKIAN PROVERB

If music be the food of love, play on.

WILLIAM SHAKESPEARE
Twelfth Night (1601-02)

Music, moody food
Of us that trade in love.

WILLIAM SHAKESPEARE
Antony and Cleopatra (1606-07)

Seasoning is in Cookery what chords are in music.

LOUIS EUSTACHE UDE
The French Cook (1813)

In the domain of victuals, as in that of music, remote
tones often combine into exquisite harmonies.

H.L. MENCKEN
in the Baltimore Evening Sun (1910)

Music with dinner is an insult both to the cook and the
violinist.

G.K. CHESTERTON
(1874-1936)

M U S I C

Let us return to our muttons.

ANONYMOUS
Maistre Pierre Patelin (1450)

Flesh of a mutton is food for a glutton.

RANDLE COTGRAVE
French-English Dictionary (1611)

Of all birds give me mutton.

THOMAS FULLER
Gnomologia (1732)

There are 72 ways of cooking lamb. Of these only 18 or 19
are palatable.

YUAN MEI
The Menu (1797)

M U T T O N

There was an old man of Tobago,
Who lived on rice, gruel, and sago;
Till, much to his bliss,
His physician said this—
To a leg, sir of mutton you may go.
JOHN MARSHALL
Anectdotes and Adventures of Fifteen Gentleman (1822)

The leg of mutton of Wales beats the leg of mutton of any other country.
GEORGE BORROW
Wild Wales (1862)

On Monday we've mutton, with damper and tea;
On Tuesday, tea, damper and mutton,
Such dishes I'm certain all men must agree
Are fit for peer peasant and glutton.
REVEREND FRANCIS LANCELOTT
On Monday We've Mutton (c. 1900)

NATURE

And the ravens brought him bread and flesh in the morning, and bread and flesh in the evening; and he drank of the brook.
II KINGS 17:5
(c. 500 B.C.)

Nature indeed will have her due, but yet whatsoever is beyond necessity is superfluous and not necessary. It is not her business to gratify the palate, but to satisfy a craving stomach.
SENECA
On the Happy Life (c. 58 A.D.)

Every investigation which is guided by principles of nature fixes its ultimate aim entirely on gratifying the stomach.
ATHENAEUS
The Gastronomers (c. 200 A.D.)

Nature delights in the most plain and simple diet. Every animal, but man, keeps to one dish.
JOSEPH ADDISON
in The Spectator (1711)

The hours we pass with happy prospects in view are more pleasing than those crowned with fruition. In the first case, we cook the dish to our appetite; in the latter Nature cooks it for us.
OLIVER GOLDSMITH
The Vicar of Wakefield (1766)

In compelling man to eat that he may live, Nature gives an appetite to invite him, and pleasure to reward him.
ANTHELME BRILLAT-SAVARIN
The Physiology of Taste (1825)

Among the great whom Heaven has made to shine,
How few have learned the art of arts—to dine!
Nature, indulgent to our daily need,
Kind-hearted mother! taught us all to feed;
But the chief art—how rarely Nature flings
This choicest gift among her social kings!
OLIVER WENDELL HOLMES
The Banker's Secret (1855)

The air was a sort of diet drink . . .
HENRY DAVID THOREAU
The Maine Woods (1864)

Eating is ignoble. Nature should have managed it differently.
ANTHONY TROLLOPE
Ayala's Angel (1881)

The whole of nature, as has been said, is a conjugation of the verb to eat, in the active and passive.
WILLIAM RALPH INGE
Outspoken Essays (1919)

Certain it is that no synthetic diet that I have been able to devise has equalled in health-sustaining qualities one composed of the fresh foodstuffs as nature provides them.
SIR ROBERT MCCARRISON
Nutrition and National Health (1944)

The act of putting into your mouth what the earth has grown is perhaps your most direct interaction with the earth.
FRANCES MOORE LAPPE
Diet for a Small Planet (1971)

I do not know of a flowering plant that tastes good and is poisonous. Nature is not out to get you.
EUELL GIBBONS
(1911-1975)

N E V E R E A T...

Rice affected by the weather or turned a man must not eat, nor fish that is not sound, nor meat that is high. He must not eat anything discolored or that smells bad. He must not eat what is overcooked, nor what is undercooked, nor anything that is out of season. He must not eat what has been crookedly cut, nor any dish that lacks its proper seasoning. The meat that he eats must not be enough to make his breath smell of meat rather than of rice. As regards wine, no limit is laid down; but he must not be disorderly.
CONFUCIUS
Analects (c. 500 B.C.)

Never eat anything bigger than your head.
B. KLIBAN
Never Eat Anything Bigger Than Your Head and Other Drawings (1976)

Never eat anything at one sitting that you can't lift.
MISS PIGGY (AS TOLD TO HENRY BEARD)
Miss Piggy's Guide to Life (1981)

I will never eat fish eyeballs, and I do not want to taste anything commonly kept as a house pet, but otherwise I am a cinch to feed.
LAURIE COLWIN
Home Cooking (1988)

Macrows: Take and make a thin foil of dough, and carve it in pieces, and cast them on boiling water, and seeth it well. Take cheese and grate it and butter cast beneath and above . . . and serve forth.

ANONYMOUS
The Forme of Cury (c. 1390)

No man is lonely while eating spaghetti—it requires too much attention.

CHRISTOPHER MORLEY
(1890-1957)

It is a very great mistake to suppose, as a few English cooks still do, that spaghetti and macaroni should be soaked in water before cooking.

ELIZABETH DAVID
(1913 -)

Everything you see I owe to spaghetti.

SOPHIA LOREN
(1934 -)

NOODLES

Jaded my appetite, I loathe my food,
And curse each hateful meal in peevish mood.

OVID
The Invalid (c. 5 A.D.)

I hate a man who swallows ⌈his food⌉, affecting not to know what he is eating. I suspect his taste in higher matters.

CHARLES LAMB
Essays of Elia (1823)

Dr. Middleton misdoubted the future as well as the past of the man who did not, in becoming gravity, exult to dine. That man he deemed unfit for this world and the next.

GEORGE MEREDITH
The Egoist (1879)

NOT INTERESTED

Taking food and drink is a great enjoyment for healthy people, and those who do not enjoy eating seldom have much capacity for enjoyment or usefulness of any sort.
CHARLES W. ELIOT
The Happy Life (1896)

One of the great disadvantages of being a coward is that one is constantly having to eat things that one does not wish to eat.
ROBERT LYND
The Blue Lion (1923)

I say it's spinach and I say the hell with it.
E.B WHITE
cartoon caption in The New Yorker (1928)

Like everything else, meals are tiresome, but it is no use to make a fuss, because nothing else will be less tiresome.
BERTRAND RUSSELL
The Conquest of Happiness (1930)

I do not eat for the sake of enjoyment.
MOHANDAS GANDHI
(1869-1948)

We lived for days on nothing but food and water.
W.C. FIELDS
(1879-1946)

In a restaurant I order everything I don't want, so I have a lot to play around with while everybody else is eating.
ANDY WARHOL
The Philosophy of Andy Warhol (1975)

Eating and sleeping are a waste of time.
GERALD FORD
(1913 -)

I no longer prepare food or drink with more than one ingredient.
CYRA McFADDEN
(1937 -)

It is so beautifully arranged on the plate—you know someone's fingers have been all over it.
JULIA CHILD
(1912 -)

Food is to eat, not to frame and hang on the wall.
WILLIAM DENTON
in the New York Times (1987)

The way I feel about it is: Beat me or feed me, but don't tease me.
JEFF SMITH
in the Boston Globe (1987)

Nothing is on the plate and everything is on the bill.
PAUL BOCUSE
in Chicago magazine (1989)

Take any back-to-the-land garden grubfest from the 1960's, cut the portions in half, and shuffle the remainder around your plate in a pentangle or triskelion pattern and—voila! You've got nouvelle cuisine.
TAD TULEJA
Quirky Quotations (1992)

I'm not a big proponent of nouvelle cuisine—the little bitty portions squarely centered on a very large plate. Makes me angry just to look at it.
SHELBY FOOTE
in Bon Appetit (1993)

NUMBERS

I write these precepts for immortal Greece,
That round a table delicately spread,
Three, or four, may sit in choice repast,
Or five at most. Who otherwise shall dine,
Are like a troop marauding for their prey.
ARCHESTRATUS
Pleasant Living (350 B.C.)

The number of guests at dinner should not be less than the number of the Graces nor exceed that of the Muses, i.e., it should begin with three and stop at nine.
MARCUS TERENTIUS VARRO
(116-27 B.C.)

The more the merrier; the fewer, the better fare.
JOHN PALSGRAVE
L'Eclair (1530)

Crowd not your table: let your numbers be not more than seven, and never less than three.
WILLIAM KING
The Art of Cookery (1708)

Five is the very awkwardest of all possible numbers to sit down to table.
JANE AUSTEN
Mansfield Park (1814)

The best number for a dinner party is two—myself and a damn good head waiter.
NUBAR GULBENKIAN
in the London Daily Telegraph (1965)

Gastronomical perfection can be reached in these combinations: one person dining alone, usually upon a couch or a hillside; two persons, of no matter what sex or age, dining in a good restaurant; six people, of no matter what sex or age, dining in a good home.
M.F.K. FISHER
(1908-1992)

Heavenly Father, bless us,
And keep us all alive,
There's ten of us to dinner
And not enough for five.
ANONYMOUS

Seven make a banquet; nine make a clamor.
ANONYMOUS

We are all dietetic sinners; only a small percent of what we eat nourishes us; the balance goes to waste and loss of energy.
SIR WILLIAM OSLER
(1849-1919)

The extra calories needed for one hour of mental effort would be completely met by the eating of one oyster cracker or one half of a salted peanut.
FRANCIS G. BENEDICT
The Energy Requirement of Intense Mental Effort (c. 1935)

We are indeed much more than we eat, but what we eat can nevertheless help us to be much more than what we are.
ADELLE DAVIS
Let's Get Well (1965)

The longer I work in nutrition, the more convinced I become that for the healthy person all foods should be delicious.
ADELLE DAVIS
(1904-1974)

NUTS

Who will eat the kernel of the nut must break the shell.
JOHN GRANGE
The Golden Aphroditis (1577)

Across the walnuts and the wine.
ALFRED, LORD TENNYSON
The Miller's Daughter (1832)

No man in the world has more courage than the man who can stop after eating one peanut.
CHANNING POLLOCK
(1880-1946)

Don't eat too many almonds. They add weight to the breasts.
SIDONIE COLETTE
Gigi (1945)

I hate television. I hate it as much as peanuts. But I can't stop eating peanuts.
ORSON WELLES
(1915-1985)

Pistachio nuts, the red ones, cure any problem.
PAULA DANZIGER
The Pistachio Prescription (1978)

In Bali, women are forbidden to touch coconut palms lest the fertility of the tree be drained off into the fertility of the woman, apparently considered less important.
WAVERLEY ROOT
Food (1980)

Eat coconuts while you have your teeth.
INDIAN PROVERB

A man cannot marry if he does not have cashews.
JAMAICAN PROVERB

He who cracks the coconut must eat the cream.
KENYAN PROVERB

He who plants a coconut tree plants vessels and clothing, food and drink, a habitation for himself, and a heritage for his children.
SAMOAN PROVERB

The harder the shell of a nut, the less is there in its center.
WELSH PROVERB

O A T S

Titania: Or say, sweet love, what thou desirest to eat.
Bottom: Truly a peck of provender: I could munch your
          good dry oats.
WILLIAM SHAKESPEARE
A Midsummer Night's Dream (1595-96)

A grain which in England is generally given to horses, but in Scotland supports the people.
SAMUEL JOHNSON
Dictionary of the English Language (1775)

How often had Shukhov in his youth fed oats to horses! Never had it occurred to him that there'd come a time when his whole soul would yearn for a handful of them.
ALEXANDER SOLZHENITSYN
One Day in the Life of Ivan Denisovich (1962)

How say you to a fat tripe finely broil'd?
WILLIAM SHAKESPEARE
The Taming of the Shrew (1593-94)

O F F A L

Tripe's good meat if it be well wiped.
JOHN RAY
English Proverbs (1670)

Kidneys cooked for an hour are tough; after a day they become tender.
YUAN MEI
The Menu (1797)

Tripe broth is better than no porridge.
H.G. BOHN
Handbook of Proverbs (1855)

Leopold Bloom ate with relish the inner organs of beasts and fowls. He liked thick giblet soup, nutty gizzards, a stuffed roast heart, liver slices fried with breadcrumbs, fried hencod's roe. Most of all he liked grilled mutton kidneys which gave to his palate a fine tang of scented urine.
JAMES JOYCE
Ulysses (1922)

Tripe, like certain alluring vices, is enjoyed by societies two extremes, the topmost and the lowermost strata, while the multitudinous middle classes of the world look upon it with genteel disdain and noses tilted. Patricians relished tripe in Babylon's gardens, plebians have always welcomed it as something good and cheap, and always the peasant cook has taught the prince how to eat it.
VARIOUS AUTHORS
Wise Encyclopedia of Cookery (1951)

O L I V E S

It is quite affecting to observe how much the olive tree is to the country people. Its fruit supplies them with food, medicine and light; its leaves, winter fodder for the goats and sheep; it is their shelter from the heat and its branches and roots supply them with firewood. The olive tree is the peasant's all-in-all.

FREDRIKA BREMER
(1801-1865)

The whole Mediterranean, the sculpture, the palms, the gold beads, the bearded heroes, the wine, the ideas, the ships, the moonlight, the winged gorgons, the bronze men, the philosophers—all of it seems to rise in the sour, pungent smell of these black olives between the teeth. A taste older than meat, older than wine. A taste as old as cold water.

LAWRENCE DURRELL
(1912-1990)

Thou art like olives: it is needful to beat thee.

ARAB PROVERB

O N I O N S

As often as you have eaten the strong-smelling shoots of Tarentine leeks give kisses with shut mouth.

MARTIAL
Epigrams (c. 95 A.D.)

Eat no onions nor garlic, for we are to utter sweet breath.

WILLIAM SHAKESPEARE
A Midsummer Night's Dream (1595-96)

By this leek, I will most horribly revenge.
I eat and eat, I swear.

WILLIAM SHAKESPEARE
Henry V (1598-99)

If thou hast not a capon feed on an onion.

JOHN RAY
English Proverbs (1670)

An honest laborious Country-man, with good Bread, Salt and a little Parsley, will make a contented Meal with a roasted Onion.
JOHN EVELYN
Acetaria (1699)

Onions can make ev'n heirs and widows weep.
BENJAMIN FRANKLIN
Poor Richard's Almanac (1734)

How beautiful and strong those buttered onions come to my nose!
CHARLES LAMB
Letter to Thomas Manning (1800)

Let onions lurk within the bowl
And scarce-suspected, animate the whole.
SYDNEY SMITH
A Receipt for Salad (1810)

The kitchen, reasonably enough, was the scene of my first gastronomic adventure. I was on all fours. I crawled in to the vegetable bin, settled on a giant onion and ate it, skin and all. It must have marked me for life, for I have never ceased to love the hearty flavor of raw onions.
JAMES BEARD
Delights and Prejudices (1964)

What a thrill—
My thumb instead of an onion.
SYLVIA PLATH
Cut (1966)

He who counts the onions and garlic shouldn't eat the stew.
ARMENIAN PROVERB

Onions, smoke, and a shrew make a good man's eyes water.
DANISH PROVERB

Live in a place and eat of its onions.
EGYPTIAN PROVERB

Lentils without onions are like a dance without music.
GREEK PROVERB

However good garlic is, it will not be as good as an onion.
NIGERIAN PROVERB

Onion and garlic are born brothers.
RUSSIAN PROVERB

OYSTERS

The oyster is unseasonable and unwholesome in all months that have not the letter R in their name.
RICHARD BUTTES
Diet's Dry Dinner (1599)

The world's mine oyster,
Which I with sword will open.
WILLIAM SHAKESPEARE
The Merry Wives of Windsor (1600-01)

Oysters . . . are ungodly, because they are eaten without grace; uncharitable, because they leave naught but shells; and unprofitable, because they must swim in wine.
ANONYMOUS
Tarlton's Jests (1611)

He was a very valiant man who first adventured on eating of oysters.
THOMAS FULLER
History of the Worthies of England (1662)

The gravest fish is an oyster.
ALLAN RAMSAY
Scots Proverbs (1737)

Oysters are a cruel meat because we eat them alive; they are an uncharitable meat, for we leave nothing to the poor.
JONATHAN SWIFT
Polite and Ingenious Conversation (1738)

An oyster may be crossed in love.
R.B. SHERIDAN
The Critic (1779)

I beg a thousand pardons, my friend, but permit me to
finish this last dozen of oysters.
ARMAND LOUIS DE GONTAUT
to his executioner (1793)

The oyster loves the dredging song
For they come of a gentle kind.
SIR WALTER SCOTT
The Antiquary (1816)

'It's a wery remarkable circumstance, sir,' said Sam, 'that
poverty and oysters always seem to go together.'
CHARLES DICKENS
Pickwick Papers (1836-37)

An oyster, that marvel of delicacy, that concentration of
sapid excellence, that mouthful before all other mouthfuls,
who first had faith to believe it, and courage to execute?
The exterior is not persuasive.
HENRY WARD BEECHER
Eyes and Ears (1862)

He had often eaten oysters, but had never had enough.
W.S. GILBERT
The 'Bab' Ballads (1866-71)

Bismarck also confesses a weakness for fried oysters; this,
in my opinion, is treason to gastronomy.
JULES HOCHE
Bismarck at Home (1888)

Mr. President, people up in this part of the country never
have learned to fry oysters as well as we have done down
our way.
LOUISIANA SENATOR HUEY LONG
in a filibuster oration (1935)

A flaccid, moping, debauched mollusk, tired from too
much love and loose-nerved from general world conditions,
can be a shameful thing served raw upon the shell.
M.F.K. FISHER
Consider the Oyster (1941)

The Louisiana oyster in winter is still a solace to the man
of moderate means.
A.J. LIEBLING
The Earl of Louisiana (1961)

If you don't love life you can't enjoy an oyster; there is a
shock of freshness to it and intimations of the ages of
man, some piercing intuition of the sea and all its weeds
and breezes.
ELEANOR CLARK
The Oysters of Locmariaquer (1964)

I have always believed that New Orleans jazz can be
exported; it's the oyster loaves that won't travel.
CALVIN TRILLIN
Alice, Let's Eat (1978)

I will not eat oysters. I want my food dead—not sick, not
wounded—dead.
WOODY ALLEN
(1935 -)

I prefer my oysters fried;
That way I know my oysters died.
ROY BLOUNT, JR.
(1941 -)

An oyster is a fish built like a nut.
ANONYMOUS

P A L A T E The pleasures of the palate deal with us like Egyptian
thieves who strangle those whom they embrace.
SENECA
(4 B.C.-65 A.D.)

In their palate alone is their reason of existence.
JUVENAL
Satires (c. 120 A.D.)

Everybody loves to have things which please the palate put in their way, without trouble or preparation.

SAMUEL JOHNSON
Boswell's Life of Johnson (1778)

A man's palate can, in time, become accustomed to anything.

NAPOLEON BONAPARTE
To Gaspard Gourgaud at Saint Helena (1815-18)

The palate craves enjoyment; and that craving, being a natural one, must be recognized as such. But what I insist upon is this; namely, that gratifying the palate shall not rank among the chief occupations or the chief enjoyments of life, for it has usurped those positions long enough.

A.M. DIAZ
Papers Found in the School Master's Trunk (1875)

To the trained palate the flavor of food comes in bits and pieces, like words in a sentence.

HSIANG JU LIN AND TSUIFENG LIN
Chinese Gastronomy (1969)

Pastry is poisoned bread. Never eat pastry. Be a plain man, and stick to plain things.

HERMAN MELVILLE
Israel Potter (1855)

PASTRY

The Queen of Hearts, she made some tarts,
All on a summer day;
The Knave of Hearts, he stole those tarts,
And took them quite away!

LEWIS CARROLL
Alice's Adventures in Wonderland (1865)

Peter Piper pick'd a peck of pickled peppers.
Where is the peck of pickled peppers Peter Piper pick'd?

J.K. PAULDING
Konigsmarke (1823)

PEPPERS

The speed with which hot peppers spread around the globe is unequalled in the annals of food.
RICHARD SCHWEID
Hot Peppers (1980)

The Negro woman is the pepper, and everyone receives nourishment from her.
BRAZILIAN PROVERB

Pepper has a beautiful face with an ugly temper.
ETHIOPIAN PROVERB

A little pepper burns a big man's mouth.
JAMAICAN PROVERB

Rub an old woman's back, and she will let you taste her pepper pot.
JAMAICAN PROVERB

Be as wary of a lovely woman as you would be of a red pepper.
JAPANESE PROVERB

The red pepper, though small, is hot.
KOREAN PROVERB

PICKLES

Hunger is the best Pickle.
BENJAMIN FRANKLIN
Poor Richard's Almanac (1750)

As long as the great American picnic-goer likes pickles, you may as well provide them, for the relief of possible bilious tendencies . . .
MRS. S.D. POWER
Anna Maria's House-Keeping (1884)

If you lift the lid the smell will come up to meet you, but if you stir it on a clear day and it gives off hot gases, start all over again.
ANONYMOUS
ancient Chinese pickle recipe

It is then in the midst of a forest or wood, with thickly tufted trees, where a rural feast ought to be held; everything ought to be transported thither in large baskets, which we will suppose is a cold dinner, but which the fire of good wine and your amiable pleasantries will not be long in warming. The zest of your enjoyment and your wit ought to render the dinner exquisite, though even in itself it should not be worth much.

D. HUMBERGIUS SECUNDUS
Tales of the Table, Kitchen and Larder (1836)

Meals are always eaten indoors, except when, once or twice a year, fantastic folk, wishing to try a short vicissitude and fit of incongruity, choose to share them with the ants and earwigs in the open air.

A LADY
The Lady's Companion (1851)

Picnics have a special enjoyment of their own; and we cannot but regret that with the advance of civilization this good old custom bids fair to be lost. . . . Have we gained in true enjoyment by increasing elegance, and requiring no one at present to bring anything but their best dress, their best looks, and their best spirits? We think not, and plead for the good old-fashioned picnic of other days.

SARAH JOSEPHA HALE
Manners: or Happy Homes & Good Society All the Year Around (1868)

Some persons bring upon the campground food that is entirely unsuitable to such occasions, rich cakes and pies, and a variety of dishes that would derange the digestion of a healthy labouring man. Nothing should be taken except the most healthful articles, cooked in a simple manner, free from all spices and grease.

ELLEN G. WHITE
Counsels on Diet and Food (1870)

There is no more wholesome or satisfactory method of entertainment—cheap or dear—than an afternoon tea or noon-day lunch in the woods in fine summer weather.
MARION HARLAND
The Cottage Kitchen (1883)

He got out the luncheon-basket and packed a simple meal, in which, remembering the stranger's origin and preferences, he took care to include a yard of long French bread, a sausage out of which the garlic sang, some cheese which lay down and cried, and a long-necked straw-covered flask wherein lay bottled sunshine shed and garnered on far Southern slopes.
KENNETH GRAHAME
The Wind in the Willows (1908)

The Mole begged as a favor to be allowed to unpack [the luncheon-basket] all by himself; and the Rat was very pleased to indulge him, and to sprawl at full length on the grass and rest, while his excited friend shook out the tablecloth and spread it, took out all the mysterious packets one by one and arranged their contents in due order, still gasping, 'O my! O my!' at each fresh revelation.
KENNETH GRAHAME
The Wind in the Willows (1908)

Like a good pioneer, father hankered to eat outdoors. And he ate outdoors, come gale, come zephyr. . . . I can see father and all of us out there under the oaks even yet. . . . Father smiling and eating hugely and shouting out between mouthfuls—'Yes, Sir! This is the way to live! Out in the air, out where a man belongs!'
ROBERT P. TRISTRAM COFFIN
Mainstays of Maine (1944)

Of late the cook has had the surprising sagacity to learn from the French that apples will make pies; and it's a question, if, in the violence of his efforts, we do not get one of apples, instead of having both of beef-steak which I prefer.
GEORGE WASHINGTON
(1779)

I often wish that all my causes were apple pie causes.
JOHN SCOTT
Lord Eldon (1751-1838)

What is a roofless cathedral compared to a well-built pie?
WILLIAM MAGINN
(1793-1842)

Lorde Dudley was so fond of apple pie that he could not dine comfortably without it. On one occasion at a grand dinner he missed his favorite dish and could not resist saying audibly, 'God bless my soul! No apple pie!'
JULIA C. ANDREWS
Breakfast, Dinner & Tea (1860)

The pie is an English institution which, planted on American soil, forthwith ran rampant and burst forth into an untold variety of genera and species.
HARRIET BEECHER STOWE
(1811-1896)

But I, when I undress me
Each night, upon my knees,
Will ask the Lord to bless me,
With apple pie and cheese.
EUGENE FIELD
Apple Pie and Cheese (1889)

The most conventional customs cling to the table. Farmers who wouldn't drive a horse too hard expect pie three times a day.
ELLA H. RICHARDS
The Healthful Farmhouse (1906)

Eat a smearkase pie and you will languish in longing and discontent until you eat another.

H.L. MENCKEN
in the Baltimore Evening Sun (1910)

Mince meat pie . . . is sheer cacophony.

H.L. MENCKEN
in the Baltimore Evening Sun (1910)

There is something pathetic and almost tragic about a race which seriously regards the pumpkin pie as a delicacy.

H.L. MENCKEN
in the Baltimore Evening Sun (1910)

There is something in the red of a raspberry pie that looks as good to a man as the red in a sheep looks to a wolf.

EDGAR WATSON HOWE
Sinner Sermons (1926)

Black bottom pie is so delicate, so luscious, that I hope to be propped up on my dying bed and fed a generous portion. Then I think I should refuse outright to die, for life would be too good to relinquish.

MARJORIE KINNAN RAWLINGS
Cross Creek Cookery (1942)

'Who in hell,' I said to myself, 'wants to try to make pies like Mother makes, when it's so much simpler to let Mother make 'em in the first place?'

HARRIET ARNOW
The Dollmaker (1954)

A big man, a big pie.

LATVIAN PROVERB

P O I

I think there must be as much of a knack in handling poi as there is in eating with chopsticks. The forefinger is thrust into the mess and stirred quickly round several times and drawn as quickly out, just as if it were poulticed; the head is thrown back, the finger inserted in the

mouth, and the delicacy stripped off and swallowed—the eye closing gently, meanwhile, in a languid sort of ecstasy.
MARK TWAIN
Mark Twain in Hawaii (1866)

A universal food for natives, poi has not often won the affection of passing visitors, many of whom have hit independently on the same description of its taste, that it is like stale library paste.
WAVERLEY ROOT AND RICHARD DE ROCHEMONT
Eating in America (1976)

P O R K

And the swine . . . is unclean to you. Of their flesh shall ye not eat.
LEVITICUS 11:7-8
(c. 700 B.C.)

Yes, to smell pork; to eat of the habitation which your prophet the Nazarite conjured the devil into. I will buy with you, sell with you, talk with you, walk with you, and so following; but I will not eat with you, drink with you, nor pray with you. What news on the Rialto?
WILLIAM SHAKESPEARE
The Merchant of Venice (1596-97)

There was lately a man that, if pork, or anything made of swine's flesh, were brought into the room, he would fall into a convulsive, sardonic laughter; nor can he for his heart leave as long as that object is before him, so that, if it should not be removed, he would certainly laugh himself to death.
INCREASE MATHER
Remarkable Providences (1684)

A chine of honest bacon would please my appetite more than all the marrow-puddings, for I like them better plain, having a very vulgar stomach.
JOHN DRYDEN
(1631-1700)

Hogs' lard is the very oil that moves the machinery of life.
DR. JOHN S. WILSON
Godey's Lady's Book (1860)

Now the possum is good eating,
When it's cooked with taters call'd the yam;
But there's nothing yet that suits me
Just as well as good old sweet ham.
HENRY HART
Good Sweet Ham (c. 1875)

The aroma of frying bacon beats orange blossoms.
EDGAR WATSON HOWE
(1853-1937)

It was a great contradiction in economics that southern
farmers liked pork and disliked hogs.
THOMAS D. CLARK
Pills, Petticoats and Plows: The Southern Country Stores (1944)

It is almost impossible to find a great vintage ham nowa-.
days; the art is becoming a lost one in a too-hurried age.
VARIOUS AUTHORS
The North Carolina Guide (1955)

I believe that eating pork makes people stupid.
DAVID STEINBERG
(1942 -)

And then there was pork.
JOHN EGERTON
Southern Food (1987)

The most exquisite peak in culinary art is conquered when
you do right by a ham. The making of a ham dinner, like
the making of a gentleman, starts a long, long time before
the event.
ANONYMOUS

Kill a pig and eat a year; kill an ox and eat a week.
ITALIAN PROVERB

If you saw what the hog ate, you would never eat hog meat.
JAMAICAN PROVERB

Fresh pork and new wine bring an early death.
SPANISH PROVERB

Nor do I say it is filthy to eat potatoes. I do not ridicule
the using of them as sauce. What I laugh at is the idea . . .
of the cultivation of them in lieu of wheat adding to the
human sustenance of a country. . . . I now dismiss the
Potato with the hope that I shall never again have to write
the word, or see the thing.
WILLIAM COBBETT
A Year's Residence in the United States of America (1819)

POTATOES

Now God refused to come down to earth in the form of
potato flour: that was an undeniable, indisputable fact.
J.K. HUYSMANS
(1848-1907)

What I say is that, if a man really likes potatoes, he must
be a pretty decent sort of fellow.
A.A. MILNE
Not That It Matters (1920)

If you have formed the habit of checking on every new
diet that comes along, you will find, mercifully, they all
blur together, leaving you with only one definite piece of
information: french-fried potatoes are out.
JEAN KERR
The Snake Has All the Lines (1960)

And then I saw the menu, stained with tea and beautifully written by a foreign hand, and on top it said—God I
hated that old man—it said 'Chips with everything'. Chips
with every damn thing. You breed babies and you eat chips
with everything.
ARNOLD WESKER
Chips with Everything (1962)

My idea of heaven is a great big baked potato and someone to share it with.
OPRAH WINFREY
(1954 -)

The best part of a potato is underground.
ENGLISH PROVERB

The miser's wedding—a potato and a herring.
IRISH PROVERB

The stupidest peasants get the largest potatoes.
SWEDISH PROVERB

PUDDING

The proof of the pudding is in the eating.
MIGUEL DE CERVANTES
Don Quixote (1605-15)

Eat your pudding, slave, and hold your tongue.
MATTHEW PRIOR
(1664-1721)

And solid pudding against empty praise.
ALEXANDER POPE
The Dunciad (1728)

'Live like yourself,' was soon my lady's word,
And lo! two puddings smok'd upon the board.
ALEXANDER POPE
Moral Essays (1733)

One solid dish his week-day meal affords,
An added pudding solemniz'd the Lord's.
ALEXANDER POPE
Moral Essays (1733)

Little a love of fame can brook delay, a love of pudding less.
EDWARD JENNER
The Placid Man (1770)

I sing the sweets I know, the charms I feel,
My morning incense, and my evening meal,
The sweets of Hasty Pudding.
JOEL BARLOW
The Hasty Pudding (1792)

Hallo! A great deal of steam! The pudding was out of the
copper. A smell like a washing-day! That was the cloth. A
smell like an eating-house and a pastrycook's next door to
each other, with a laundress's next door to that. That was
the pudding.
CHARLES DICKENS
A Christmas Carol (1843)

After that they had boiled jam roll and apple dumpling, as
the fancy took them, for if you wanted a change of food
from the Puddin', all you had to do was to whistle twice
and turn the basin round.
NORMAN LINDSAY
The Magic Pudding (1918)

Cold pudding settles love.
ENGLISH PROVERB

A hungry dog eats dirty puddings.
ENGLISH PROVERB

Those that eat black pudding will dream of the devil.
ENGLISH PROVERB

Better some of the pudding than none of the pie.
ENGLISH PROVERB

If a woman can't make a good noodle pudding, divorce
her.
JEWISH PROVERB

If you eat pudding on the Sabbath, you'll be full all week.
JEWISH PROVERB

RECIPES One certainly cannot learn the technical details of cookery entirely from books; but if the cooks, celebrated and obscure, of the past had believed that written recipes were unnecessary, we should now be in a sad plight indeed.
ELIZABETH DAVID
French Provincial Cooking (1960)

I feel a recipe is only a theme, which an intelligent cook can play each time with variation.
JEHANE BENOIT
Enjoying the Art of Canadian Cooking (1974)

I refuse to believe that trading recipes is silly. Tunafish casserole is at least as real as corporate stock.
BARBARA GRIZZUTI HARRISON
(1934 -)

Recipes without the author, without the cuisine to which they were once a living, seamless part, die.
JOHN THORNE
Simple Cooking (1987)

RELIGION And thus shall ye eat it; with your loins girded, your shoes on your feet, and your staff in your hand; and ye shall eat it in haste: it is the Lord's passover.
EXODUS 12:11
(c. 700 B.C.)

If ye shall harken diligently to my commandments. . . . I will give you the rain of your land in his due season . . . that thou mayest gather in thy corn, and thy wine, and thine oil.
DEUTERONOMY 11:13-14
(c. 650 B.C.)

Go thy way, eat thy bread with joy, and drink thy wine with a merry heart; for God now accepteth thy works.
ECCLESIASTES 9:7
(c. 200 B.C.)

Every man should eat and drink, and enjoy the good of all
his labour, it is the gift of God.
ECCLESIASTES 3:13
(c. 200 B.C.)

Whether therefore ye eat, or drink, or whatsoever ye do,
do all to the glory of God.
I CORINTHIANS 10:31
(c. 35 A.D.)

Take, eat: this is my body, which is broken for you: this
do in remembrance of me.
I CORINTHIANS 11:24
(c. 35 A.D.)

Whose God is their belly, and whose glory is in their
shame.
PHILIPPIANS 3:19
(c. 60 A.D.)

Jesus said unto them, I am the bread of life: he that
cometh to me shall never hunger; and he that believeth on
me shall never thirst.
JOHN 6:35
(c. 115 A.D.)

It is meant before we partake of food to bless the Maker of
all things, and to sing when we drink.
CLEMENT OF ALEXANDRIA
Paedagogus (c. 190 A.D.)

He who is a slave to the belly seldom worships God.
SA'DI
Golestan (1258)

Now, God be with you, my dear children: I have break-
fasted with you and shall sup with my Lord Jesus Christ.
ROBERT BRUCE
(1274-1329)

My heart is Catholic, but my stomach Lutheran.
DESIDERIUS ERASMUS
Familiar Colloquies (1518)

If a man eats and drinks only to satisfy himself, that is not praiseworthy: He should eat and drink to preserve life, in order to serve his Creator.
JOSEPH CARO
The Prepared Table (c. 1550)

He that eateth well, drinketh well; he that drinketh well, sleepeth well; he that sleepeth well, sinneth not; he that sinneth not goeth straight through Purgatory to Paradise.
WILLIAM LITHGOW
Rare Adventures (1609)

We don't call a man mad who believes that he eats God, but we do the one who says he is Jesus Christ.
CLAUDE ADRIEN
De L'Esprit (1758)

Sermons on diet ought to be preached in the churches at least once a week.
G.C. LICHTENBERG
Reflections (1799)

The general prayer should be for a full stomach, and the individual for one that works well; for on that basis only are we a match for temporal matters, and able to contemplate eternal.
GEORGE MEREDITH
The Ordeal of Richard Feverel (1859)

Our God is great and the cook is his prophet.
JEROME K. JEROME
The Idle Thoughts of an Idle Fellow (1889)

You can't make a good Christian out of a hungry man.
BOOKER T. WASHINGTON
Solving the Negro Problem (1900)

I can't talk religion to a man with bodily hunger in his eyes.
GEORGE BERNARD SHAW
Major Barbara (1907)

Cooking is one of those arts which most require to be done
by persons of a religious nature.
ALFRED NORTH WHITEHEAD
(1861-1947)

To a man with an empty stomach food is God.
MOHANDAS GANDHI
(1869-1948)

Where you eat is sacred.
MEL BROOKS
(1926 -)

Beware of a religious teacher who is a glutton.
INDIAN PROVERB

He who eats and drinks, but does not bless the Lord, is
a thief.
JEWISH PROVERB

How just is our Lord: The rich He gives food—and the
poor He gives appetite.
JEWISH PROVERB

Sleep in the beds of Christians but don't eat their food; eat
the food of Jews but don't sleep in their beds.
MOORISH PROVERB

The belly is the foremost of the gods.
NIGERIAN PROVERB

RESTAURANTS

The halls of the professor and the philosopher are de-
serted, but what a crowd there is in the cafes!
SENECA
Moral Letters (c. 63 A.D.)

He ordered as one to the menu born.
O. HENRY
(1862-1910)

God made the wicked Grocer
For a mystery and a sign.
That men might shun the awful shops
And go to inns to dine.
G.K. CHESTERTON
Song Against Grocers (1915)

They sat at a corner table in the little restaurant, eating
with gusto and noise after the manner of simple-hearted
people who like their neighbors to see and know their
pleasures.
JEAN RHYS
The Left Bank (1927)

I've known what it is to be hungry, but I always went
right to a restaurant.
RING LARDNER
(1885-1933)

Automat—The first restaurant to make it possible for the
poor man to enjoy food served under glass.
FRED ALLEN
(1894-1956)

Whenever I go to a restaurant I don't know, I always ask
to meet the chef before I eat. For I know that if he is
thin, I won't eat well. And if he is thin and sad, there is
nothing for it but to run.
FERNAND POINT
(1897-1955)

Poor Japhy, it was here I finally found out his Achilles
heel. This little tough guy who wasn't afraid of anything
and could ramble around mountains weeks alone and run
down mountains, was afraid of going into a restaurant
because the people in it were too well dressed. I got mad
and said, 'What you afraid of, Japhy, what's the difference? You may know all about mountains, but I know
where to eat.'
JACK KEROUAC
The Dharma Bums (1958)

If you are really hungry you go into a self-service cafeteria and finish the meal of someone who left a lot on the plate.
ABBIE HOFFMAN
Steal This Book (1971)

The murals in restaurants are on a par with the food in museums.
PETER DE VRIES
Madder Music (1977)

Great restaurants are, of course, nothing but mouth-brothels.
FREDERIC RAPHAEL
in The Sunday Times Magazine (1977)

There is one almost infallible way to find honest food at just prices in blue-highway America: count the wall calendars in a cafe.

No calendar: Same as interstate pit stop.
One calendar: Preprocessed food assembled in New Jersey.
Two calendar: Only if fish trophies present.
Three calendar: Can't miss on the farm-boy breakfasts.
Four calendar: Try the ho-made pies too.
Five calendar: Keep it under your hat, or they'll franchise.
WILLIAM LEAST HEAT-MOON
Blue Highways (1982)

The key to a successful restaurant is dressing girls in degrading clothes.
MICHAEL O'DONOGHUE
IN PLAYBOY (1983)

Sit-down, simple-fare, low-cost restaurants are important to building community spirit. They are the common man's country clubs, where the affairs of the town get discussed and chewed over. . . . They are, of course, among the many non-chain small businesses which are being pressed into oblivion in our society.
LARRY MCGEHEE
in his syndicated column (1984)

The diner is everybody's kitchen.

RICHARD GUTMAN
in Smithsonian (1986)

Today's patron is more sophisticated than in the past and recognizes items of value on the menu. Failure to change prices as product and labor costs change may encourage patrons to take advantage of prices advantageous to them.

JACK E. MILLER
Menu Pricing and Strategy (1987)

The American restaurant is never merely a place to eat. It is a place to go, to see, to experience, to hang out in, to seduce in, and to be seduced.

JOHN MARIANI
America Eats Out (1991)

Being a restaurant critic is sort of like being put out to stud. There's no denying that the basic activity is highly pleasurable, but when you have to do it when and with whom somebody else tells you, it loses a lot of its appeal.

COLMAN ANDREWS
Everything on the Table (1992)

An inn-keeper does not object to greedy appetites.

CHINESE PROVERB

When going to an eating house, go to one that is filled with customers.

CHINESE PROVERB

R I C E Rice is the best food for the soldier.

NAPOLEON BONAPARTE
To Gaspard Gourgaud at Saint Helena (1815-18)

Rice obtained by crookedness will not boil up into good food.

CHINESE PROVERB

Talk does not cook rice.

CHINESE PROVERB

Though there are a hundred ways to cook rice, there are only three religions.
CHINESE PROVERB

Thunder will not strike one when eating rice.
CHINESE PROVERB

Give rice to the aged, and add mud to a ruinous wall.
INDIAN PROVERB

No treasure is equal to rice.
INDIAN PROVERB

A man who has time eats rice with a needle.
JAMAICAN PROVERB

Boiled rice doesn't grow on trees.
JAPANESE PROVERB

It is not every day that a delicious rice cake falls into the open mouth.
JAPANESE PROVERB

One meal without rice mars domestic happiness for a week.
JAPANESE PROVERB

Sunshine and rice may be found everywhere.
JAPANESE PROVERB

Who could ever weary of moonlit nights and well-cooked rice?
JAPANESE PROVERB

When the curry is tasty, the rice will be raw.
MALAYSIAN PROVERB

When the rice crop is abundant, don't look down upon potato and taro.
VIETNAMESE PROVERB

S A L A D In a good salad there should be more oil than vinegar or salt.
SAINT FRANCIS DE SALES
Introduction to the Devout Life (1609)

Oh, herbaceous treat!
'Twould tempt the dying anchorite to eat;
Back to the world he'd turn his fleeting soul,
and plunge his fingers in the salad bowl.
SYDNEY SMITH
A Receipt for Salad (1810)

According to the Spanish proverb, four persons are wanted
to make a good salad: a spendthrift for oil, a miser for
vinegar, a counselor for salt, and a madman to stir it all up.
ABRAHAM HAYWARD
The Art of Dining (1852)

Salad, and eggs, and lighter fare,
Tune the Italian spark's guitar;
And, if I take Dan Congreve right,
Pudding and beef make Britons fight.
MATTHEW PRIOR
Alma (1718)

You can put everything, and the more things the better,
into salad, as into a conversation; but everything depends
upon the mixing.
CHARLES DUDLEY WARNER
My Summer in a Garden (1870)

The salad, for which, like everybody else I ever met, he
had a special receipt of his own.
GEORGE DU MAURIER
(1834-1896)

To make a good salad is to be a brilliant diplomatist—the
problem is entirely the same in both cases. To know
exactly how much oil one must put with one's vinegar.
OSCAR WILDE
Vera: or, The Nihilists (1883)

Only bear in mind, good ladies, that if you wish to eat lettuce salad with your fingers you must mix the salad with oil and vinegar, and not with that abominable ready-made white 'salad-dressing,' to look upon which is nauseating.
THEODORE CHILD
Delicate Feasting (1890)

A green salad, I firmly believe, should follow the main course of a meal, at noon or night, and should be made almost always and almost solely of fresh crisp garden lettuces tossed at the last with a plain vinaigrette.
M.F.K. FISHER
With Bold Knife & Fork (1968)

The better the salad, the worse the dinner.
ITALIAN PROVERB

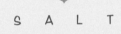

S A L T

And every oblation of thy meat offering shalt thou season with salt.
LEVITICUS 2:13
(c. 700 B.C.)

Trust no one unless you have eaten much salt with him.
CICERO
On Friendship (44 B.C.)

Salt is white and pure—there is something holy in salt.
NATHANIEL HAWTHORNE
Passages from The American Notebooks (1840)

Everything which inflames one appetite is likely to arouse the others also . . . and even salt, in any but the smallest quantity, is objectionable; it is such a goad toward carnalism that the ancient fable depicted Venus as born of the salt sea wave.
DR. DIO LEWIS
Chastity: or, Our Secret Sins (1874)

Salt is the policeman of taste: it keeps the various flavors of a dish in order, and restrains the stronger from tyrannizing over the weaker.
MALCOLM DE CHAZAL
(1902 -)

Where would we be without salt?
JAMES BEARD
(1903-1985)

They passed around candy before dinner; it was a regular welcome party. The few Hawaiian workers passed around salt. Chinese take a bit of sugar to remind them in times of bitter struggle of the sweetness of life, and Hawaiians take a few grains of salt on the tongue because it tastes like the sea, like the earth, like human sweat and tears.
MAXINE HONG KINGSTON
China Men (1980)

Before you trust a man, eat a peck of salt with him.
ANONYMOUS

Salt is what makes things taste bad when it isn't in them.
ANONYMOUS

The man who hoards his ginger and nibbles his salt is a true miser.
CHINESE PROVERB

There are six flavors, and of them all salt is the chief.
INDIAN PROVERB

All dishes need salt, but not all need spices.
JEWISH PROVERB

Meat without salt is fit only for dogs.
JEWISH PROVERB

Nothing is more useful than the sun and salt.
SPANISH PROVERB

A kiss without a beard is like broth without salt.
SILESIAN PROVERB

Salt enters into all food.
TURKISH PROVERB

SANDWICHES

Do not make a stingy sandwich
Pile the cold-cuts high
Customers should see salami
Coming through the rye.
ALLAN SHERMAN
(1924-1973)

'What do you think a citizen of Hamburg, Germany, for
instance, would say if you served him one of our ham-
burgers? You know what he would say?'
'Yes,' I said, 'he'd say it lost a lot in translation.'
ALEXANDER KING
Mine Enemy Grows Older (1960)

Too few people understand a really good sandwich.
JAMES BEARD
(1903-1985)

Life is a shit sandwich. But, man, if you've got enough
bread, you don't taste the shit.
JONATHAN WINTERS
(1925 -)

I like the philosophy of the sandwich, as it were. It typifies
my attitude to life, really. It's all there, it's fun, it looks
good, and you don't have to wash up afterwards.
MOLLY PARKIN
(1932 -)

Always it was a club sandwich, the toast brown and crisp,
the turkey moist with mayonnaise, the bacon sharp and
smoky. . . . I looked out over the boats rocking at their

moorings and lazily worked my way through each triangle. The waiter called me 'sir,' the tablecloth was white—and I was very fond of sandwiches.
VLADIMIR ESTRAGON
(1940 -)

I told ⌈Brady Bunch producers⌉ that I was globally ranked in surfing events, and that I could surf Oahu's six-foot surf with a sandwich in one hand and a Marlboro in the other.
BARRY WILLIAMS
Growing Up Brady (1992)

Go as a meat pie, come back as a sandwich.
MALAYSIAN PROVERB

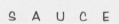

S A U C E   Wo was his cook, if his sauce was not poynaunt and sharp.
GEOFFREY CHAUCER
Canterbury Tales (c. 1395)

A crier of green sauce.
FRANCOIS RABELAIS
Gargantua (1535)

My more-having would be a sauce
To make me hunger more.
WILLIAM SHAKESPEARE
Macbeth (1605-06)

Nor do you find fault with the sauce, keen hunger being the best.
PHILIP MASSINGER
Unnatural Combat (1639)

I would eat my own father with such a sauce.
ALEXANDRE GRIMOD DE LA REYNIERE
The Gourmand's Almanac (c. 1820)

To put any kind of sauce—be it the best in the world—on such a dish as fresh sole or salmon, steak or chop is as

unpardonable as it would be to pour cologne over a bunch
of fragrant violets.
HENRY T. FINCK
Food and Flavor (1913)

Sauce for the goose is sauce for the gander.
ENGLISH PROVERB

It is the sauce that makes the fish edible.
FRENCH PROVERB

SAUERKRAUT

Rain forty days, rain forty nights;
Sauerkraut sticking out the smokestack.
ANONYMOUS
American popular song (c. 1875)

The German sauerkraut—[is] a superb victual when
properly prepared for the table. But how often, in America,
is it properly prepared? Perhaps once in 100,000 times.
Even the Germans, coming here, lose the art of handling
it as it deserves. It becomes in their hands, as in the hands
of the American cooks, simply a sort of stewed hay, with
overtones of the dishpan.
H.L. MENCKEN
in the Chicago Tribune (1926)

When, during the World War, certain super-patriots went
about the country seeking to extirpate every vestige of the
German Kultur, they quickly collided with sauerkraut and
were bested by it. Unable to induce Americans to stop
eating it, they tried to change its name to liberty cabbage,
but the only reply was a laugh, and it went on under its
original colors.
H.L. MENCKEN
in the New York American (1934)

Sauerkraut and bacon drive all care away.
GERMAN PROVERB

SAUSAGE Let them make sausages of me and serve them up to the students.
ARISTOPHANES
The Clouds (423 B.C.)

Laws are like sausages. It's better not to see them being made.
OTTO VON BISMARCK
(1815-1898)

Think of the man who first tried German sausage.
JEROME K. JEROME
Three Men in a Boat (1889)

There was never the least attention paid to what was cut up for sausage.
UPTON SINCLAIR
The Jungle (1906)

The hot dog is the reducto ad absurdum of American eating. The Sicilian in the ditch though he can never be President, knows better: he puts a slice of onion between his slabs of bread, not a cartridge filled with the sweepings of the abbatoir.
H.L. MENCKEN
in the Chicago Tribune (1926)

And now with some pleasure I find that it's seven; and must cook dinner. Haddock and sausage meat. I think it is true that one gains a certain hold on sausage and haddock by writing them down.
VIRGINIA WOOLF
A Writer's Diary (1953)

The noblest of all dogs is the hot dog: it feeds the hand that bites it.
LAURENCE J. PETER
(1919 -)

He who goes seeking other people's sausages often loses his own ham.
CZECH PROVERB

Everything has an end, except a sausage, which has two.
DANISH PROVERB

Better a sausage in hand than a ham at the butcher's.
POLISH PROVERB

'Tis a superstition to insist on a special diet. All is made at last of the same chemical atoms.
RALPH WALDO EMERSON
The Conduct of Life (1860)

SCIENCE

Science has murdered the art of eating.
H.L. MENCKEN
in the Baltimore Evening Sun (1910)

The influence of victuals upon the human soul is a matter that invites the serious consideration of physiologists and psychologists.
H.L. MENCKEN
in the Baltimore Evening Sun (1910)

We have robbed eating of its artlessness, its old impetuous daring, its old romanticism and now seek to make it a purely scientific proceeding, like a game of chess or a surgical operation.
H.L. MENCKEN
in the Baltimore Evening Sun (1910)

In our own precious cabbage patches the holometabolous insecta are the hosts of parasitic polyembryonic hymenoptera, upon the prevalence of which rests the psychic and somatic stamina of our fellow countrymen.
SIR WILLIAM OSLER
in a speech to the Classical Association at Oxford (1919)

Fifty years hence . . . we shall escape the absurdity of growing a whole chicken in order to eat the breast or wing, by growing these parts separately under a suitable medium.
WINSTON CHURCHILL
in Popular Mechanics (1932)

Foods will [by 1976] be sterilized by split-second exposures
[to atomic radiation], thus extending the shelf life of
fresh foods practically indefinitely. Fission rays will immu-
nize seeds, oats and other grains against disease.
MORRIS L. ERNST
Utopia 1976 (1955)

Our bodies are not puritanical. The pleasant habits of
eating and drinking were never meant to be subject to a
chemical equation.
MERVYN HORDER
The Little Genius (1966)

Fake food—I mean those patented substances chemically
flavored and mechanically bulked out to kill the appetite
and deceive the gut—is unnatural, almost immoral, a bane
to good eating and good cooking.
JULIA CHILD
Julia Child and Company (1978)

Food is so fundamental, more so than sexuality, aggression,
or learning, that it is astounding to realize the neglect of
food and eating in depth psychology.
JAMES HILLMAN
(1926 -)

SELF-DENIAL Let an ascetic eat no honey, no flesh, no mushrooms, nor
anything grown on plowed ground.
MANU
The Code of Manu (c. 100 B.C.)

To abstain that we may enjoy is the epicurianism of reason.
JEAN JACQUES ROUSSEAU
(1712-1778)

He may live without books—what is knowledge but grieving?
He may live without hope—what is hope but deceiving?
He may live without love—what is passion but pining?
But where is the man that can live without dining?
EDWARD R. BULWER-LYTTON
Lucile (1860)

Gave up spinach for Lent.
F. SCOTT FITZGERALD
The Crack-up (1945)

If you are willing to eat cabbage stalks, you can accomplish a hundred affairs.
CHINESE PROVERB

S E X

Eating and mating are human instincts.
MENCIUS
Book of Mencius (c. 320 B.C.)

The most violent appetites of all creatures are lust and hunger: the first is a perpetual call upon them to propagate their kind, the latter to preserve themselves.
JOSEPH ADDISON
in The Spectator (1711)

The sergeant was describing a military life. It was all drinking, he said, except that there were frequent intervals of eating and love making.
CHARLES DICKENS
Barnaby Rudge (1841)

Copulation is . . . dangerous immediately after a meal and during the two and three hours which the first digestion needs. . . .
BERNARD S. TALMEY
Love: A Treatise on the Science of Sex-Attraction (1919)

I don't know whether you've ever had a woman eat an apple while you were doing it. . . . Well you can imagine how that affects you.
HENRY MILLER
Tropic of Capricorn (1939)

No hunter of the Age of Fable
Had need to buckle in his belt;
More game than he was ever able
To take ran wild upon the veldt;

Each night with roast he stocked his table,
Then procreated on the pelt.
And that is how, of course, there came
At last to be more men than game.
ALEC DERWENT HOPE
Conversation with Calliope (1962)

Sex is like having dinner: sometimes you joke about the dishes, sometimes you take the meal seriously.
WOODY ALLEN
(1965)

People who appreciate gastronomic miracles never worry about their insides while they eat—any more than a man worries about his heart while making love.
LOUIS VAUDABLE
in Life (1966)

Eating takes a special talent. Some people are much better at it than others. In that way, it's like sex, and as with sex, it's more fun with someone who really likes it. I can't imagine having a lasting friendship with anyone who is not interested in food.
ALAN KING
(1927 -)

Great food is like great sex—the more you have the more you want.
GAEL GREENE
(c. 1940 -)

Primitive society tells us where it's at. Our business is basically sex and hunger.
HENRY G. WALTER
(c. 1980)

Chili's a lot like sex: when it's good it's great, and even when it's bad, it's not so bad.
BILL BOLDENWECK
in American Way (1982)

To as great a degree as sexuality, food is inseparable from imagination.
JEAN-FRANCOIS REVEL
Culture and Cuisine (1982)

Sex is good, but not as good as fresh sweet corn.
GARRISON KEILLOR
(1942 -)

In New Orleans, food is like sex. Everybody's interested.
ELLA BRENNAN
in Travel and Leisure (1989)

SHELLFISH

I am a shellfish just come from being saturated with the waters of the Lucrine lake, near Baiae; but now I luxuriously thirst for noble pickle.
MARTIAL
Epigrams (c. 95 A.D.)

Every year before the crab season starts, I begin to save money. People say crabs are my life, and my hoarded money is the ransom.
LI LIWENG
(1611-1676)

In Baltimore soft crabs are always fried (or broiled) in the altogether, with maybe a small jock-strap of bacon added.
H.L. MENCKEN
Heathen Days (1943)

There must be hundreds of unsung heroes and heroines who first tasted strange things growing—and think of the man who first ate a lobster. This staggers the imagination. I salute him every time I take my nutcracker in hand and move the melted-butter pipkin closer.
GLADYS TABER
Stillmeadow Daybook (1955)

There are crawfish (or crayfish, or crawdads) all over the country, but outside of Louisiana they are all but ignored—lumps of clay lacking a sculptor.
CALVIN TRILLIN
American Fried (1974)

Many shrimps, many flavors; many men, many whims.
MALAYSIAN PROVERB

SIMPLICITY

When the sun rises I go to work,
When the sun goes down, I take my rest,
I dig the well from which I drink,
I farm the soil that yields my food,
I share creation. Kings can do no more.
UNKNOWN CHINESE AUTHOR
(2500 B.C.)

Give me neither poverty or riches; feed me with food convenient for me.
PROVERBS 30:8
(c. 350 B.C.)

Plain fare gives as much pleasure as a costly diet, while bread and water confer the highest possible pleasure when they are brought to hungry lips.
EPICURUS
Letter to Menaceus (c. 290 B.C.)

The chief pleasure in eating does not consist in costly seasoning or exquisite flavor, but in yourself. Seek you for sauce in sweating.
HORACE
Satires (c. 30 B.C.)

A simple dinner in a poor man's house, without tapestries and purple, has smoothed the wrinkles from the anxious brow.
HORACE
Odes (c. 25 B.C.)

We have water and porridge; let us rival Jove himself in happiness.
SENECA
Moral Letters (c. 63 A.D.)

Their best and most wholesome feeding is upon one dish and no more . . . for surely this huddling of many meats one upon another of diverse tastes is pestiferous. But sundry sauces are more dangerous than that.
PLINY THE ELDER
Natural History (c. 79 A.D.)

⌈A parson's⌉ fare is plain and common, but wholesome; what he hath is little, but very good. It consisteth most of mutton, beef and veal.
GEORGE HERBERT
The Temple (1633)

The poor man will praise it so hath he good cause,
That all the year eats neither partridge nor quail,
But sets up his rest and makes up his feast,
With a crust of brown bread and a pot of good ale.
ANONYMOUS
An Antidote Against Melancholy (1661)

Bread and Herbs was sufficiently bless'd with all a frugal Man could need or desire.
JOHN EVELYN
Acetaria (1699)

Hard was their lodging, homely was their food;
For all their luxury was doing good.
SIR SAMUEL GARTH
Claremont (1699)

Do we find those who keep great Tables, and live deliciously, healthier and live longer than others? Nay, rather do not those who content themselves with plain Foods, and season them no farther than is requisite for the Health, do better in these Respects than the others.
DR. M.L. LEMERY
A Treatise of All Sorts of Foods (1745)

A frugal and simple diet, the most coarse and ordinary food is more palatable and agreeable to a sober man's taste and affords him treble the ease and pleasure and advantage than can possibly accrue from the richest and most delicious provision a racked invention can contrive to those of vitiated palate.

L. LESSIUS
Health and Long Life (1749)

The miser's feast is often the most splendid.

SAMUEL RICHARDSON
Sir Charles Grandison (1749)

Do not fuss with the natural state of the food just to show that you are a clever cook.

YUAN MEI
The Menu (1797)

Begin at once a life of open air,
To dig and trench and cultivate the ground,
Content yourself within the common round,
And for your dinner have the homeliest fare.

JOHANN WOLFGANG VON GOETHE
Faust, Part I (1808)

Those are happy who have been brought up in the habit of being content with humble fare, whose health is so firm that it needs no artificial adjustment; who, with the appetite of a cormorant, have the digestion of an ostrich and eagerly devour whatever is set before them without asking any questions about what it is or how it was prepared.

DR. WILLIAM KITCHINER
The Cook's Oracle (1817)

If a Canadian can keep up his supply of pork and pumpkin-pie, of molasses and sourcrout, of tea and Johnny cake—which he seldom fails to accomplish—he feels perfectly indifferent regarding those household conveniences which are not so eminently useful.

E.A. TALBOT
Five Years' Residence in the Canadas (1824)

A very spare and simple diet has commonly been recommended as most conducive to Health. Aim at the happy mean—be Liberal without being Lavish, be Prudent without being Penurious. Plenty of Good Food, plainly but properly prepared, is a Feast for an Emperor.
DR. WILLIAM KITCHINER
The Housekeeper's Ledger (1825)

A few things well ordered will never fail to give a greater appetite, and pleasure to your guest, than a crowded table badly prepared; and as there is a time for all things, there will be time to crowd your table with delicacies.
MRS. LETTICE BRYAN
The Kentucky Housewife (1839)

No one need be ashamed of plain dinners if given with a hearty welcome.
ANONYMOUS
Table Observances (1854)

I learned from my two year's experiment that it would cost incredibly little trouble to obtain one's necessary food, even in this latitude; that many a man may use as simple a diet as the animals, and yet retain health and strength.
HENRY DAVID THOREAU
Walden (1854)

Cloyed with ragouts you scorn my simple food,
And think good eating is man's only good;
I ask no more than temperance can give;
You live to eat, I only eat to live.
RICHARD GRAVES
Diogenes to Aristippus (c. 1890)

There is more simplicity in the man who eats caviar on impulse than in the man who eats Grape Nuts on principle.
G.K. CHESTERTON
(1874-1936)

How simple and frugal a thing is happiness: a glass of wine, a roast chestnut, a wretched little brazier, the sound of the sea . . .
NIKOS KAZANTZAKIS
(1883-1957)

And before he had finished, Ivy and the other children were sorry for millionaires who had only money and could not enjoy the fruits of the earth at the peak of their season.
WILMA DYKEMAN
The Far Family (1966)

Give me a platter of choice finnan haddie, freshly cooked in its bath of water and milk, add melted butter, a slice or two of hot toast, a pot of steaming Darjeeling tea, and you may tell the butler to dispense with the caviar, truffles and nightingales' tongues.
CRAIG CLAIBORNE
in the New York Times (1977)

So long as there is bread to eat, water to drink and an arm to sleep on happiness is not impossible.
CHINESE PROVERB

Eat simple food and follow your nose.
INDIAN PROVERB

SNACKS

Who can live without a snack?
SUETONIUS
Divus Claudius (c. 110 A.D.)

Very merry, and the best fritters that ever I eat in my life.
SAMUEL PEPYS
Diary (1660)

Timid roach, why be so shy?
We are brothers, thou and I.

262

In the midnight, like thyself,
I explore the pantry shelf!
CHRISTOPHER MORLEY
Nursery Rhymes for the Tender-Hearted (1920)

'Nearly eleven o'clock,' said Pooh happily. 'You're just in
time for a smackerel of something.'
A. A. MILNE
The House at Pooh Corner (1928)

Milk and then just as it comes dear?
I'm afraid the preserve's full of stones;
Beg pardon, I'm soiling the doileys
With afternoon tea-cakes and scones.
SIR JOHN BETJEMAN
How to Get on in Society (1954)

There is a charm in improvised eating which a regular
meal lacks.
GRAHAM GREENE
(1904-1991)

Romance looks more promising than in the recent past.
The outcome of a family conference makes you happy. Day
trips can provide a change of scenery without being too
expensive. Take your own snacks.
JEANE DIXON
horoscope for Sagittarius (May 8, 1994)

SOLITUDE

What I eat in my own corner without compliments or
ceremonies, though it were nothing but bread and an
onion, relishes better than turkey at other folk's tables,
where I am forced to eat leisurely, drink little, wipe my
mouth often, and can neither sneeze nor cough when I
have a mind.
MIGUEL DE CERVANTES
Don Quixote (1605-15)

Oh, the pleasure of eating my dinner alone!
CHARLES LAMB
Letter to Mrs. Wordsworth (1818)

A man should have dinner with his friends, and the commanding general has no friends.
GENERAL CURTIS LeMAY
in Look (1965)

I was alone, which seems to be indicated for many such sensual rites. The potatoes were light, whipped to a firm cloud with rich hot milk, faintly yellow from ample butter. I put them in a big warmed bowl, made a dent about the size of a respectable coffee cup, and filled it to the brim with catsup from a large, full vulgar bottle that stood beside my table mat where a wineglass would be at an ordinary, commonplace, everyday banquet. Mine was, as I have said, delicious.
M.F.K. FISHER
With Bold Knife & Fork (1968)

He who eats alone, coughs alone.
ARAB PROVERB

S O U L
F O O D

When de cabbage pot is steamin'
An' de bacon good an' fat,
When de chittlins is a-sputter'n'
So's to show you whah dey's at;
Tek away yo' sody biscuit,
Tek away yo' cake an' pie,
Fu' de glory time is comin',
An' it's 'proachin' mighty nigh,
An' you want to jump an' hollah,
Dough you know you'd bettah not,
When yo mammy says de blessin'
An de co'n pone's hot.
PAUL LAURENCE DUNBAR
When de Co'n Pone's Hot (1895)

Nashville is the turnip-greens and hog-jowl center of
the universe.
ALFRED LELAND CRABB
Nashville: Personality of a City (1960)

So much of this segregation bit is in the mind. People
aren't just segregating us. They're segregating themselves
too. Like, how many of you have ever tasted hominy grits?
Black-eyed peas? Chitlins? No law against it. . . . You try it
tomorrow, and I guarantee you won't turn one shade darker.
DICK GREGORY
From the Back of the Bus (1962)

Do black-eyed peas—as the tradition says—bring good luck
for the coming year? How is it that we believe this,
considering our present circumstances? Consider that if we
are in this condition after centuries of eating black-eyed
peas, what would our condition be if we didn't eat them?
VERTAMAE GROSVENOR
Vibration Cooking (1970)

If you want to be real technical on the subject, while all
soul food is southern food, not all southern food is 'soul.'
BOB JEFFRIES
Soul Food Cookbook (1970)

Soul food cooking is an example of how really good southern Negro cooks cooked with what they had available
to them.
BOB JEFFRIES
Soul Food Cookbook (1970)

All I want is a few ham hocks fried in bacon grease, a
little mess of turnips with sowbelly in it, and a hunk of
corn bread and I'm happy.
WYATT COOPER
Families (1975)

It'll make you limber, it'll make you quick.
ARETHA FRANKLIN
(1942 -)

S O U P Make way, my lords, and let me return to my former liberty. . . . I would rather stuff myself with gazpachos than be subject to the misery of an impertinent physician who kills me with hunger.

MIGUEL DE CERVANTES
Don Quixote (1605-15)

In taking soup, it is necessary to avoid lifting too much in the spoon, or filling the mouth so full as almost to stop the breath.

SAINT JOHN BAPTIST DE LA SALLE
The Rules of Christian Manners and Civility (1695)

Of soup and love, the first is best.

THOMAS FULLER
Gnomologia (1732)

Whoever tells a lie cannot be pure in heart—and only the pure in heart can make a good soup.

LUDWIG VON BEETHOVEN
To Mademoiselle Streicher (1817)

Soup and fish explain half of the emotions of life.

SYDNEY SMITH
(1771-1845)

But one day, one cold winter's day, he screamed out, 'Take the Soup away!'

HEINRICH HOFFMAN
Augustus (1848)

This Bouillabaisse a noble dish is—
A sort of soup, or broth, or brew,
Or hotchpotch of all sorts of fishes,
That Greenwich could never outdo;
Green herbs, red peppers, mussels, saffron,
Soles, onions, garlic, roach, and dace;
All those you eat at Terre's tavern
In that one dish of Bouillabaisse.

WILLIAM MAKEPEACE THACKERAY
Ballad of Bouillabaisse (1849)

'But the chowder; clam or cod for breakfast men?'
'Both,' says I, 'and let's have a couple of smoked herring by
way of variety.'
HERMAN MELVILLE
Moby Dick (1851)

Beautiful soup! Who cares for fish
Game, or any other dish?
Who would not give all else for two
Pennyworth only of beautiful soup?
LEWIS CARROLL
Alice's Adventures in Wonderland (1865)

Stir the wallaby stew, make soup of the kangaroo tail.
I tell you things is pretty tough since Dad got put in gaol.
ANONYMOUS
Wallaby Stew (c. 1895)

Of all the items on the menu, soup is that which exacts
the most delicate perfection and the strictest attention.
AUGUSTE ESCOFFIER
(1847-1935)

To possess a cook who makes perfect soups is to possess a
jewel of great price. A woman who cannot make soup
should not be allowed to marry . . .
P. MORTON SHAND
A Book of Food (1928)

A first-rate soup is more creative than a second-rate painting.
ABRAHAM MASLOW
(1908-1970)

A bowl of thin cabbage soup, half burned, was as welcome
to them as rain to parched earth. They'd swallowed it in
one gulp. That bowl of soup—it was dearer than freedom,
dearer than life itself, past, present, and future.
ALEXANDER SOLZHENITSYN
One Day in the Life of Ivan Denisovich (1962)

Chowder breathes reassurance. It steams consolation.
CLEMENTINE PADDLEFORD
How America Eats (1970)

In reality. . . . Ole Fritz merely wanted the recipe for her potato soup, which was wholesome, he said, and soothed his gouty bones.
GUNTER GRASS
The Flounder (1977)

My good health is due to a soup made of white doves. It is simply wonderful.
MADAME CHIANG KAI-SHEK
(1898 -)

There is nothing like soup. It is by nature eccentric: no two are ever alike, unless of course you get your soup from cans.
LAURIE COLWIN
Home Cooking (1988)

Eat bad soup with a big spoon.
ARMENIAN PROVERB

Words don't season soup.
BRAZILIAN PROVERB

It is better to let the man wait for his soup than to let the soup wait for the man.
CHINESE PROVERB

Gruel gets the gloves on, broth the rope to the sled, porridge half a fathom of wood home.
ESTONIAN PROVERB

Good soup draws the chair to it.
GHANIAN PROVERB

Old meat makes good soup.
ITALIAN PROVERB

Borscht and bread make your cheeks red.
JEWISH PROVERB

Worries go down better with soup.
JEWISH PROVERB

Cheap soup has no taste.
MONGOLIAN PROVERB

Beauty does not season soup.
POLISH PROVERB

S O U R

The fathers have eaten a sour grape, and the children's teeth are set on edge.
JEREMIAH 31:29
(c. 625 B.C.)

Sweetest nut hath sourest rind.
WILLIAM SHAKESPEARE
As You Like It (1599-1600)

Sweet appears sour when we pay.
JAMES HOWELL
Proverbs (1659)

Sweet in the on taking, but sour in the off putting.
JAMES KELLY
Complete Collection of Scottish Proverbs (1721)

I thought tamarinds were made to eat, but that was probably not the idea. I ate several, and it seemed that they were rather sour that year. They pursed up my lips, till they resembled the stem end of a tomato, and I had to take my sustenance through a quill for twenty-four hours. . . . I found, afterward, that only strangers eat tamarinds—but they only eat them once.
MARK TWAIN
Mark Twain in Hawaii (1866)

Whoever has bitten a sour apple will enjoy a sweet one all the more.
GERMAN PROVERB

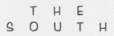

T H E
S O U T H

All over the Colony, a universal hospitality reigns; full Tables and open Doors, the kind Salute, the generous Detention, speak somewhat like the old Roast-beef ages of our Fore-fathers. . . . Strangers are sought after with Greediness, as they pass the Country, to be invited. Their Breakfast Tables have generally the cold Remains of the former Day, hash'd or fricasseed; Coffee, Tea, Chocolate, Venison-pasty, Punch, and Beer, or Cyder, upon one Board; their Dinner, good Beef, Veal, Mutton, Venison, Turkies and Geese, wild and tame, Fowls, boil'd and roasted; and perhaps somewhat more, as Pies, Puddings, etc. for Dessert: Suppers the same, with some small Addition, and a good hearty Cup to precede a Bed of Down: And this is the constant life they lead, and to this Fare every Comer is welcome.

UNKNOWN AUTHOR TRAVELING IN VIRGINIA
quoted in London Magazine (1746)

Within ten years, as many people have died prematurely in this State ⌈North Carolina⌉ from bad cookery as were slain in the ⌈Civil⌉ war.

GENERAL THOMAS L. CLINGMAN
(1875)

So Jim he got out some corn-dodgers and buttermilk, and pork and cabbage and greens—there ain't nothing in the world so good when it's cooked right . . .

MARK TWAIN
The Adventures of Huckleberry Finn (1885)

There ⌈the Mason-Dixon line⌉ is, a great crimson scar of politics across the face of the grandest country that God ever made. There it is, and there it will remain, the dividing line—between cold bread and hot biscuit.

TENNESSEE GOVERNOR ROBERT "OUR BOB" TAYLOR
(c. 1890)

The close-fisted stinginess that fed the poor slave on coarse cornmeal and tainted meat . . . wholly vanished on approaching the sacred precincts of the Great House itself.
FREDERICK DOUGLASS
Life and Times of Frederick Douglass (1892)

The Southerners are the only cooks in the United States. The real difference between the South and the North is that one enjoys itself getting dyspepsia and the other does not.
GERTRUDE ATHERTON
Senator North (1900)

That combination of onions and mushrooms, green peppers and tomatoes is the hallmark of Creole cookery. The idea of combining them thus must stand forever as Louisiana's greatest contribution to human thought.
H.L. MENCKEN
in the Baltimore Evening Sun (1910)

And the breakfast, simple as it was, I could not have had at any restaurant in Atlanta at any price. There was fried chicken, as it is fried only in the South, hominy boiled to the consistency where it could be eaten with a fork, and biscuits so light and flaky that a fellow with any appetite at all would have no difficulty in disposing of eight or ten. When I had finished, I felt that I had experienced the realization of, at least, one of my dreams of Southern life.
JAMES WELDON JOHNSON
The Autobiography of an Ex-Coloured Man (1912)

In the North man may not be able to live by bread alone; but in the South, and particularly in Charleston, he comes mighty near to it, provided the bread is hot.
HELEN WOODWARD
Two Hundred Years of Charleston Cooking (1930)

The cooking here, to speak sententiously, is grandchild to France, descendant to Spain, cousin to Italy, and also it is full fledged Southern.
MARY MOORE BREMER
New Orleans Creole Recipes (1932)

Everybody has the right to nominate whose food is the most gorgeous, and I nominate Georgia's.

OGDEN NASH
introduction to The Savannah Cook Book (1933)

If, beyond the pearly gates, I am permitted to select my place at the table, it will be among Kentuckians, and the food, I hope, will be Kentucky style. Eating dinner in Kentucky is more than a physiological refueling of the human body, it is a joyous social ritual.

THOMAS D. CLARK
The Kentucky (1941)

Travelers in the South who have heard of the delights of Southern cuisine are about as likely to find them as they are to be hit by a meteor—unless they have some Southern cousins or belong to a Southern country Sunday school.

WILLIAM T. POLK
Southern Accent (1953)

Many Southern ladies had Negro cooks to help them; and just how much we owe to their skill I have no way of knowing except that almost all of the finest Southern dishes are of their creating or at least bear their special touch, and everyone who loves good cookery should thank them from the bottom of his heart.

DUNCAN HINES
Food Odyssey (1955)

Usually a short distance from the manor, the ⌈plantation⌉ kitchen was full of the cook's wares: pots, kettles, waffle irons, swinging cranes, bake ovens, scales, iron firedogs holding rotating spits. This was the spot in which south-ern cooking had its inspiration and consummation.

MARSHALL FISHWICK
in the American Heritage Cookbook (1964)

To the serious traveler and eater, Virginia means two things above all: history and ham.

EUGENE WALTER
American Cooking Southern Style (1971)

As I drove in she was walking into the house with eggs for breakfast and homemade biscuits ready for baking. Somehow in rural Southern culture, food is always the first thought of neighbors when there is trouble. That is something they can do and not feel uncomfortable. It is something they do not have to explain or discuss or feel self-conscious about. 'Here, I brought you some fresh eggs for your breakfast. And here's a cake. And some potato salad.' It means, 'I love you. And I am sorry for what you are going through and I will share as much of your burden as I can.' And maybe potato salad is a better way of saying it.

WILL D. CAMPBELL
Brother to a Dragonfly (1977)

We had the first of a very relaxed and informal series of meals with our family. Earlier, when Rosalynn was visiting the White House, some of our staff asked the chef and cooks if they thought that they could prepare the kind of meals which we enjoyed in the South, and the cook said, 'Yes, Ma'am, we've been fixing that kind of food for the servants for a long time!'

JIMMY CARTER
entry in White House diary (1977)

Real Southern food, despite what its crass promoters and its bigoted detractors say, is not always fried, nor is it typically greasy or heavy or monotonous.

KATHRYN TUCKER WINDHAM
Southern Cooking to Remember (1978)

During the last third of the nineteenth century and well into the following one, a southern country store was likely to have, in a corner, a long counter equipped with bottles of pepper sauce, catsup, vinegar, well-worn knives and forks, cracked plates, a mechanical cheese cutter, and boxes of crackers. Here many a rural Southerner first met 'bought' foods—canned oysters, sardines, salmon, or link sausages from a midwestern packing plant. A particular favorite of the farmers was sardines seasoned with pepper sauce and eaten with salt crackers.

RICHARD J. HOOKER
Food and Drink in America (1981)

True Southern cooking has its foundations in the country kitchen. It is characterized by the gracious willingness to share a meal with strangers as well as loved ones, which is something you will find everywhere people have known hard times.

NATHALIE DUPREE
Cooking of the South (1982)

The fact that snow is important to Eskimos is supposedly indicated by the seven or twelve or however many different words they have for it. What, then, are we to make of the hundred-plus expressions for cornbread of various kinds that one folklorist uncovered in South Carolina alone? Obviously, food is and has been important to Southerners—in part, perhaps, because some have never had enough, and there have been times when no one had enough.

JOHN SHELTON REED
in the Georgia Historical Quarterly (1982)

When it comes to fried chicken, let's not beat around the bush for one second. To know about fried chicken you have to have been weaned and reared on it in the South. Period.

JAMES VILLAS
American Taste (1982)

Southern cooking is born of these three parents—European, African, and Native American.

BILL NEAL
Bill Neal's Southern Cooking (1985)

Southern cooking is primarily home cooking, not chef's art. It certainly ain't nouvelle or precious. It's just good food, fit for savoring, not simply pretty to look at.

NATHALIE DUPREE
New Southern Cooking (1986)

A Charlestonian is like a Chinaman; he eats rice and
worships his ancestors.
ANONYMOUS

SPICES

Make haste, my beloved, and be like a gazelle or a young
stag upon the mountain of spices!
SONG OF SOLOMON 8:14
(c. 200 B.C.)

If you beat spice it will smell the sweeter.
THOMAS FULLER
Gnomologia (1732)

If you carry a nutmeg in your pocket you'll be married to
an old man.
JONATHAN SWIFT
Polite and Ingenious Conversation (1738)

Anyone who has tasted this spice ⌈nutmeg⌉ no longer
desires others, just as anyone who has made love with a
Chinese woman no longer desires to make love with
other women.
CURNONSKY
(1873-1956)

The older ginger and cinnamon become, the more pungent
is their flavor.
CHINESE PROVERB

He who has spice enough may season his meat as he
pleases.
ENGLISH PROVERB

Man can live without spices, but not without wheat.
JEWISH PROVERB

If you slaughter a buffalo, don't spare the spices.
THAI PROVERB

S P I R I T S   If I had a thousand sons the first human principle I would teach them should be to forswear thin potations and to addict themselves to sack ⌈sherry⌉.

WILLIAM SHAKESPEARE
2 Henry IV (1597-98)

Better belly burst than good liquor be lost.

JAMES HOWELL
Proverbs (1659)

Claret is the liquor for boys; port for men; but he who aspires to be a hero must drink brandy.

SAMUEL JOHNSON
Boswell's Life of Johnson (1779)

A mixture of brandy and water spoils two good things.

CHARLES LAMB
(1775-1834)

I'm the very infant that refused its milk before its eyes were open, and called out for a bottle of old rye. W-h-o-o-p! I'm that little cupid!

MORGAN NEVILLE
The Last of the Boatmen (1829)

A soft drink turneth away company.

OLIVER HERFORD
(1863-1935)

Wines and liquors were created by God, not to take the place of castor oil and aspirin, but to make the human race happy.

H.L. MENCKEN
in American Mercury (1927)

There is nothing like bourbon to warm the heart, to reduce the anomie of the late twentieth century, to cut the cold phlegm of Wednesday afternoons.

WALKER PERCY
Esquire (1975)

A generous and noble spirit cannot be expected to dwell in the breasts of men who are struggling for their daily bread.
DIONYSIUS OF HALICARNASSUS
Antiquities of Rome (c. 20 B.C.)

To him who is stinted of food a boiled turnip will relish like a roast fowl.
SA'DI
Golestan (1258)

To eat well is no whoredom, and to starve is no gentility.
THOMAS FULLER
Gnomologia (1732)

A man may be as easily starved in Leadenhall Market as in the deserts of Arabia.
HENRY FIELDING
Tom Jones (1749)

And famish'd people must be slowly nurst,
And fed by spoonfuls, else they always burst.
LORD BYRON
Don Juan (1823)

It takes much more than you think to starve a man. Starvation is very little when you are used to it. Some people even live on it quite comfortably, and make their daily bread of it.
WILLIAM MAKEPEACE THACKERAY
Catherine: A Story (1839-40)

The eye, can it feast when the stomach is starving?
Pray less of your gilding and more of your carving.
PETER EGERTON WARBURTON
On a Mean Host (c. 1875)

Poverty is an anomaly to rich people; it is very difficult to make out why people who want dinner do not ring the bell.
WALTER BAGEHOT
Literary Studies (1878)

My piece of bread only belongs to me when I know that everyone else has a share, and that no one starves while I eat.
LEO TOLSTOY
(1828-1910)

Love and business and family and religion and art and patriotism are nothing but shadows of words when a man is starving.
O. HENRY
Heart of the West (1907)

Our first act as free men was to throw ourselves on the provisions. We thought only of that. Not of revenge, not of our families. Nothing but bread.
ELIE WIESEL
Night (1960)

I've never known a country to be starved into democracy.
VERMONT SENATOR GEORGE D. AIKEN
(1892-1984)

If sometimes our poor people have had to die of starvation, it is not that God didn't care for them, but because you and I didn't give, were not an instrument of love in the hands of God, to give them that bread, to give them that clothing; because we did not recognize him, when once more Christ came in distressing disguise, in the hungry man, in the lonely man, in the homeless child, and seeking for shelter.
MOTHER TERESA
A Gift for God (1975)

America is an enormous frosted cupcake in the middle of millions of starving people.
GLORIA STEINEM
(1934 -)

To the starving a blow from a skewer of meat is more acceptable than a caress from the hand of a maiden.
CHINESE PROVERB

Though your threshing-floor grind a hundred thousand
bushels of corn, not for that reason will your stomach
hold more than mine.
HORACE
Satires (c. 30 B.C.)

A great step toward independence is a good-humoured
stomach.
SENECA
(4 B.C.-65 A.D.)

Our stomachs
Will make what's homely savoury.
WILLIAM SHAKESPEARE
Cymbeline (1609-10)

A hungry stomach cannot hear.
JEAN DE LA FONTAINE
Fables (1668)

Why, at this rate, a fellow that has but a groat in his
pocket may have a stomach capable of a ten-shilling ordinary.
WILLIAM CONGREVE
(1670-1729)

So if unprejudiced you scan
The goings of this clock-work, man,
You find a hundred movements made
By fine devices in his head:
But 'tis the stomach's solid stroke
That tells his being what's o'clock.
MATTHEW PRIOR
Alma (1718)

My stomach serves me instead of a clock.
JONATHAN SWIFT
Polite and Ingenious Conversation (1738)

This eating and drinking takes away a body's stomach.
JONATHAN SWIFT
Polite and Ingenious Conversation (1738)

Thought depends absolutely on the stomach, but in spite of that, those who have the best stomachs are not the best thinkers.
VOLTAIRE
(1694-1778)

The stomach is a slave that must accept everything that is given to it, but which avenges wrongs as slyly as does the slave.
EMILE SOUVESTRE
(1806-1854)

The stomach sets us to work.
GEORGE ELIOT
Felix Holt the Radical (1866)

Lazy foks' stummucks don't git tired.
JOEL CHANDLER HARRIS
Uncle Remus: Legends of the Old Plantation (1881)

No one can worship God or love his neighbor on an empty stomach.
WOODROW WILSON
in a speech (1912)

If your stomach disputes you, lie down and pacify it with cool thoughts.
SATCHEL PAIGE
How to Keep Young (1953)

Bread, soup—these were my whole life. I was a body. Perhaps less than that even: a starved stomach. The stomach alone was aware of the passage of time.
ELIE WIESEL
Night (1960)

A dainty stomach beggars the purse.
ANONYMOUS

One with a full stomach will not learn anything.
ARMENIAN PROVERB

A full gut supports moral precepts.
BURMESE PROVERB

The mouth should always consult with the stomach.
CHINESE PROVERB

When the stomach is concerned, wisdom withdraws.
EGYPTIAN PROVERB

It is easier to fill the stomach than the eye.
GERMAN PROVERB

There is no caste system among stomachs.
GHANIAN PROVERB

One laughs when joyous, sulks when angry, is at peace
with the world when the stomach is satisfied.
HAWAIIAN PROVERB

If the stomach be empty, blushing is of no consequence.
INDIAN PROVERB

If your stomach is not strong, do not swallow cactus seed.
JAMAICAN PROVERB

If the stomach be not strong, do not eat cockroaches.
NIGERIAN PROVERB

Poor folk seek meat for their stomachs, and rich folk
stomachs for their meat.
SCOTTISH PROVERB

You know not what man's stomach can contain.
SENEGALESE PROVERB

And men sit down to that nourishment which is called   S U P P E R
supper.
WILLIAM SHAKESPEARE
Love's Labour's Lost (1594-95)

If ever I ate a good supper at night,
I dream'd of the devil, and wak'd in a fright.
CHRISTOPHER ANSTEY
The New Bath Guide (1766)

It was a saying of his that no man was sure of his supper
until he had eaten it.
OLIVER GOLDSMITH
She Stoops to Conquer (1773)

For my part now, I consider supper as a turnpike through
which one must pass, in order to get to bed.
OLIVER EDWARDS
Boswell's Life of Johnson (1778)

I take my little porringer
And eat my supper there.
WILLIAM WORDSWORTH
We Are Seven (1798)

Your supper is like the Hidalgo's dinner, very little meat
and a great deal of tablecloth.
HENRY WADSWORTH LONGFELLOW
The Spanish Student (1840)

The cup, the cup itself, from which our Lord
Drank at the last sad supper with his own.
ALFRED, LORD TENNYSON
The Holy Grail (1869)

Rooster set about preparing our supper. Here is what he
brought along for 'grub': a sack of salt and a sack of red
pepper and a sack of taffy—all this in his jacket pockets—
and then some ground coffee beans and a big slab of salt
pork and one hundred and seventy corn dodgers. I could
scarcely credit it. The 'corn dodgers' were balls of what I
would call hot-water cornbread. Rooster said the woman
who prepared them thought the order was for a wagon
party of marshalls.
CHARLES PORTIS
True Grit (1968)

I had to stand to reach plates across the table, but I intended
to do the supper in.
WILLIAM LEAST HEAT-MOON
Blue Highways (1982)

On her mind was the supper she wanted to fix for Paul
D—something difficult to do, something she would do just
so—to launch her newer, stronger life with a tender man.
Those little bitty potatoes browned on all sides, heavy on
the pepper; snap beans seasoned with rind; yellow squash
sprinkled with vinegar and sugar. Maybe corn cut from
the cob and fried with green onions and butter. Raised
bread, even.
TONI MORRISON
Beloved (1987)

Who goes to bed supperless tosses all night.
ITALIAN PROVERB

I am glad that my Adonis hath a sweet tooth in his head.   S W E E T S
JOHN LYLY
Euphues and His England (1580)

A wilderness of sweets.
JOHN MILTON
Paradise Lost (1667)

Stolen sweets are best.
COLLEY CIBBER
The Rival Fools (1709)

He rolls it under his tongue as a sweet morsel.
MATTHEW HENRY
Commentary on the Bible (1710)

Sweet things are bad for the teeth.
JONATHAN SWIFT
Polite and Ingenious Conversation (1738)

And still she slept an azure-lidded sleep,
In blanched linen, smooth, and lavender'd,

While he from forth the closet brought a heap
Of candied apple, quince, and plum, and gourd,
With jellies soother than the creamy curd,
And lucent syrops, tinct with cinnamon;
Manna and dates, in argosy transferr'd
From Fez; and spiced dainties, every one,
From silken Samarcand to cedar'd Lebanon.
JOHN KEATS
The Eve of St. Agnes (1820)

After the bitter comes the sweet.
CHINESE PROVERB

If you can't give sugar, talk sugar.
INDIAN PROVERB

The gods give everything to the eater of sugar.
INDIAN PROVERB

Sweets stay long in the stomach.
JAPANESE PROVERB

He who eats the sweets of life should be able to bear the
bitters of it.
LEBANESE PROVERB

THE TABLE

The joys of the table are superior to all other pleasures,
notably those of personal adornment, of drinking and of
love, and those procured by perfumes and by music.
CHAMSEDDINE MOHAMED EL HASSAN EL BAGHDADI
Kitabe el-tibah (1226)

Consider your table as a table before the Lord: Chew well
and hurry not.
MOSES DE LEON
Sefer ha-zohar (c. 1275)

The table robs more than a thief.
GEORGE HERBERT
Jacula Prudentum (1651)

Keep a good table and look after the ladies.
NAPOLEON BONAPARTE
instructions to Abbe de Pradt (c. 1820)

The table is the only place where we do not get weary during the first hour.
ANTHELME BRILLAT-SAVARIN
The Physiology of Taste (1825)

Many a one has been comforted in their sorrow by seeing a good dish come upon the table.
ELIZABETH GASKELL
(1810-1865)

Who would ever dine, however hungry, if required to eat everything brought on the table?
EDWARD BELLAMY
Looking Backward (1883)

It is at table that everything happens.
PIERRE BUSSAC
(1921 -)

The dinner table is the center for the teaching and practicing not just of table manners but of conversation, consideration, tolerance, family feeling, and just about all the other accomplishments of polite society except the minuet.
JUDITH MARTIN
Miss Manners' Guide for the Turn-of-the-Millenium (1989)

At the table one never grows old.
ITALIAN PROVERB

T A S T E

All men's tastes are alike; we are not dogs or horses. Were it not so, how would Iya ⌈a famous cook⌉ have become famous?
MENCIUS
Book of Mencius (c. 320 B.C.)

285

One man's meat is another man's poison.
OSWALD DYKES
English Proverbs (1709)

Why is not a rat as good as a rabbit? Why should men eat shrimps and neglect cockroaches?
HENRY WARD BEECHER
Eyes and Ears (1862)

I might glorify my bill of fare until I was tired; but after all, the Scotchman would shake his head and say, 'Where's your haggis?' and the Fijian would sigh and say, 'Where's your missionary?'
MARK TWAIN
A Tramp Abroad (1879)

To be without a sense of taste is to be deficient in an exquisite faculty, that of appreciating the qualities of food, just as a person may lack the faculty of appreciating the quality of a book or a work of art. It is to want a vital sense, one of the elements of human superiority.
GUY DE MAUPASSANT
(1850-1893)

He who cannot eat horsemeat need not do so. Let him eat pork. But he who cannot eat pork, let him eat horsemeat. It is simply a question of taste.
NIKITA KHRUSHCHEV
in the New York World-Telegram (1964)

Gastronomy is a matter of words and taste as well as food.
HSIANG JU LIN AND TSUIFENG LIN
Chinese Gastronomy (1969)

Tolerance of messiness, of course, is based partly on familiarity with the mess; there are undoubtedly Midwestern tourists on Fisherman's Wharf who would think nothing of being up to their elbows in fried chicken or barbecued ribs but recoil at taking apart a Dungeness crab.
CALVIN TRILLIN
Alice, Let's Eat (1978)

Tea has a myriad of shapes. If I may speak vulgarly and rashly, tea may shrink and crinkle like a Mongol's boots. Or it may look like the dewlap of a wild ox, some sharp, some curling as the eaves of a house. It can look like a mushroom in whirling flight just as clouds do when they float out from behind a mountain peak. Its leaves can swell and leap as if they were being lightly tossed on wind-disturbed waters. Others will look like clay, soft and malleable, prepared for the hand of the potter and will be as clear and pure as if filtered through wood. Still others will twist and turn like the rivulets carved out by a violent rain on newly tilled fields—those are the very finest of teas.

Lu Yu
The Classic of Tea (c. 770 A.D.)

There are also teas like the husk of bamboo, hard of stem and too firm to steam or beat. They assume the shape of a sieve. Then there are those that are like the lotus after frost. Their stem and leaves become sere and limp, their appearance so altered that they look like piled-up rubble. Such teas are old and barren of worth.

Lu Yu
The Classic of Tea (c. 770 A.D.)

The way of tea is nothing but this;
Boil water, infuse tea, and drink.
That is all you need to know.

Sen no Rikyu
(1521-91)

Chrysanthemum
silence—monk
sips his morning tea.

Matsuo Basho
(1644-1694)

Retired to their tea and scandal, according to their ancient custom.
WILLIAM CONGREVE
The Double Dealer (1694)

Tea! thou soft, thou sober, sage, and venerable liquid, thou female tongue-running, smile-soothing, heart-opening, wink-tippling cordial, to whose glorious insipidity I owe the happiest moments of my life, let me fall prostrate.
COLLEY CIBBER
The Lady's Last Stake (1707)

The infusion of a Chinese plant sweetened with the pith of an Indian cane.
JOSEPH ADDISON
in The Spectator (c. 1712)

Here thou, great Anna! whom three realms obey,
Dost sometimes counsel take—and sometimes tea.
ALEXANDER POPE
The Rape of the Lock (1714)

Love and scandal are the best sweeteners of tea.
HENRY FIELDING
Love in Several Masques (1728)

A hardened and shameless tea-drinker, who has for twenty years diluted his meals with only the infusion of this fascinating plant; whose kettle has scarcely time to cool; who with tea amuses the evening, with tea solaces the midnight, and with tea welcomes the morning.
SAMUEL JOHNSON
in Literary Magazine (1757)

You can taste and feel, but not describe, the exquisite state of repose produced by tea, that precious drink which drives away the five causes of sorrow.
EMPEROR CHIEN LUNG
(1710-1799)

We love our cup of tea full well; but love our freedom more.
ANONYMOUS
ballad popular in the wake of the Boston Tea Party (c. 1774)

Tea possesses an acrid astringent quality, peculiar to most leaves and exterior bark of trees, and corrodes and paralyzes the nerves.
JESSEY TORREY
The Moral Instructor (1819)

Tea, though ridiculed by those who are naturally coarse in their nervous sensibilities . . . will always be the favorite beverage of the intellectual.
THOMAS DE QUINCEY
Confessions of an English Opium-Eater (1822)

Free yourselves from the slavery of tea and coffee and other slopkettle.
WILLIAM COBBETT
Advice to Young Men (1829)

Polly put the kettle on, we'll all have tea.
CHARLES DICKENS
Barnaby Rudge (1841)

'Take some more tea,' the March Hare said to Alice, very earnestly.

'I've had nothing yet,' Alice replied in an offended tone, 'so I can't take more.'

'You mean you can't take less,' said the Hatter: 'it's very easy to take more than nothing.'
LEWIS CARROLL
Alice's Adventures in Wonderland (1865)

Under certain circumstances there are few hours in life more agreeable than the hour dedicated to the ceremony known as afternoon tea.
HENRY JAMES
Portrait of a Lady (1881)

Is there no Latin word for Tea? Upon my soul, if I had known that I would have let the vulgar stuff alone.
HILAIRE BELLOC
On Nothing (1908)

The cosy fire is bright and gay,
The merry kettle boils away
And hums a cheerful song.
I sing the saucer and the cup;
Pray, Mary, fill the teapot up,
And do not make it strong.
BARRY PAIN
The Poets at Tea: Cowper (c. 1910)

'Come, little cottage girl, you seem
To want my cup of tea;
And will you take a little cream?
Now tell the truth to me.'

She had a rustic, woodland grin
Her cheek was soft as silk,
And she replied, 'Sir, please put in
A little drop of milk.'
BARRY PAIN
The Poets at Tea: Wordsworth (c. 1910)

Stands the Church clock at ten to three?
And is there honey still for tea?
RUPERT BROOKE
The Old Vicarage, Grantchester (1912)

It has been well said that tea is suggestive of a thousand
wants, from which spring the decencies and luxuries of
civilization.
AGNES REPPLIER
To Think of Tea! (1932)

Ah, there's nothing like tea in the afternoon. When the
British Empire collapses, historians will find that it had
made but two invaluable contributions to civilization—this
tea ritual and the detective novel.
AYN RAND
The Fountainhead (1943)

I myself'd gotten the water from the stream, which was
cold and pure like snow and the crystal-lidded eyes of heaven.

Therefore, the tea was by far the most pure and thirst-quenching tea I ever drank in all my life, and it made you want to drink more and more, it actually quenched your thirst and of course it swam around hot in your belly.

'Now you understand the Oriental passion for tea,' said Japhy. 'Remember that book I told you about the first sip is joy the second is gladness, the third is serenity, the fourth is madness, the fifth is ecstasy.'

JACK KEROUAC
The Dharma Bums (1958)

There are those who love to get dirty
and fix things.
They drink coffee at dawn,
beer after work.

And those who stay clean,
just appreciate things,
At breakfast they have milk
and juice at night.

There are those who do both,
they drink tea.

GARY SNYDER
There are those who love to get dirty (c. 1975)

Iced tea is too pure and natural a creation not to have been invented as soon as tea, ice, and hot weather crossed paths.

JOHN EGERTON
Side Orders (1990)

The first cup of tea is nothing, the second is enough, and the third is senseless.

AFGHAN PROVERB

When a man is in great haste he is apt to drink his tea with a fork.

CHINESE PROVERB

Even a cup of tea will stay hunger for a time.
JAPANESE PROVERB

Rather cold tea and cold rice than cold words and cold looks.
JAPANESE PROVERB

THIRST

Ho, everyone that thirsteth, come ye to the waters, and he that hath no money; come ye, buy, and eat; yea, come, buy wine and milk without money and without price.
ISAIAH 55:1
(c. 700 B.C.)

It is wretched business to be digging a well just as thirst is mastering you.
PLAUTUS
(254-184 B.C.)

Let his thirst be quenched, and nature is satisfied, no matter whence it comes, or whether he drinks in gold, silver, or in the hollow of his hand.
SENECA
On the Happy Life (c. 58 A.D.)

Let your boat of life be light, packed with only what you need—a homely home and simple pleasures, one or two friends, worth the name, someone to love and someone to love you, a cat, a dog, and a pipe or two, enough to eat and enough to wear, and a little more than enough to drink; for thirst is a dangerous thing.
JEROME K. JEROME
Three Men in a Boat (1889)

They speak of my drinking, but never think of my thirst.
SCOTTISH PROVERB

If I should eat this fruit ⌈a tomato⌉, cut in slices in a
pan with butter and oil, it would be injurious and harmful
to me.

PIETRO ANTONIO MICHIEL
(c. 1575)

In Spaine and those hot regions they use to eate the
Apples ⌈tomatoes⌉ prepared and boiled with pepper, salt,
and oyle: but they yeeld very little nourishment to the
body, and the same naught and corrupt.

JOHN GERARD
Gerard's Herball (1597)

Chops and Tomata sauce. Yours, Pickwick.

CHARLES DICKENS
Pickwick Papers (1836-37)

⌈Tomatoes⌉ will not lose their raw taste in less than three
hours cooking.

ELIZA LESLIE
Directions for Cookery (1848)

To lift off the cover of a tomato-y mixture and let it
bubble up mushroom and basil under my nose does a lot
to counteract the many subtle efforts a part of me makes
to punish myself for all those worst of my shortcomings—
those I can neither name nor find a shape for. Terrible
brown ghosts with sinews like bedsprings.

MARY VIRGINIA MICKA
The Cazenovia Journal (1986)

The truly remarkable side to the world's tomatomania is
that it was able to develop and spread in an atmosphere of
almost universal tomatophobia. Out of initial ignorance
grew ultimate passion.

RAYMOND SOKOLOV
Why We Eat What We Eat (1991)

TRAVEL

No bread . . . no water doth a man any good out of his own country.

THOMAS NASHE
The Unfortunate Traveller (1594)

Why do they always put mud into coffee on board steamers? Why does the tea generally taste of boiled boots?

WILLIAM MAKEPEACE THACKERAY
The Kickleburys on the Rhine (1850)

I know what wages beauty gives,
How hard a life her servant lives,
Yet praise the winters gone:
There is not a fool can call me friend,
And I may dine at journey's end
With Landor and with Donne.

WILLIAM BUTLER YEATS
To a Young Beauty (1919)

I've run more risk eating my way across the country than in all my driving.

DUNCAN HINES
Adventures in Good Eating (1936)

Then all around from far away across the world
he smelled good things to eat
so he gave up being king of where the wild things are.

MAURICE SENDAK
Where The Wild Things Are (1963)

· He who goes for a day in the forest should take bread for a week.

CZECH PROVERB

When you travel in a country of corn-ears, take a sickle with you.

ETHIOPIAN PROVERB

Born but to banquet and to drain the bowl.

HOMER
Odyssey (c. 800 B.C.)

He is a very valiant trencherman; he hath an excellent stomach.

WILLIAM SHAKESPEARE
Much Ado About Nothing (1598-99)

Great eaters and great sleepers are incapable of anything else that is great.

HENRY IV OF FRANCE
(1553-1610)

He was a man of an unbounded stomach.

WILLIAM SHAKESPEARE
Henry VIII (1612-13)

There are wholesale eaters who can devour a leg of mutton and trimmings at a sitting.

THOMAS HOOD
Review of Arthur Coningsby (1838)

We hadn't been south of Thirty-fifth Street, east of Fifth Avenue or north of Fifty-ninth. But we'd been thorough. We'd had pizza, coconut juice, pastrami, pig's feet, paella, and Him Soon York, and Lamaar had been sick on the corner of Broadway and Forty-fourth Street.

WILLIAM PRICE FOX
Hello New York (1968)

Then a roadsign:

SWAMP GUINEA'S FISH LODGE

ALL YOU CAN EAT!

An arrow pointed down a county highway. I would gorge myself. A record would be set. They'd ask me to leave. An embarassment to all.

WILLIAM LEAST HEAT-MOON
Blue Highways (1982)

Michael Lotito (b. 1950) of Grenoble, France, known as Monsieur Mangetout, has been eating metal and glass since 1959. Gastroenterologists have X-rayed his stomach and described his ability to consume two pounds of metal per day as unique. His diet since 1966 has included 10 bicycles, a supermarket cart, seven TV sets, six chandeliers, a low-calorie Cessna light aircraft, and a computer. He is said to have provided the only example in history of a coffin ending up inside a man.

THE GUINNESS BOOK OF RECORDS (1994)

T U R T L E

A plate of turtle green and glutinous.

ROBERT BROWNING
The Pied Piper of Hamelin (1842)

'Of all the things I ever swallow—
Good well dress'd turtle beats them hollow—
It almost makes me wish, I vow,
To have two stomachs, like a cow!'
And lo! as with the cud, an inward thrill
Upheaved his waistcoat and disturb'd his frill,
His mouth was oozing, and he work'd his jaw—
'I almost think that I could eat one raw.'

THOMAS HOOD
The Turtles (1842)

Turtle makes all men equal.

BENJAMIN DISRAELI
(1804-1881)

As for me, give me turtle or give me death. What is life without turtle? nothing. What is turtle without life? nothinger still.

ARTEMUS WARD
(1834-1867)

Let housewives make a skillet of my helm.
WILLIAM SHAKESPEARE
Othello (1604-05)

They say fingers were made before forks, and hands
before knives.
JONATHAN SWIFT
Polite and Ingenious Conversation (1738)

The frightful manner of feeding with their knives, till the
whole blade seemed to enter into the mouth; and the still
more frightful manner of cleaning the teeth afterwards
with a pocket-knife.
FRANCES TROLLOPE
Domestic Manners of the Americans (1832)

At the root of many a woman's failure to become a great
cook lies her failure to develop a workmanlike regard
for knives.
ROBERT FARRAR CAPON
(1976)

An ill cook should have a good cleaver.
ENGLISH PROVERB

VEGETABLES

My new province is a land of bamboo groves:
Their shoots in spring fill the valleys and hills . . .
I put the shoots in a great earthen pot
And heat them up along with boiling rice.
The purple nodules broken—like an old brocade;
The white skin opened—like new pearls.
Now every day I eat them recklessly . . .
PO CHU-I
Eating Bamboo Shoots (c. 825 A.D.)

After the chrysanthemums
Besides the daikon
There is nothing.
MATSUO BASHO
(1644-1694)

A cucumber should be well sliced, and dressed with pepper and vinegar, and then thrown out, as good for nothing.
SAMUEL JOHNSON
Boswell's Life of Johnson (1773)

I stick to asparagus, which seems to inspire gentle thoughts.
CHARLES LAMB
Essays of Elia (1823)

The taro root looks like a thick, or, if you please, corpulent sweet potato, in shape, but it is of a light purple color when boiled. When boiled, it answers as a passable substitute for bread.
MARK TWAIN
Mark Twain in Hawaii (1866)

Cauliflower is nothing but cabbage with a college education.
MARK TWAIN
(1835-1910)

I hate with a bitter hatred the names of lentils and haricots—those pretentious cheats of the appetite, those tabulated humbugs, those certificated aridites calling themselves human food!
GEORGE GISSING
The Private Papers of Henry Ryecroft (1903)

Cabbage: A familiar kitchen-garden vegetable about as large and wise as a man's head.
AMBROSE BIERCE
The Devil's Dictionary (1906)

There's someone at every party who eats all the celery.
KIN HUBBARD
(1868-1930)

For every mess of asparagus that you eat, a human back somewhere must ache.
H.L. MENCKEN
in Smart Set (1921)

There is an idea prevalent that anybody can cook sweet potatoes. This is a very great mistake . . .
GEORGE WASHINGTON CARVER
Tuskegee Institute Bulletin Number 38 (1922)

The green and gold of my delight—Asparagus with Hollandaise.
THOMAS AUGUSTINE DALY
(1871-1948)

The first zucchini I ever saw, I killed it with a hoe.
JOHN GOULD
Monstrous Depravity (1963)

I have no truck with lettuce, cabbage, and similar chloro-phyll. Any dietician will tell you that a running foot of apple strudel contains four times the vitamins of a bushel of beans.
S.J. PERELMAN
(1904-1979)

Vegetables are interesting but lack a sense of purpose when unaccompanied by a good cut of meat.
FRAN LEBOWITZ
Metropolitan Life (1978)

I do not like broccoli and I haven't liked it since I was a little kid and my mother made me eat it. And I'm Presi-dent of the United States, and I'm not going to eat any more broccoli.
GEORGE BUSH
(1924 -)

If Elvis Presley had eaten green vegetables he'd still be alive.
IAN DURY
(1942 -)

Plant carrots in January, and you'll never have to eat carrots.
ANONYMOUS

The one who constantly eats vegetable roots can do anything.
CHINESE PROVERB

When eating bamboo shoots, remember the man who planted them.
CHINESE PROVERB

He who can't get bacon must be content with cabbage.
DANISH PROVERB

The gardener's dog neither eats cabbage himself nor lets anyone else eat it.
FRENCH PROVERB

Rhubarb and patience work wonders.
GERMAN PROVERB

Only in dreams are the carrots as big as bears.
JEWISH PROVERB

VEGETARIANISM

Nebuchadnezzar . . . was driven from men, and did eat grass as oxen.
DANIEL 4:33
(c. 165 B.C.)

Oh, how criminal it is for flesh to be stored away in flesh, for one greedy body to grow fat with food gained from another, for one live creature to go on living through the destruction of another living thing! And so in the midst of the wealth of food which Earth, the best of mothers, has produced, it is your pleasure to chew the piteous flesh of slaughtered animals!
OVID
Metamorphoses (c. 10 A.D.)

Kill creatures that work you harm, but even in the case of
these let killing suffice. Make not their flesh your food,
but seek a more harmless nourishment.
OVID
Metamorphoses (c. 10 A.D.)

Take not away the life you cannot give, for all things
have an equal right to live. Kill noxious creatures, where
'tis sin to save; this only just prerogative we have. But
nourish life with vegetable food, and shun the sacrilegious
taste of blood.
OVID
Metamorphoses (c. 10 A.D.)

If meat make my brother to offend, I will eat no flesh
while the world standeth, lest I make my brother to
offend.
I CORINTHIANS 8:13
(c. 35 A.D.)

It is good neither to eat flesh, nor to drink wine, nor
anything whereby thy brother stumbleth, or is offended,
or is made weak.
ROMANS 14:21
(c. 55 A.D.)

In the latter times some shall depart from the faith, giving
heed to seducing spirits, and doctrines of devils . . . commanding to abstain from meats, which God hath created to
be received with thanksgiving of them which believe and
know the truth.
I TIMOTHY 4:1-3
(c. 60 A.D.)

It engenders choler, planteth anger;
And better 'twere that both of us did fast,
Since, of ourselves, ourselves are choleric,
Than feed it with such oven-roasted flesh.
WILLIAM SHAKESPEARE
The Taming of the Shrew (1593-94)

Their soul abhorred all manner of meat: and they were
even hard at death's door.
THE BOOK OF COMMON PRAYER 107:18
(1662)

But from the mountain's grassy side
A guiltless feast I bring;
A scrip with herbs and fruit supplied,
And water from the spring.
OLIVER GOLDSMITH
Edwin and Angelina (1765)

Persons living entirely on vegetables are seldom of a plump
and succulent habit.
WILLIAM CULLEN
First Lines of the Practice of Physic (1774)

All wholesome food is caught without a net or a trap.
WILLIAM BLAKE
(1757-1827)

There is no disease, bodily or mental, which adoption of
vegetable diet and pure water has not infallibly mitigated,
wherever the experiment has been fairly tried.
PERCY BYSSHE SHELLEY
Queen Mab (1813)

I have no doubt that it is a part of the destiny of the
human race, in its gradual improvement, to leave off
eating animals, as surely as the savage tribes have left off
eating each other when they come in contact with the
more civilized.
HENRY DAVID THOREAU
Walden (1854)

I have a friend, a vegetarian seer,
By name Elias Baptist Butterworth,
A harmless, bland, disinterested man.
GEORGE ELIOT
A Minor Prophet (1865)

Most vigitaryans I iver see looked enough like their food to be classed as cannybals.

FINLEY PETER DUNNE
Mr. Dooley's Philosophy (1900)

Vegetarianism is harmless enough, though it is apt to fill a man with wind and self-righteousness.

SIR ROBERT HUTCHINSON
Food and the Principles of Dietetics (c. 1910)

So I gave him all the pork
That I had, upon a fork
Because I am myself a vegetarian.

G.K. CHESTERTON
The Logical Vegetarian (1915)

A man of my spiritual intensity does not eat corpses.

GEORGE BERNARD SHAW
(1856-1950)

If your eyes are set wide apart you should be a vegetarian, because you inherit the digestive characteristics of bovine and equine ancestry.

DR. LINARD WILLIAMS
(1932)

I have known many meat eaters to be far more non-violent than vegetarians.

MOHANDAS GANDHI
Non-Violence in Peace and War (1948)

Vegetarian: A person who eats only side dishes.

GERALD LIEBERMAN
The Greatest Laughs of All Time (1961)

Vegetarians have wicked, shifty eyes and laugh in a cold, calculating manner. They pinch little children, steal stamps, drink water, favor beards.

J.B. MORTON
in the London Daily Express (c. 1965)

Don't eat anything that has a face. Don't eat anything that has sexual urges, that has a mother and father or that tries to run away from you.

JOHN ROBBINS
A Diet for a New America (1987)

I'm not a vegetarian because I love animals; I'm a vegetarian because I hate plants.

A. WHITNEY BROWN
(1952 -)

Every vegetarian knows what a pig looks like.

CHINESE PROVERB

If you become a vegetarian you separate from your ancestors and cut off posterity.

CHINESE PROVERB

WAITERS/ WAITRESSES

The last man in the world whose opinion I would take on what to eat would be a doctor. It is far safer to consult a waiter, and not a bit more expensive.

ROBERT LYND
Solomon in All His Glory (1923)

We can go to any restaurant at all and be made uncomfortable by the waiters, waiters seeming to be a breed gifted in making guests ill at ease. They are always older, wearier, and wiser than we are; and they have us at a disadvantage because we are sitting down and they are standing up. We should very much like to discover a restaurant where we would be allowed to stand up to our food, and the waiters be compelled to sit down, so we could lord it over them.

E.B. WHITE
Every Day Is Saturday (1934)

When the waitress puts the dinner on the table, the old men look at the dinner. The young men look at the waitress.

GELETT BURGESS
(1866-1951)

Security is a smile from a headwaiter.
RUSSELL BAKER
(1925 -)

'Waitperson' is surely one of the most preposterous and cumbersome of the supposedly 'nonsexist' neologisms with which our language has been saddled in recent years. The next time somebody announces himself or herself at your table as a 'waitperson,' just ask to see his or her driveperson's license.
COLMAN ANDREWS
Everything on the Table (1992)

Hunger and cold deliver a man up to his enemy.
JOHN RAY
English Proverbs (1670)

W   A   R

Some men are born to feast, and not to fight;
Whose sluggish minds, e'en in fair honor's field,
Still on their dinner turn—
Let such pot-boiling varlets stay at home,
And wield a flesh-hook rather than a sword.
JOANNA BAILLIE
Basil (1811)

An army marches on its stomach.
NAPOLEON BONAPARTE
(1769-1821)

I offer hunger, thirst, forced marches, battles, and death. Let him who loves his country in his heart and not with his lips only, follow me.
GIUSEPPE GARIBALDI
Garibaldi's Defense of the Roman Republic (1911)

Before the war, while travel had had the glamour of the rich and while sex had had the allure of the forbidden, food was thought to be pretty dull stuff. Food was fodder or fuel or whatever liquid or solid it was that came in cans. But during the war our boys in the trenches found

themselves dreaming of thick ribs and T-bones as well as
of slender waists and ankles of fair creatures left behind. It
took us by surprise that the memory of a last hot dog
could be as powerful as the memory of a first kiss.
BETTY FUSELL
Masters of American Cookery (1983)

W A T E R

Stolen waters are sweet, and bread eaten in secret is
pleasant.
PROVERBS 9:17
(c. 350 B.C.)

There is no small pleasure in pure water.
OVID
(43 B.C.-17 A.D.)

He that drinks water drinks phlegm.
JOHN FLORIO
Second Fruites (1591)

Water taken in moderation cannot hurt anybody.
MARK TWAIN
(1835-1910)

Some say delicacies are the mainstay of life; others that
water is.
MAORI PROVERB

Water is the king of food.
NIGERIAN PROVERB

W I N E

Wine gives strength to weary men.
HOMER
Iliad (c. 800 B.C.)

The blood of grapes.
GENESIS 49:11
(c. 700 B.C.)

He shall separate himself from wine and strong drink, and shall drink no vinegar of wine, or vinegar of strong drink, neither shall he drink any liquor of grapes, nor eat moist grapes, or dried.
NUMBERS 6:3
(c. 700 B.C.)

All the Jews returned out of all places whither they were driven, and came to the land of Judah, to Gedaliah, unto Mizpah, and gathered wine and summer fruits very much.
JEREMIAH 49:12
(c. 625 B.C.)

When men drink wine they are rich, they are busy, they push lawsuits, they are happy, they help their friends.
ARISTOPHANES
The Knights (424 B.C.)

Boys should abstain from all use of wine until their eighteenth year, for it is wrong to add fire to fire.
PLATO
Laws (360 B.C.)

Look not upon the wine when it is red, when it giveth his color in the cup, when it moveth itself aright. At the last it biteth like a serpent, and stingeth like an adder. Thine eyes shall behold strange women, and thine heart shall utter perverse things.
PROVERBS 23:31-33
(c. 350 B.C.)

Wine unlocks secrets, bids hopes be certainties, thrusts cowards into the fray, takes loads off anxious hearts, teaches new accomplishments. The life-giving wine cup . . . whom has it not made free even in the pinch of poverty?
HORACE
Epistles (c. 20 B.C.)

Drink no longer water, but use a little wine for thy stomach's sake and thine often infirmities.
I TIMOTHY 5:23
(c. 60 A.D.)

And [Jesus] took the cup, and gave thanks, and gave it to
them, saying, Drink ye all of it; for this is my blood of
the new testament, which is shed for many for the
remission of sins. But I say unto you, I will not drink
henceforth of this fruit of the vine, until that day when
I drink it new with you in my Father's kingdom.
**MATTHEW 26:27-29
(c. 75 A.D.)**

Toward evening, about supper-time, when the serious
studies of the day are over, is the time to take wine.
**CLEMENT OF ALEXANDRIA
Paedagogus (c. 190 A.D)**

Wine brings sorrow to man.
**TALMUD: SANHEDRIN
(c. 200 A.D.)**

At the third cup I penetrate the Great Way;
A full gallon—Nature and I are one . . .
But the things I feel when wine possesses my soul
I will never tell those who are not drunk.
**ANONYMOUS
The Book of Wine (c. 1050)**

Wine, though bitter, sweetens all bitterness.
**MOSES IBN EZRA
(1060-1139)**

If wine turns sour, place a little bag of charred peas within
the jar.
**MADAME WU
A Housewife's Handbook (c. 1160)**

A truce with thirst, a truce with hunger;
they're strong, but wine and meat are stronger.
**FRANCOIS RABELAIS
Gargantua (1535)**

Diogenes was asked which wine he liked best; and he answered as I would have done when he said: 'Somebody else's.'
**MICHEL DE MONTAIGNE
(1533-1592)**

He that drinks wine drinks blood.
JOHN FLORIO
Second Fruites (1591)

Wine . . . is a great increaser of the vital spirits: it very greatly comforteth a weak stomack, helpeth concoction, distribution and nutrition, mightily strengtheneth the natural heat, openeth obstruction, discusseth windiness, taketh away sadness, and other hurt of melancholy.
TOBIAS VENNER
Via recta (1620)

Wine is sure proof that God loves us and wants us to be happy.
BENJAMIN FRANKLIN
Poor Richard's Almanac (1732)

Never spare the parson's wine, nor the baker's pudding.
BENJAMIN FRANKLIN
Poor Richard's Almanac (1733)

Wine . . . is one of the noblest cordials in nature.
JOHN WESLEY
Journal (1771)

This is one of the disadvantages of wine: it makes a man mistake words for thoughts.
SAMUEL JOHNSON
Boswell's Life of Johnson (1778)

Wine gives great pleasure, and every pleasure is of itself a good.
SAMUEL JOHNSON
Boswell's Life of Johnson (1778)

No nation is drunken where wine is cheap. . . . It is, in truth, the only antidote to the bane of whiskey.
THOMAS JEFFERSON
Letter to Monsieur de Neuville (1818)

O for a beaker of the warm South,
Full of the true, the blushful Hippocrene,

With beaded bubbles winking at the brim,
And purple-stained mouth.
JOHN KEATS
Ode to a Nightingale (1819)

A meal without wine is like a day without sunshine.
ANTHELME BRILLAT-SAVARIN
The Physiology of Taste (1825)

Wine is earth's answer to the sun.
MARGARET FULLER
in Lydia Marie Child's Letters from New York (1845)

God made the waters, man made the wines.
VICTOR HUGO
Les Contemplations (1856)

Wine . . . is a food.
OLIVER WENDELL HOLMES
address to the Massachusetts Medical Society (1860)

'Have some wine,' the March Hare said in an encouraging
tone. Alice looked all round the table, but there was
nothing on it but tea. 'I don't see any wine,' she remarked.
'There isn't any,' said the March Hare.
LEWIS CARROLL
Alice's Adventures in Wonderland (1865)

Wine is the drink of the gods. Milk is the drink of
babies, tea the drink of women. And water is the drink
of beasts.
JOHN S. BLACKIE
(1809-1895)

Wine is the most healthful and hygienic of beverages.
LOUIS PASTEUR
(1822-1895)

Now and then it is a joy to have one's table red with wine
and roses.
OSCAR WILDE
De Profundis (1897)

And Noah he often said to his wife when he sat down
    to dine,
'I don't care where the water goes if it doesn't get into
    the wine.'
G.K. CHESTERTON
Wine and Water (1915)

I believe that it will be a long time before any genuine
understanding of and gift for wines, in the Continental
sense, will show itself in the American people.
H.L. MENCKEN
in American Mercury (1928)

It's a Naïve Domestic Burgundy, Without Any Breeding,
But I Think You'll be Amused by its Presumption.
JAMES THURBER
cartoon caption in The New Yorker (1937)

A good general rule is to state that the bouquet is better
than the taste, and vice versa.
STEPHEN POTTER
One-upsmanship (1952)

Wine is a part of society because it provides a basis not
only for a morality but also for an environment; it is an
ornament in the slightest ceremonials of French daily life,
from the snack . . . to the feast.
ROLAND BARTHES
Mythologies (1957)

To take wine into our mouths is to savor a droplet of the
river of human history.
CLIFTON FADIMAN
The Joys of Wine (1975)

Wine tastes like gasoline.
COLONEL HARLAND SANDERS
(1890-1980)

One wine writer once likened a champagne to 'a young
girl in a long white dress in a summer garden.' Another,

more succinct but just as imaginative, pondered a wine for a while then pronounced: 'It has broad shoulders and very narrow hips.' Still others resort to arcane flummery such as 'It starts well and has a pleasant finish, but it dies on the middle palate.' One of the more creative wine experts around once sipped a glass, raised his head, and said, 'Marigolds.' Then he took another sip and said, 'I was wrong. Not marigolds. Dwarf marigolds.'

FRANK J. PRIAL
in the New York Times (c. 1978)

Excellent wine generates enthusiasm. And whatever you do with enthusiasm is generally successful.

PHILIPPE DE ROTHSCHILD
(1980)

What is the definition of a good wine? It should start and end with a smile.

WILLIAM SOKOLIN
(1984)

He who drinks wine after his soup should never be asked for advice.

ANONYMOUS

Wine and meat attract many friends.

CHINESE PROVERB

Wine wears no breeches.

ENGLISH PROVERB

Good wine makes the horse go.

FRENCH PROVERB

White meat, white wine; red meat, red wine.

FRENCH PROVERB

Wine on milk is good; milk on wine is poison.

FRENCH PROVERB

Good wine is milk for the aged.

GERMAN PROVERB

After melon, wine is a felon.
ITALIAN PROVERB

Wine and late rising are shortcuts to poverty.
JAPANESE PROVERB

Wine is the best of all medicines and the worst of all poisons.
JAPANESE PROVERB

Wine, in moderation, unfolds a man's brain; a teetotaler rarely possesses great wisdom.
JEWISH PROVERB

Wine is the greatest medicine.
JEWISH PROVERB

All wine would be port if it could.
PORTUGUESE PROVERB

Good wine and a loving wife are two sweet poisons to a man.
RUMANIAN PROVERB

W O M E N

The woman whom thou gavest to be with me, she gave me of the tree, and I did eat.
GENESIS 3:12
(c. 700 B.C.)

Her that ruled the roost in the kitchen.
THOMAS HEYWOOD
The History of Women (1624)

Flattery is dearer to a woman than her food.
SAMUEL RICHARDSON
Sir Charles Grandison (1749)

Women cannot make a good book of cookery.
SAMUEL JOHNSON
Boswell's Life of Johnson (1778)

What say you to such a supper with such a woman?
LORD BYRON
Letter on the Rev. W.L. Bowles's Strictures on Pope (1821)

Though we eat little flesh and drink no wine,
Yet let's be merry: we'll have tea and toast;
Custards for supper, and an endless host
Of syllabubs and jellies and mince pies,
And other such lady-like luxuries.
PERCY BYSSHE SHELLEY
Letter to Maria Gisborne (1824)

From my greenest youth, when I used to play about and make dirt-pies with my brothers and sisters, I had a stirring ambition to be useful in my generation; and it was ever my opinion as long ago as I can remember, that nothing in the whole circle of female duties was so useful and becoming to a modest and virtuous woman as a practical knowledge of the mysteries of cookery.
PRUDENCE SMITH
Modern American Cookery (1831)

It is not beneath the solicitude of a good wife, who would not suffer any abatement in the affection of which she is the object, constantly to provide a neat and well-dressed repast.
MRS. N.K.M. LEE
The Cook's Own Book (1832)

All American ladies should know how to clear starch and iron; how to keep plate and glass; how to cook dainties; and, if they understand the making of bread and soup likewise, so much the better.
HARRIET MARTINEAU
Society in America (1836)

A kitchen without a female cook is like a flowerless garden, a waveless sea, a sailless ship.
ALEXIS SOYER
The Gastronomic Regenerator (1846)

Woman is nearer the vegetable than man.
GEORGE MEREDITH
The Ordeal of Richard Feverel (1859)

The idea occurred to me that woman might not have been created mainly for the purpose of getting three meals a day.
A.M. DIAZ
Papers Found in the School Master's Trunk (1875)

Woman does not understand what food means, and yet she insists upon being a cook!
FRIEDRICH NIETZSCHE
Beyond Good and Evil (1886)

Good dinners are so much rarer than good women: and far more piquant.
G.B. BURGIN
Which Woman? (1907)

Man wants good dinners. It is woman's province to provide them.
M.E.W. SHERWOOD
The Art of Entertainment (1892)

No mean woman can cook well, for it calls for a light head, a generous spirit, and a large heart.
PAUL GAUGUIN
(1848-1903)

To remove sugar from the kitchen were to deprive alimentation of many of its benefits and pleasures, as well as to rob woman of much of her allurement.
GEORGE H. ELLWANGER
The Pleasures of the Table (1902)

When a well bred girl expects to wed, 'tis well to remember that men like bread.
GOLD MEDAL FLOUR ADVERTISEMENT
in Ladies' Home Journal (1903)

We are taught that man most loves and admires the domestic type of woman. This is one of the roaring jokes

of history. The breakers of hearts, the queens of romance, the goddesses of a thousand devotees, have not been cooks.
CHARLOTTE PERKINS GILMAN
The Home (1903)

The theory that the man who raises corn does a more important piece of work than the woman who makes it into bread is absurd. The inference is that the men alone render useful service. But neither man nor woman eats these things until the woman has prepared it.
IDA M. TARBELL
The Business of Being a Woman (1912)

It's certain that fine women eat
A crazy salad with their meat.
WILLIAM BUTLER YEATS
A Prayer for My Daughter (1919)

Women have no wilderness in them,
They are provident instead,
Content in the tight hot cell of their hearts
To eat dusty bread.
LOUISE BOGAN
Women (1922)

Ever since Eve started it all by offering Adam the apple, woman's punishment has been to have to supply a man with food and then suffer the consequences when it disagrees with him.
HELEN ROWLAND
A Guide to Men (1922)

There is nothing I hate more than to see a woman, hot, tired, and untidy from cooking a dinner I am supposed to eat. It takes all the pleasure out of the meal.
G.F. SCOTSON-CLARK
Eating Without Fears (1924)

Whoever can toss up, day in and day out, as many meals as may be required, make them edible and varied and as effortless as possible, is a good cook, plenty good enough for

you and me. And unsung females are doing just this all
the time.
ALEXANDER WRIGHT
How to Live without a Woman (1937)

There is no spectacle on earth more appealing than that of
a beautiful woman in the act of cooking dinner for someone she loves.
THOMAS WOLFE
The Web and the Rock (1939)

The man who fights a worthwhile fight
Must lean upon the skillet,
And she who wants her man to win
Must know just how to fill it.
For soggy bread and tasteless food
Might do to stuff a mummy,
But winners in the fight of life
Win not with heart but tummy.
BERTA CRENSHAW WHITE
untitled (c. 1940)

There is one thing more exasperating than a wife who can
cook and won't and that's a wife who can't cook and will.
ROBERT FROST
(1874-1963)

Naturally I like to cook, and it's a damned good thing that
I do, because my wife went to Smith.
JOHN KEATS
in The Artists' and Writers' Cookbook (1961)

In old China, in modest homes, the wife who cooked well
was considered a pearl of great price. She was valued more
for her culinary skill than for her beauty. Beauty fades,
but a good cook improves with age. Her husband would
never think of leaving her, since he couldn't bear the
prospect of a future without her food.
DR. LEE SU JAN
The Fine Art of Chinese Cooking (1962)

Zee always went naked in the house, except for the brassiere she wore when it was her turn to get dinner. Once, cooking French-fried potatoes in a kettle of boiling fat, she had come within an inch of crisping her most striking features.
GEORGE SUMNER ALBEE
(1905-1964)

We connive to keep the calories down and feel triumphant when we get compliments on a low-calorie meal from the man we are trying to please.
LADY BIRD JOHNSON
(1912 -)

Many women are poor cooks only because their native greatness has been beaten down by ingratitude.
ROBERT FARRAR CAPON
The Supper of the Lamb (1969)

Women are like cheese strudels. When first baked, they are crisp and fresh on the outside, but the filling is unsettled and indigestible; in age, the crust may not be so lovely, but the filling comes at last into its own.
ROBERT FARRAR CAPON
The Supper of the Lamb (1969)

Most of our grandmothers were no great shakes in the kitchen. They spent more time there than women do today, but what came out of their hard work was often no match for what a new bride can turn out today.
JAMES TRAGER
The Food Book (1970)

When men reach their sixties and retire, they go to pieces. Women go right on cooking.
GAIL SHEEHY
(1937 -)

Woman's appetite is twice that of a man, her intelligence four times, and her desires eight times.
BURMESE PROVERB

Women, melons, and cheese should be chosen by weight.
SPANISH PROVERB

And no meat offering, which ye shall bring unto the Lord, shall be made with leaven: for ye shall burn no leaven, nor any honey, in any offering of the Lord made by fire.

LEVITICUS 2:11
(c. 700 B.C.)

A little leaven leaveneth the whole lump.

GALATIANS 5:9
(c. 50 A.D.)

Three things are good in a little measure, and bad in large: yeast, salt, and hesitation.

TALMUD: BERAKOTH
(c. 200 A.D.)

The Evil Impulse is like a cake of yeast: placed in one spot, it ferments throughout.

MOSES DE LEON
Sefer ha-zohar (c. 1275)

Y E A S T

319

AUTHOR INDEX

MARCH EGERTON'S fondness for both food and holidays is perhaps partly explained by his having arrived in this world during the long Thanksgiving weekend of 1964. He was raised in Nashville by a clan of accomplished and somewhat bookish cooks before moving on to Chapel Hill, North Carolina, Seattle, Washington and the Hawaiian island of Oahu, where he authored a best-selling, off-the-beaten-path dining guide. He now lives and eats in Portland, Oregon.